Published by STS Publications
Studium Theologicum Salesianum
26, Rehov Shmuel Hanagid
P.O.B.7336
9107202 Jerusalem (Israel)

ISBN:978-965-7690-38-3

Michal Vojtáš

Reviving
Don Bosco's
Oratory

Salesian Youth Ministry,
Leadership and Innovative
Project Management

Abbreviations

ACG   Acts of the General Council of the Salesian Society

ACS   Acts of the Superior Council of the Salesian Society

Const. Constitutions of the Society of Saint Francis de Sales

EPC   Educative and Pastoral Community

FMA   Daughters of Mary Help of Christians

FSE   Faculty of Sciences of Education at the Salesian Pontifical University

GC   General Chapter of the Society of Saint Francis de Sales

MBO Management by Objectives

Reg.   General Regulations of the Society of St Francis de Sales

SDB   Salesians of Don Bosco (also Salesian Society or Society of Saint Francis de Sales)

SEPP Salesian Educative and Pastoral Project

SGC   Special General Chapter of the Society of Saint Francis de Sales

UPS   Salesian Pontifical University

YM   Youth Ministry

The methods can become defective also through the infiltration of prejudices or arbitrary theories. The temptation to mix in with them some unnecessary ideological suppositions is unfortunately a real one. The new evangelization demands a search for methods which can make an efficacious contribution to education in and of the faith, following integrally the Church's deposit of faith and ensuring the presence of well-founded certainties that are well defined, simple and solid, and stronger than the rationalistic misgivings that can arise.

Fr. Egidio Viganò

Introduction

The "Salesians of Don Bosco" (SDB) are the largest Catholic religious order with a primary focus on youth ministry and education. If we
observe its action in synergy with the whole Salesian Family, uniting
more than 30 congregations, institutes, associations and movements, we
can state that the Salesian Youth Ministry influences millions of young
people worldwide through schools, youth centres, parishes, missionary
centres, informal activities, volunteering, and animation. Leadership
styles, governance models and project management methodologies are
therefore phenomena influencing concretely a vast and diverse educational and pastoral network. Here I would like to pose that were felt at
the beginning of the journey which progresses with this publication: How
were the main ideas of the Salesian Youth Ministry, the Leadership models and the Project Management methodologies developed? What was
their theoretical background? What is the central idea that organizes the
whole system? And, of course, how can we offer better ministry and education for the young of the third millennium? These fundamental
questions, and the respective efforts to answer them, organize the whole
publication.

The first chapter outlines the development of some key ideas. During
the post-Vatican II update of the Salesian mission, the Congregation had
to deal with the complexity of services, the insistent need of inculturation
and with the uncertainty of the future. The Salesian Educational and Pastoral Project (SEPP) was therefore one of the central issues and
instruments of Youth Ministry, decentralization, inculturation and operational effectiveness. The change from a faithful and often repetitive
education according to pre-Vatican II models towards a critical, culture-
sensible and future-centered approach to youth ministry brought developments connected with multiple risks.

The second chapter analyzes the main theoretical and organizational
perspectives. The particular post-Vatican II context and expectations
have influenced the Salesian Youth Ministry with many fruitful concepts

of pastoral theology and educational sciences. It could, however, mark the design with some exaggerated tendencies of the late '60s, '70s and '80s: an anthropocentric world vision, a technically designed project management method, a weak appreciation of tradition, an accentuated socio-political dimension of youth ministry, a radical idea of decentralization and inculturation, etc. After a period of initial enthusiasm about the effectiveness of the planned educational and pastoral action, however, a moment of disillusion was reached. The almost impossible translation from "paper to life", the linguistic ambiguity of the term "project", the exaggerated multiplication of interconnected projects, a constant production of texts to be implemented, a too technical methodology, or too short implementation times are just some of the symptoms of a general discomfort around the desired "project mentality".

The third chapter follows the path of some significant indications that connect the difficulties with the Salesian Leadership and Project Management to the anthropological model and the design paradigm underlying the SEPP theories. So we turn back to the original and permanent criterion for any renewal – the experience of Don Bosco in the first Salesian house, the Valdocco Oratory. We locate it within different organizational studies of consecrated life and, phenomenologically, read the evolution of the leadership and management qualities of "Don Bosco in the Oratory" in course of his life.

Don Bosco's experience, new and innovative leadership concepts and some solid bases of the Salesian Youth Ministry are sewn creatively together in the fourth chapter. The first concepts were contemplated upon four years ago, but then we felt the need for prototyping and experimentation in the field. Feedbacks from the academics, practitioners, students, leadership seminars and from the process consulting at Borgo Don Bosco in Rome were useful for developing an actionable proposal. First, we created an integral anthropological and methodological framework. Then six typical virtues of a Salesian educator were developed at the level of action mentality, shared leadership and operative management qualities.

Finally, we proposed five steps of a project cycle that merges planning, community building and discernment. We will follow the red thread of an integral anthropology, which incorporates deeper spiritual and vocational dynamics into the practical planning to create a transformational path for the entire Educative and Pastoral Community.

The ideas and experiments expressed in this publication have been transformative and formative for me and for those who have shared in the journey. I would like to thank the Faculty members of the Pontifical Salesian University for their fraternal support, inspiration, dialogue and research suggestions. In a special way, I would like to remember with gratitude Francesco Casella, Jerome Vallabaraj, Michele Pellerey, Aldo Giraudo and Rossano Sala. In addition, my gratitude goes to Peter Michael Senge, the founder of Society for Organizational Learning, Beth Jandernoa from the Presencing Institute, Lumír Šarman from Franklin-Covey, Reiner von Leoprechting from ProAction Learning, and the members of the SOL Rome creative group. Putting into practice the shared ideas has greatly contributed to the development of this book. In particular, I would like to mention my friends from the Salesian Family of Slovakia: the former provincial Karol Gabo Maník and my colleagues Filip Vagač, Slávka Brigantová and Ján Mihálik. Last but not the least, my acknowledgements go to the Educative and Pastoral Community of Borgo Don Bosco, especially to the rector Stefano Aspettati that co-created and put into practice the methodology presented in this book (see Appendix 3). Thanks to Joe Boenzi, Cassius Correya, Patrick Lepcha and Miriam Bicková for terminological suggestions and orthographic corrections. These people remembered, and those not explicitly mentioned, have become a part of a shared and witnessed project of life, through research, education, ministry and trust in Providence.

Michal Vojtáš, SDB
Faculty of Education Sciences
Salesian Pontifical University
Rome, October 1st 2017

1. Historical Evolution of the Salesian Youth Ministry

Education and youth ministry can be considered, among other criteria, in their dual temporal sense, as an appeal to the heritage of past experiences or an outreach to possible future development. The dimension of the tradition, translated in a faithful reproduction of the faith-culture model in the first hundred years of the Salesian Congregation, tended to marginalize almost automatically any critical attitude towards the traditional Salesian Youth Ministry model that had its strong roots in the praxis of St. John Bosco (1815-1888) and in the faith-culture paradigms of the Restauration.[1] In a generalized way, we can state that in the 1960s there was a change of emphasis from a loyal and often repetitive education to a critical pedagogical-pastoral approach. Juan Edmundo Vecchi, a key figure of the Salesian Youth Ministry from 1978 to 2002, expressed it in the following words: "In the last 40 years we should register a significant innovation: education seen as a projection into the future. It is a dimension that has been less relevant before".[2]

The future in those years was imagined through the lens of *aggiornamento* (bringing up to date) of the ecclesiastical culture, the pastoral paradigm of Vatican II, the freedom of expression, the anthropocentric point of view, the progress of science, the critical approach to the social reality with a communitarian accent, the understanding of youth as a political force, the social commitment and the equality and self-determination of nations. It is understandable that the youth ministry of the sixties and seventies put a strong emphasis on the projection into the future. The educative and pastoral projects were adopted as an instrument that seemed appropriate to manage the future. It was an option that, as

---

[1] See P. STELLA, *Don Bosco. Religious Outlook and Spirituality*, Salesiana Publishers, New Rochelle NY 1996.

[2] J.E. VECCHI, *I guardiani dei sogni con il dito sul mouse. Educatori nell'era informatica*, Rettore Maggiore dei Salesiani di Don Bosco intervistato da Carlo di Cicco, LDC, Leumann TO 1999, p. 21.

we will see, was not exempt from risks and reductions. In the first chapter of this study we would like to survey the fundamental traits of frequently nonlinear evolution of the post-Vatican II Salesian Youth Ministry model from the 1960s up to today.

1.1 The Pastoral Echoes of Vatican II in the 19th General Chapter (1965)

The centenary of the Salesian Congregation was celebrated in 1959. In the same year Pope John XXIII convoked the Second Vatican Ecumenical Council. This coincidence strengthened the anticipations of the Salesians about a turning point in the years to come. The Rector Major Renato Ziggiotti was invited to participate in the Council as a member of the Commission for the Religious. The Rector Major evaluated this experience as a great school and a stimulus for the commitment to the Salesian apostolic vocation.[3] The Council's influence on the Salesian youth ministry model can be considered from interrelated aspects: the pastoral content of the Magisterium and the practical ways in which the pastoral efforts were intended to be put into practice.

1.1.1 General Chapter Methodology

The way and the method of realization of the GC19, influenced by the Council, changed the Salesian Chapter paradigm regarding the duration, the depth of the issues, and the openness to the human sciences. The work of the Chapter held in Rome in the new Salesian University continued for 53 days, setting a record compared to previous General Chapters that lasted an average of ten days. The GC19 created a space for open discussion that did not cover the different points of view of the assembly members. In fact, the newly elect Rector Major Luigi Ricceri, feeling the

---

[3] See R. ZIGGIOTTI, *Lettera del Rettor Maggiore*, in ACS 44 (1963) 229, 5-6.

atmosphere of polarized tension between adaptation to the new challenges and fidelity to the charism, intervened: "Dear Brothers... ours must be an atmosphere of charity. [...] We must realize this union of charity at all costs. I have said already, union together in charity. Such union presupposes understanding [...] my 'opponent' in the order of ideas – to understand the man who thinks other than I do, to know him as my brother, in our common father Don Bosco. [...] We have to be convinced, by reason of that same deep understanding of yet another thing – in our houses and communities there are today psychological situations existing and malaise which cannot be ignored. They are the result of our living and suffering in the life of Society and the Church at the present time".[4]

The accumulation of tension and the necessary drive to change the course is understandable if we comprehend the way of dealing with the issues caused by the changed post-World War II context. Pietro Braido describes the previous General Chapter 18 in 1958 as one that "does not seem to feel the deep transformations that occurred in the previous six years. As for the oratories, the use of social media and entertainment, and even more the boarding schools, the speeches were almost identical to those of previous chapters, reflecting echoes of the regulatory provisions made in the 1920s and later".[5]

Another element of change of the GC19 was the invitation of 19 experts, including two lay Salesians. Almost all the experts were scholars (mostly specialists in education) and only a few were "full- time" educators. The term "expert", therefore, has a scholarly emphasis in the Salesian context, leaving behind the role of a facilitator or of a good practitioner.[6] The emphasis on the academic dimension of the "experts" in

---

[4] GC19 (1965), pp. 313-314. See also the letter of Fr. Ricceri about dialogue in ACS 48 (1967) 247.

[5] P. BRAIDO, *Le metamorfosi dell'Oratorio Salesiano tra il secondo dopoguerra e il Post-concilio Vaticano II (1944-1984)*, in «Ricerche Storiche Salesiane» 49 (2006) 2, 319.

[6] The expert as facilitator is proposed, on the other hand, by the classic *Lexikon der Pastoraltheologie* edited by Karl Rahner: "What concerns all, must also be decided by all. In accordance with this legal basis, in principle everyone is competent regarding the pastoral planning [...] The task of the experts and managers is to enable persons to plan

the Congregation was strengthened in the 80s through the cooperation between the Youth Pastoral Department and the Faculty of Sciences of Education (FSE) at the Salesian Pontifical University in Rome (UPS).

1.1.2 Implications for the Youth Ministry

The GC19 was the first Chapter that expressed an awareness of the changes that took place in the educational and pastoral context of the post-war period. Its pastoral attempts can be summarized in four areas: reorganization of the central structures of the government; downsizing of the structures; focus on qualification; formation of adults and some practical educative applications.

First, at the level of the General Council, the Councillor for the Youth and Parish Ministry was experimentally introduced. His area of influence united three former Councillors' fields: schools, vocational training and oratories-parishes. Six Regional Councillors were instituted in order to decentralize the leadership and the pastoral ministry. The changes to the General Council tended to enhance the specificity of the regions and, at the same time, to hold together the different educational and pastoral dimensions and structures.[7]

The second area of reflections concerned the "downsizing", a concept that had a good fortune during the GC19, because of a widespread need of the Congregation. The general principle was the simplification of extensive houses and the consolidation of small communities. As for the type of educational structure, the boarding schools seemed to be in crisis from the perspective of both the Salesians and the students.[8] The Chapter

---

for themselves the necessary changes and implement them". See N. HEPP, *Piano pastorale*, in K. RAHNER et al. (Eds.), *Dizionario di Pastorale*, Queriniana, Brescia 1979, pp. 567-568.

[7] See GC19 (1965), pp. 23-26.

[8] 72% of Salesian Past Pupils in Italy would have preferred education in a family context with an average level of parenting compared to a well-organized boarding school education with specifically prepared educators. Among the more negative aspects of Salesian boarding school education were mentioned: unrealistic preparation to life,

then revalued the "primordial" structure of the oratory, "fittingly brought up to date and reshaped [...] so that it may attract and serve as many young people as possible, with a variety of subsidiaries (youth centres, clubs, various associations, courses, night schools)".[9] Oratory was seen already at that time as "a pastoral instrument of approach to all young people opening out in this spirit of missionary dialogue, to all the youth of the parish, area, city – to include those of no faith at all".[10]

A third theme resounding in the GC19 was summarized in the key word "qualification" of the Salesians. It meant primarily the acquisition of the required skills for the mission in "today's world". Luigi Ricceri made an appeal saying: "By now every manifestation of our activity claim qualified people in the field of theology, liturgy, philosophy, education, science, technology, instruction, art, recreation and management". It seems that the attention to the qualification, together with the option to resize the structures to a human scale, was an application of the anthropological turn of the Council.[11]

The last nucleus of the reflection focused on the educational and pastoral issues, still called by the traditional term "apostolate". The reflection on the Christian formation of the adults was added to the youth ministry topic. Among the traditional areas of the adult apostolate, such as assistance to the FMA, the Cooperators, the Past Pupils and the Mission *ad gentes*, six new areas were inserted: parish ministry; adult catechesis; family apostolate; lay teachers' formation; working class ministry; and social communication. Some more concrete educational and pastoral issues still reflected the dominance of the boarding school

---

suppression of personality, too many compulsory religious practices, excessive discipline and un-readiness to engage in relations with the other sex. See P.G. GRASSO, *La Società Salesiana tra il passato e l'avvenire. Risultati di un'inchiesta tra ex allievi Salesiani*, Edizione extra-commerciale riservata, Roma 1964, pp. 45-152.
[9] GC19 (1965), p. 103.
[10] GC19 (1965), p. 137.
[11] See GC19 (1965), pp. 9-10.

paradigm and its poor compatibility with the desire for freedom of expression lived by the young generation of the late 1960s.[12] The actual concerns of the confreres were linked almost exclusively to the life in boarding school: a lively discussion about the compulsory attendance of daily masses or the themes of sexual education, co-education, free time and holiday management of the interns.[13]

1.1.3 Execution of Pastoral Conclusions and Recommendations

Undoubtedly, GC19 was a beginning of a new journey in the Congregation. In 1982 Egidio Viganò spoke about many "anticipatory directions"[14] of the Chapter and in 2010 Pascual Chávez Villanueva saw the GC19 as a representation of "the first collective stock-taking by the communities in the Congregation with regard to the changes taking place in the areas of youth, and the need to reformulate the traditional educative-pastoral praxis".[15] Given the importance of the GC19, it becomes useful therefore to study not only the contents of the discussion but also the "impact history" of the new ideas.[16]

The Rector Major Luigi Ricceri presented the Acts of the GC19 highlighting some criteria for the application of its conclusions. The first

---

[12] The boarding school paradigm is noticeable in the presentation of the GC19 by the Rector Major that omits the boarding school in the part about the downsizing of the structures and also in the heterogeneous structure of the documents IX - XIX, which describe boarding schools (and schools with an attached boarding structure) as the only structures for youth apostolate. See GC19 (1965), pp. 9-13 and pp. 101-201.

[13] See GC19 (1965), pp. 188-189; 194-198 and 336-338.

[14] E. VIGANÒ, *Il Capitolo Generale XXII*, in ACS 63 (1982) 305, 10.

[15] P. CHÁVEZ VILLANUEVA, *"And he took pity on them, because they were like sheep without a sheperd, and he set himself to teach them at some length" (Mk 6,34). Salesian Youth Ministry*, in ACG 91 (2010) 407, 6-7.

[16] The "impact history" or the "history of effects" (ger. *Wirkungsgeschichte*) is a key concept of Hans-Georg Gadamers' hermeneutical theory. In the present publication we will be using it as an interpretative category to capture the semantic nuances of the key concepts such as education, youth ministry, pastoral ministry, project, plan, significance, etc., which are linked closely with the context in which they arose, with interpretations in subsequent Salesian documents and, last but not least, with the way they were (or were not) carried out.

criterion was "to mould in ourselves a mentality rather than set up an inventory of injunctions to be carried out".[17] The second was intended especially for superiors who should use a prudent gradual approach to the application of the Chapter. Gradual application should not be improvised, but guided by the norms issued by superiors to prevent the danger of arbitrary interpretations and dispersion. Dialogue is emphasized as a superior's key skill in order to foster collaboration at various levels. Resizing the structures served as the third criterion of the GC19. The downsizing of educational structures was not concerned about the effectiveness of the activity of the community but about paying attention to the authentic good of the confreres. The Rector Major wrote: "Before moving on to increase already existing activities in number and size we should all of us feel a preoccupation for the man, the religious, the Salesian, the one who plays the leading part in this whirlwind drama [...] The apostolate is a delicate spiritual work. It cannot be effective if one's soul is tired out".[18]

Paradoxically, it seems that the post-conciliar transformation implied too many human resources. This happened right around the time of the first serious demographic crisis of the Salesian personnel, the signs of which date back to the beginnings of the 60s.[19] Peter Braido noted that after the GC19, only at the global level, "there were nearly thirty structural units to be worked on: manuals and regulations to be composed, committees to be set up, centres and offices to be organized at the General Government level to be erected and studies on particular issues to be carried out".[20] To get to a certain decentralization, many resources were used in creating a more structured organization. The configuration of the Provincial Conferences (in geographical regions) was to be built and set up. Six years later, Luigi Ricceri evaluated the situation of the Salesian

---

[17] GC19 (1965), p. 6.
[18] GC19 (1965), pp. 9-10.
[19] See the letters of Fr. Ziggiotti in ACS 44 (1963) 233 and 234.
[20] BRAIDO, *Le metamorfosi dell'Oratorio Salesiano*, 336.

staff in terms of "serious and sometimes almost chronic haemorrhage suffered by various provinces, simultaneously with the ageing of personnel and the inability to cope any longer with tasks previously carried out".[21] In his estimation, "for every two to three Salesians one should be a leader".[22]

The most immediate effects of the GC19 in the educative-pastoral area was the election of Gaetano Scrivo, former superior of the Roman province, as the Councillor for Youth Ministry and the establishment of the Youth Ministry Centre in Turin with Michel Mouillard working as the delegate. The medium of information diffusion was the magazine *Note di Pastorale Giovanile* (Youth Ministry Notes), whose first issue was published in 1967.

The new term Youth Ministry was introduced to the GC19 and was applied in some decisions about general and regional structures. But the pre-conciliar "youth apostolate" mentality linked to the boarding schools was still shared by the majority of the confreres.[23] The change of mentality and the personalization evoked by Ricceri required more time and maturation. In 1982 the Rector Major Egidio Viganò made a remark in regard to this paradigm shift: "The perception of the needs of the Council was [...] rather limited; not all, in fact, had even had a chance to grasp the profound renewed ecclesiology of the Vatican II. However, the Chapter Assembly had breathed the atmosphere".[24] In that sense, some key principles of the youth ministry, such as respect for the young, the sense of freedom, social awareness, adherence to today's world, and the principle of graduality would be developed only in the '80s in terms of dimensions, methodology, tools and educational pastoral mentality.

---

[21] L. RICCERI, *Presentation of the "Report on the General State of the Congregation"*, in SGC (1972), p. 615.

[22] See *Idem*, p. 619.

[23] See S. FRIGATO, *Educazione ed evangelizzazione. La riflessione della Congregazione Salesiana nel Postconcilio*, in A. BOZZOLO – R. CARELLI (Eds.), *Evangelizzazione e educazione*, LAS, Roma 2011, pp. 70-72.

[24] VIGANÒ, *Il Capitolo Generale XXII*, 9.

One year after closing the Chapter, the Apostolic Letter Motu Proprio *Ecclesiae sanctae*, which announced a Special General Chapter (SGC) for all religious institutes, suspended the application of the ambitious conclusions of the GC19. All operational and creative efforts were shifted to the preparation of the Special General Chapter that stated after six years: "Much of GC19 remained on paper".[25] The greatest effects of GC19 were, therefore, the change of the Salesian General Chapter paradigm towards a greater openness and dialogue, the embracing of the Vatican II mentality, the simultaneous establishment of a global management structure that enabled more dialogue and participation (Regions), and finally giving value to experts-scholars in different fields of the Salesian life. The most worrisome side effect of the GC paradigm shift was expressed by Vecchi: "The GC19 did not have a satisfactory operational translation [...]; the mentality and the operational practice did not experience major changes at the grass root level of the Congregation".[26]

1.2 The Post-Vatican II and the Special General Chapter (1966-72)

The late 1960s were characterized by the growing self-awareness of the young who emerged as a new generation and a political force according to the underlying ideological-critical vision. This process was catalyzed by the phenomena of underdevelopment of the "third world"; oppression of the underprivileged; racial discrimination; wars for world domination; educational and cultural subordination to the economic systems. In the intellectual world, the Marxist ideology, the criticism of mass society dynamics of the Frankfurt School, and the critical pedagogy of the oppressed often linked with the theology of liberation resurfaced with new strength.

---

[25] SGC (1972), n. 393.
[26] J.E. VECCHI, *Pastorale, educazione, pedagogia nella prassi Salesiana*, in *Il cammino e la prospettiva 2000*, Documenti PG 13, SDB, Roma 1991, p. 10.

The *Zeitgeist* of that period was described as the "civil rights move-ment" in the USA, "contestation" in Italy and France, and in the Spanish-speaking countries a more "revolutionary" lexicon was used. The youth movement adopted an anti-establishment ethos fighting academic, indus-trial, and capitalist oppression. The ideal and utopian world to be built was seen through the lenses of participation, decentralization, dialogue, social awareness, freedom, justice and new ethics. There were different paradoxes, on the one hand, between the proclamation of the principle of dialogue and peace, and the actual ways of protesting and ideologically dividing the world into separate "classes" on the other. All these ideals and paradoxes were interpreted within the economic, technological and mass-media developments of the post-war period. After some years, the mid-1970s energy crisis tested strongly the utopian idealism of the move-ment's prospects. In the Salesian context, the post-Ricaldonian traditionalist Salesian mindset, the Vatican II paradigm shift and the proximity to the feelings of the young generation can explain the strong controversies of those years. The post-conciliar period can be effectively called a real crisis era in the Church and in the Salesian Congregation.[27]

1.2.1 The Crisis and the Special General Chapter Preparations

The Rector Major Luigi Ricceri (1965-77), the sixth successor of Don Bosco, gathered the results of the work done by his predecessors. In fact, in 1967 the Salesians reached the peak number of 21,614 members and 1,196 novices. But there was also a double crisis: one arising from the same world expansion of the Congregation, not always purified and con-trolled; and another deriving from the cultural and ecclesial context concurrent with the celebration of the Vatican II. Gradually, but inexo-rably, the new situation became evident in Europe and America. The

---

[27] See M. WIRTH, *Da Don Bosco ai nostri giorni. Tra storia e nuove sfide (1815-2000)*, LAS, Roma 2000, pp. 447-449; M. TOLOMELLI, *Il Sessantotto. Una breve storia*, Carocci, Roma 2008 e A. BERNHARD – W. KEIM (Eds.), *1968 und die neue Restaura-tion*, Jahrbuch für Pädagogik 2008, Peter Lang, Frankfurt am Main 2009.

1968 movement implied a contestation of young Salesians, which reached its peak during the years 1969-70. The Salesian Pontifical University in Rome became a visualizer of everything that was blistering in different countries, especially in Latin America.[28]

The crisis in the Salesian context was evident especially in the rapid decline in vocations and desertions of the Salesians during the formation and also increased priest laicization requests. The number of Salesians in the decade 1968-77 fell by about a quarter. The demographic crisis was only the most visible effect of a religious order that was in a strong process of transformation. On the one hand, there was the opening of new forms of apostolate, a substantial number of new initiatives in the pastoral field, especially in the context of dialogical opening to the world and the commitment for the underprivileged. On the other, there were lively discussions and polarizations between the "progressists" and the "fundamentalists" and, in the specific field of the youth ministry, between the "pastoralists" (new school) and the "educators" (old school).[29]

In the first six years of his mandate, Fr. Ricceri had concentrated his attention on the almost impossible realization of the conclusions of the GC19 and he made every effort to balance decentralization and unity in the Congregation.[30] We can state that the Congregation experienced the paradox of the "decentralization from the centre" which stands for the

---

[28] See R. ALBERDI – C. SEMERARO, *Società Salesiana di San Giovanni Bosco*, in G. PELLICCIA – G. ROCCA (Eds.), *Dizionario degli istituti di perfezione*, vol. 8, San Paolo, Roma 1988, pp. 1690-1691 and WIRTH, *Da Don Bosco ai nostri giorni*, p. 532.

[29] See WIRTH, *Da Don Bosco ai giorni nostri*, pp. 527-532; F. DESRAMAUT – M. MIDALI *L'impegno della Famiglia Salesiana per la giustizia*. Colloqui sulla vita Salesiana 7. Jünkerath 24-28 agosto 1975, LDC, Leumann (TO) 1976.

[30] In his abundant publication of letters, Luigi Ricceri defended his right and duty of directing, animating, and indicating the right way, promptly correcting the errors, reporting abuses, defining at times the right positions, so that everyone at a given moment can know the path to be walked on with the necessary clarity. See ACS 54 (1973) 269 and ACS 54 (1973) 270.

primary involvement of the hierarchy in the implementation of a complex decentralized model with some specific limits and guidelines decided in Rome.[31]

Roman directives were not followed automatically also under the influence of the decentralization paradox that produced a certain pushback from the provinces on the periphery. Riccardo Tonelli, the director of the magazine *Note di Pastorale Giovanile* (Youth Ministry Notes) and one of the prominent figures of the post-Vatican II Youth Ministry model stated: "These were the years of change. There was, in fact, the beginning and the consolidation of a very original model of culture, of reflection, and of socio-political planning [...] Of course, because of the urgency of the problems [...] it was not always easy to proceed with the necessary tranquility and balance".[32]

In the letter of October 1968, the Rector Major described a complex 9-stage and 15-step process which should be realized within the first months of 1971. An important step was the publication of the proposals sent by the Provincial Chapters held in 1969. The publication was edited by the pre-SGC Commissions, divided into four volumes, and published with the subtitle of *The X-ray of the Congregation*.[33] It gave an insight on the type of problems and on the prevailing mindset of the confreres. A majority of provinces expressed the idea of rethinking and restructuring, but the concrete implementation proposals differed in almost every province. The preferred ways of the restructuration were decentralization, expert consulting and rational planning, themes that returned like a refrain from different provinces. The editors of the *X-ray* noted that the

---

[31] See S. KÜHL, *Sisyphos im Management. Die vergebliche Suche nach der optimalen Organisationsstruktur*, Wiley, Weinheim 2002, pp. 36-39; 65-88 and 131-166.

[32] R. TONELLI, *Ripensando quarant'anni di servizio alla pastorale giovanile*, intervista a cura di Giancarlo De Nicolò, in «Note di Pastorale Giovanile» 43 (2009) 5, 14-15.

[33] See CGS-COMMISSIONI PRECAPITOLARI CENTRALI, *Ecco ciò che pensano i Salesiani della loro congregazione oggi. "Radiografia"* delle relazioni dei Capitoli Ispettoriali speciali tenuti in gennaio-maggio 1969, 4 vols, Istituto Salesiano Arti Grafiche, Castelnuovo D. Bosco (AT) 1969.

Provincial Chapters were continually talking about "integration", "coordination", "planning", and "projects". The decentralization of the government had to be established by setting up other institutions, departments, teams, groups and commissions, following the path opened by the GC19 in 1965.[34] Reflecting the climate of the time, there was an almost naive trust in planning, in scientific solutions and in dialogical confrontation, not taking into account the necessary human resources needed to make it all happen. This planning mindset was not only a Salesian "obsession", the aforementioned Pastoral Dictionary speaks very clearly: "By means of science and management, man is now able to plan, manipulate and change the environment and the society [...] These means are available also to the Church, in order to plan consciously the future and develop a proper strategy".[35] In those years as in GC19, the concrete Youth Ministry issues were almost completely sidelined. We consider it one of the paradoxes of the Vatican II "pastoral turning point" that was intended to be carried out through a new set of government and ministry structures and little was done about pastoral formation of the personnel.

1.2.2 Special General Chapter

The general goal of the SGC was to "rediscover in depth our own identity in the light of today's reality".[36] The specific purpose of the SGC was to formulate a new text of the Constitutions and Regulations that would conform to the Vatican II guidelines. Therefore, it is understandable that operational pastoral issues remained a secondary theme and the search for solutions was practically delegated to the provinces following the decentralization logic.

The identity of the Salesian educational and pastoral activity was expressed in terms "mission" and "ministry". The Mission referred

---

[34] See *Ecco ciò che pensano i Salesiani*, vol. 1, p. 108.
[35] HEPP, *Piano pastorale*, in RAHNER et al. (Eds.), *Dizionario di Pastorale*, p. 567.
[36] SGC (1972), p. VIII (The translation is ours in order to maintain the original meaning).

primarily to the salvation of the poor and abandoned young people without reference to the activities and structures, in order to emphasize its integrity in opposition with the variety of activities. The relationship between the mission and the pastoral ministry was defined as follows: "The 'pastoral ministry' is a practical realization of the mission under the guidance of the 'pastors'."[37] The Salesian Youth Ministry was further updated with the christocentric and ecclesiocentric views of the Vatican II. From this horizon, the SGC stated the absolute priority of the Youth Ministry with the need to update all activities, communities and structures according to this new "pastoral" mindset.[38] In the Acts of the SGC one can read some courageous formulations like: "the existence of a purely mechanical and pastorally inefficacious work which merely wears out the confreres is inadmissible".[39] The pastoral ministry became theoretically an integral key that connects human promotion and evangelization.[40]

As a first step, the Special Chapter participants needed a criterion for the renewal efforts in order to balance the return to the sources with the adaptation to the changed conditions of the times. This was found in the formula: "Don Bosco in the Oratory". It did not entail a reference to the concept of the oratory structure, but to the person of Don Bosco, who had carried out his ministry in the chronologically well-defined Valdocco Oratory. First it was a simple Sunday oratory, later it became the "Oratory" in its entirety, with a secondary school, vocational training centre, boarding facilities and annexed places for cultural and recreational free-time activities. The ideal criterion was represented by Don Bosco in the

---

[37] SGC (1972), n. 23. We are using the term "pastoral ministry" to unify the different translations of the Italian term *"pastorale"*. The English translation uses different terms: "pastoral action", "pastoral work" or "pastoral apostolate".

[38] See SGC (1972), n. 180.

[39] SGC (1972), n. 398 (The translation is ours in order to maintain the original meaning). The reference to an inefficacious work is to be linked to the traditional boarding houses. See FRIGATO, *Educazione ed evangelizzazione*, in BOZZOLO – CARELLI (Eds.), *Evangelizzazione e educazione*, p. 73.

[40] See SGC (1972), n. 61.

Oratory, in which the Oratory has to be intended as "the matrix, the synthesis, the sum total of all the genial apostolic creations of our Founder, the mature fruit of all his efforts"[41] and Don Bosco, "faithful and dynamic, docile and creative, firm but at the same time flexible at the same time stands out as a model of behaviour for all his sons".[42]

The Salesian rethinking effort in a pastoral key, according to the Council, and the accentuation of social engagement sidelined implicitly the concept of "education", which should be a distinctive characteristic of the Congregation according to the GC19. We agree with a posterior Vecchi's assessment of the SGC: "There are many educational ideas and inspirations scattered here and there. Still, many complements, mediations, and reorganizational efforts are needed to make the ideas become applicable by operators and embraced by beneficiaries".[43] Note also the varied use of the term "education" according to the context. It can be linked to evangelization, care, instruction or socialization, but it can also mean any type of intervention that requires a certain level of expertise. Despite the diminished importance of the educational dimension, we must acknowledge the importance of a newly introduced term of the "educative community", a term that will have its later development. As conceived by the SGC, the educative community was to be composed of Salesians, lay educators, young people and parents who regularly plan and review their action in a family atmosphere of co-responsibility.[44]

1.2.3 Application of the SGC guidelines

We can agree with Viganò that the SGC with its more than 200 days of work in the new headquarters in Rome was "an intense effort of the confreres to enter in a new mindset. It was certainly one of the strongest

---

[41] SGC (1972), n. 195.
[42] SGC (1972), n. 197.
[43] See VECCHI, *Pastorale, educazione, pedagogia*, in *Il cammino e la prospettiva 2000*, p. 18.
[44] See SGC (1972), n. 395.

moments of the Salesian community reflection in the history of the Congregation [...] It made a huge and largely successful work, even judged positively by non-Salesian scholars and specialists".[45]

The SGC emphasized the identity of the Salesians, following the renewal of the Vatican II, rather than the operational responses to the needs of youth. However, at the end of nearly every document there was a chapter called "operational guidelines". For example, the section dealing with the Salesian mission contained over 50 specific instructions. Some of them regarded the necessity of studies and qualification opportunities for confreres, the Youth Ministry structural change, the criteria for institutional downsizing, the creation of research and study centres, the creation of teams and planning of meetings at different levels. The difficulty of applying these conclusions was reinforced by the diversity of the content and the style of the SGC documents. The Rector Major Fr. Ricceri perceived this risk and in his presentation intervened against a manipulative use of the documents: "sometimes there may appear a lack of homogeneity, this in no way lessens their validity, for there is always a global oneness between the individual documents".[46] The application of numerous tasks was also operationally complicated because of the principle of decentralization, which left an "ample scope for the creativity and initiatives of the individual provinces".[47]

Another point of view on the execution of the SGC guidelines can be seen in the *Report on the State of the Congregation* from 1977 and in the Provincial Chapter reports. The descriptions present an image of many different initiatives that were poorly coordinated with the risk of dispersion or contrast among them. Some strong individuals or small groups acted as protagonists but it seems they failed to involve the majority of

---

[45] See VIGANÒ, *Il Capitolo Generale XXII*, pp. 10-11.
[46] SGC (1972), pp. X-XI. Interesting interpretation is to be noted in the translation of "*organicità*" as "oneness".
[47] SGC (1972), n. 759.

the communities in the provinces. It is understandable given the complexity of the youth phenomenon, pluralism of settings and different interpretation theories.

The "general institutional downsizing", which both GC19 and SGC insisted on, could have been the most concrete indicator of changes at different levels. After some years, Juan E. Vecchi interpreted the Report on the State of the Congregation and came to a strong conclusion: "The failed experience of a 'general downsizing' seems to bring the provinces towards a long-term progressive policy, which consists of partial reductions, developments and changes of communities; creation of some new service or human resources displacement".[48] It seems that new proposals and initiatives, which demanded new and prepared personnel, were simply added to the existing activities, sometimes producing only a deceptive façade change. Later, the GC23 in 1990 would resume the discussion on the new-old structures in a perspective of "significance". Recently, also the mid-term provincial chapters after the GC27 have had to discuss the criteria of "structures management" with an accent on the numerical consistency of the communities. It must be noted that long-term helplessness in the institutional resizing has led to the weakening of communities and to the work overload of the confreres active in different types of ministry. As seen by the Rector Major Luigi Ricceri, and often reaffirmed afterwards, the work overload often leads to activism and to a faith that is "rather epidermal, superficial, is only an information, an external fact, a cliché, that does not explode from the inside to become vitality".[49]

---

[48] VECCHI, *Verso una nuova tappa di PG Salesiana*, in *Il cammino e la prospettiva 2000*, p. 79.

[49] L. RICCERI, *Lettera del Rettor Maggiore*, in ACG 51 (1970) 260, 14. See also A. GIRAUDO, *Interrogativi e spinte della Chiesa del postconcilio sulla spiritualità Salesiana*, in C. SEMERARO (Ed.), *La spiritualità Salesiana in un mondo che cambia*, Salvatore Sciascia, Caltanissetta 2003, pp. 138-141.

1.3 Educative and Pastoral Project Logic of Viganò and Vecchi (1978-90)

GC21, held from the end of October 1977 until February 1978, could have brought to fruition some of the big number of proposals indicated by SGC. The previous turbulent six-year period was characterized by a non-coordinated rise of many initiatives despite the ongoing demographic crisis. With regard to the central structures, some developments can be mentioned. In 1973 the Salesian Pontifical Athenaeum became the Salesian Pontifical University (UPS), an intellectual centre that would play an important role in the '70s and '80s. Noteworthy is the European Conference on "Don Bosco's Educational System Between an Old and a New Pedagogy" with about 300 participants (some of them from America and Asia) and the "European Youth Week" which evaluated different educational and pastoral experiences.[50] In that period, the Centre for Don Bosco Studies at the UPS published 37 volumes of *Opere edite* that summed up all the works published by Don Bosco and, in this way, contributed to the deepening and sharing of knowledge about the Founder. In the logic of decentralization of the government, we could mention three meetings of Luigi Ricceri and some General Council members with the Provincials and delegates from different continents in 1975.

During the GC21, the seventh successor of Don Bosco was to be elected. In the second ballot Egidio Viganò, former Councillor for Formation, was chosen. Braido characterizes the personality of Viganò as a "multifaceted figure, a personality with lucid, penetrating intelligence and a strong disciplined passion; a visionary leader and an illuminated,

---

[50] See *Il sistema educativo di Don Bosco tra pedagogia antica e nuova*. Atti del convegno europeo Salesiano sul Sistema Preventivo di Don Bosco, svoltosi a Roma dal 31 dicembre 1973 al 5 gennaio 1974, LDC, Leumann (TO) 1974 and *A servizio dell'educazione. La Facoltà di Scienze dell'Educazione dell'Università Pontificia Salesiana*, a cura di G. Malizia ed E. Alberich, LAS, Roma 1984.

imaginative and firm legislator".[51] In his letters, the new Rector Major emphasized the rising of spiritual superficiality and proposed an apostolic interiority as a fruit of the "grace of unity". Already in the closing address to the GC21 he introduced the concept of the "oratorian heart", linking it with the spirit of initiative and pastoral creativity of every Salesian presence.[52] Thanks to his leadership and governance abilities, the Congregation became more peaceful and united in thought and in action as compared to the previous fifteen-year period.[53]

1.3.1 SEPP as the Actualization of the Preventive System

The work of GC21 focused on the Salesian education and youth ministry. The document "Salesians Evangelizers of the Young" can be considered as the first treatise on Salesian education and evangelization. In fact, the themes that had been developed by this Chapter determined the priority themes for the Chapters of the next three decades: the close relationship between education and evangelization; the Salesian community as the animating nucleus of the Educative and Pastoral Community (EPC); the Salesian Educative and Pastoral Project (SEPP); and the theme of oratorian "criterion" or "heart" developed particularly by Viganò in terms of preference for young people linked with the traditional Salesian motto *Da mihi animas, cetera tolle*.

The Chapter, recognizing "the actual risk of educational disaffection",[54] confirmed the close link between education and evangelization in reference to Don Bosco, the Salesian tradition and to *Evangelii Nuntiandi* (1975). The strong connection of the two moments was translated as a plan of practical commitment for the salvation of the young. "As sharers of the evangelizing activity of the Church we believe in Don

---

[51] BRAIDO, *Le metamorfosi dell'Oratorio Salesiano*, p. 350.
[52] See GC21 (1978), nn. 565-568.
[53] See WIRTH, *Da Don Bosco ai giorni nostri*, p. 466.
[54] FRIGATO, *Educazione ed evangelizzazione*, in BOZZOLO – CARELLI (Eds.), *Evangelizzazione e educazione*, p. 77.

Bosco's charism and hence in our particular way of evangelizing the young. This we do in a realistic way by means of the Salesian Educational Project, the 'Preventive System', rethought and reactivated".[55]

With regaining the educational dimension, which balanced the relationship between education and pastoral ministry, we see the emergence of an epistemological and methodological axiom for the following years: "We are well aware that education and evangelization are specifically distinct activities of their class, but there is nevertheless a strict connection between them on the practical plane of existence".[56] The document specifies that education and evangelization, "in themselves, are not chronologically successive, nor divergent, but they cover two major aspects of the human vocation, that is outlined in the plan of God." Riccardo Tonelli witnessed the risk to perceive education and evangelization in the logic of "before and after", which was unfortunately implemented in some contexts.[57] The risk of passing from autonomy to separation between education and evangelization is perceived in Viganò's letter about the SEPP. He recalls the need for unity of vocation, motivation, fundamental option for Christ, concrete action, proposing a practical possibility of a "Christian education".[58] The solution to bring together these two dimensions "on the practical level of existence" has been often neglected because of both diversity of the contexts in which the Congregation carries out its mission, and employing of the few remaining Salesians in organizational and administrative tasks.[59] Still it seems that the theme of the Salesian Educative and Pastoral Project was vital for its practical implications and attracted a lot of educators, pastors, scholars and leaders from the late '70s to the '90s. Let us now see the

---

[55] GC21 (1978), n. 14. See also nn. 4, 81 and 569.
[56] GC21 (1978), n. 14.
[57] See TONELLI, *Ripensando quarant'anni*, pp. 41-42.
[58] See E. VIGANÒ, *The Letter of the Rector Major Rev. Fr. Egidius Viganò on the Preventive System*, The Salesian Publication – The Citadel, Madras, pp. 40-60.
[59] See GC21 (1978), nn. 14 and 85.

beginnings and the development of the reflection about these very particular "projects" or "plans".

The rethinking of the Salesian education and youth ministry through
the SEPP was distributed by the General Chapter in the "content" section
(the situation, objectives and means of realization) and in a section about
the style and the "spirit" (the attitudes of educators and the characteristics
of the environment). As we will see in the next paragraphs, the first section had a good translation in a series of practical brochures (called
Handouts) published by the Youth Ministry Department under the guidance of the newly elected Councillor Juan Edmundo Vecchi. The second
section about the spirit or style, always vital to the Salesian Youth Ministry, was neglected and it seems that this lapse would lead to serious
questions and practical difficulties.

1.3.2 Salesian Educative and Pastoral Project as an Operational Tool

In the closing address of GC21 Viganò presented the Salesian Educative and Pastoral Project as a new understanding of the Preventive
System of Don Bosco. He did not see it exclusively from a theoretical
pedagogical perspective that only reorganizes the contents and the vocabulary: "If anyone were to think that this system is something only
theoretical or secondary, I do not hesitate to say that he would show very
clearly that he has understood neither the heart of Don Bosco nor the
sensitivity of the present moment for the Congregation".[60] The Rector
Major contemplated the Salesian Educative and Pastoral Project to be the
unifying point of the six-year plan. In this sense, he proposed to study, to
learn, to analyze the educational heritage of Don Bosco and to translate
it into practice in the areas or environments of the Salesian evangelization.[61]

---

[60] GC21 (1978), n. 569.
[61] See GC21 (1978), n. 571.

The GC21 once again emphasized the aspect of decentralization and attention to the unique realities of each context and the SEPP became its main instrument: "Every province (or group of provinces) will draw up an educational project suited to the local conditions as a basis for planning and evaluating its various works in line with the basic options made by the Congregation: oratories, youth centres, day and boarding schools, residences for students and artisans, parishes, missions, etc. To foster unity within decentralization, the Youth Ministry Department, in the light of the Salesian experience and self-evaluation, will draw up the broad outlines of this project (objectives, content, method, characteristics...) with due regard to the diversity of geographical and cultural situations".[62]

The dissemination of decisions and of information was designed by the Chapter in an obvious logic "from the centre to the periphery", starting from the Chapter's decisions, then continuing with the instructions of the Youth Ministry Department, with the subsequent processing of the Provincial SEPP and finally concluding the series with the work of a local SEPP. This logic is understandable in a Chapter assembly but it is not necessarily the best for specific purposes. It realized the paradox of "centralization through decentralization" with a number of practical implications that have been part of the later "impact history" of the Salesian project management mindset.[63] Having proposed the sequence of the implementation of projects from the largest structure to the smaller units has induced the Salesians to adopt an imitation (copy/paste) mindset. The General Chapter documents and decisions were often linguistically adjusted by the Provincial Chapters and the local SEPP often reproduced faithfully the contents of the Provincial project as the

---

[62] GC21 (1978), n. 105. N.B. in order to maintain uniformity of terms, we translated "plan" and "master plan" as "project", and "Department for the Youth Apostolate" as "Youth Ministry Department".
[63] See KÜHL, *Sisyphos im Management*, pp. 131-166.

community had to be tuned with it. We think that the mentality, the implications and the risks would have been definitely different, if the
proposed projects started locally and followed a more "inductive" logic.

Six months after the closing of GC21, the Rector Major sent a circular
letter which presented a summary of the Chapter's results regarding the
Salesian Educational and Pastoral Projects and reaffirmed that reassem-
bling "the synthesis of the preventive system at the level of ideas and of
praxis [...] is one of the programmatic requirements of the six-year period"[64] and it should include every Salesian and every community.
According to Viganò, the Salesian way of composing the SEPP means:
- "to call together individuals for study and reflection,
- to focus attention on the social and ecclesial phase of our work,
- to search with creativity ways and solutions of situations, [...]
- to unite the community with a unified criterion to which all members
  can aspire and by which each can recognize one another, [...]
- to assure integrity and to free ourselves from sectionalism and im-
  provisation".[65]

Juan Edmundo Vecchi, the Councillor for Youth Ministry elected
during GC21, noted that "since 1978, there is proliferation of motivation
literature, production of handouts and practical models. The first steps
involved the animation at the provincial level, which local communities
were struggling to adopt".[66]

---

[64] See VIGANÒ, *Letter on the Preventive System*, 1978, pp. 66-67.
[65] VIGANÒ, *Letter on the Preventive System*, 1978, pp. 67-68.
[66] Cfr. VECCHI, *Pastorale, educazione, pedagogia*, in *Il cammino e la prospettiva 2000*,
p. 26. The pastoral projects and planning experiences in a wider Church context were
very similar. Various dioceses elaborated projects for their youth ministry. The design,
however, was heterogeneous, the interventions were of different sizes and different
autonomy, sometimes they were the result of long preparation, sometimes they ap-
peared in the diocesan synods, were more extended or too synthetic. We can agree with
Giuseppe Angelini who, in 1979, spoke of the youth ministry in Italy as a "fine dust
cloud made of extremely varied practical experiences, very diversified and generally
poorly developed in theoretical-practical reflection". See G. ANGELINI, *Pastorale giovanile e prassi complessiva della Chiesa*, in FACOLTÀ TEOLOGICA DELL'ITALIA
SETTENTRIONALE, *Condizione giovanile e annuncio della fede*, La Scuola, Brescia

1.3.3 SEPP in the Youth Ministry Department Handouts (1978-80)

Various studies, manuals and handouts about the project management, produced by the Youth Ministry Department from the 1970s until today, have been influenced by the ambiguity of the multiple semantic functions of the word "project". The ambiguity of the term has two main sources: the use of the expression "project" in the Italian language and its dual use in the Salesian documents. These are, obviously, linked to the difficulty of translation into other languages. In Italian, the term "*progetto*" has two different denotations: a more precise one, signifying an ordered and detailed work plan; and the other, more indeterminate significance, understanding "project" as only a vague idea or a generic purpose for the future which can be hardly implemented in an operative way.

In the other Neo-Latin languages the word "project" retains both meanings, though in some cases the Salesian documents' translations choose "plan" or "design". Also, the semantic relationship between "project" and "*ideario*" was not always clear in the Salesian environments, especially in the Spanish-speaking countries. The Spanish word "*ideario*" which was also used by the GC21 does not have an Italian term that exactly matches.[67] It indicates the guiding principles of an Educational Project linked to an inspiring "memory", a term often used by Vecchi to indicate "tradition". A major problem is found in the English and German contexts where the terms "project" and "project management" have, almost exclusively, the sense of a structured and precise work plan with a clear methodology. In sciences of education the terms "educational design" or "instructional design" were also used. The German term for "project" is "*Projekt*", but the Salesians in the German-speaking countries adopted a more linguistically appropriate solution and

---

1979, p. 81. See also A. DEL MONTE, *Una Chiesa giovane per annunciare il vangelo ai giovani*, in «Il Regno-documenti» 3 (1979) 63-76 e G. COSTA, *Pastorale giovanile in Italia. Un dossier*, La Roccia, Roma 1981.
[67] See GC21 (1978), n. 84.

did not translate the term SEPP as *"Projekt"*, but as *"Pastoralkonzept"* (pastoral draft) or *"Leitlinien"* (guidelines). These terms express better the very nature of the documents produced in the Salesian contexts under the name of "project".[68]

We can also note that the use of the term "project" in the Salesian environments emphasizes two different aspects. GC21, on the one hand, stressed the theoretical aspect, so the Salesian educational project was envisioned as a re-interpretation of the Preventive System of Don Bosco;[69] and on the other hand, it highlighted the operational and practical application that examines programming of goals, processes, strategies and means.[70] We consider critically the Salesian term "project" as a conceptual container in which the quantity of the contents is inversely proportional to the accuracy required by the operational needs of the project management methodology.[71]

Handout No.1: Methodology of the SEPP (1978)

The first Youth Ministry Handout was published in December 1978, ten months after the closing of the GC21. Prior to more detailed studies, this document should have been fairly simple in order to accompany the

---

[68] For the ambivalences and the background of the term "project" see G. MORANTE, *Progetto educativo*, in Z. TRENTI et al. (Eds.), *Religio. Enciclopedia tematica dell'educazione religiosa*, Piemme, Casale Monferrato (AL) 1998, pp. 752-753. For the importance of cultural diversity paradigm in project management and leadership see the in-depth analysis in R.D. LEWIS, *When Cultures Collide. Leading across cultures*, Nicholas Brealey International, Boston ³2006, pp. 3-80.

[69] See GC21 (1978), nn. 14, 4 and 81.

[70] See GC21 (1978), nn. 105 and 127-161.

[71] As an emblematic example see the letter of E. VIGANÒ, *Riprogettiamo insieme la santità*, in ACS 63 (1982) 303, 3-28, which uses the Italian term "progetto" in expressions such as: there is to re-*project* our holiness together; man as *project* willed by God; re-*project* in us the capacity for conversion, expiation and prevention; a larger *project* in which God intervenes as Father: it is a vast *project* of love and victory; *project* of the Father; divine *project* of redemption, etc.

"first steps towards a project".[72] The text, containing 25 pages plus the addendum, is brief but substantial and the composition reveals the expert touch of the Councillor Juan E. Vecchi. As an education sciences scholar and the Regional Councillor of South America, Vecchi had abundant experience in educational projects and curriculum design.

Although the Congregational "Big Scheme" had a top-down structure starting with the General Chapters and descending to the local communities, Vecchi's proposal privileged the Provincials and their Youth Ministry delegates to play the role of promoters and facilitators of the local community SEPP. Comparing the Handout to Vecchi's lecture at a 1978 conference on the Preventive System, we understand the theoretical framework of the document.[73] He emphasizes the real dynamics in the communities and the necessary integration of the "bottom-up" logic. The Provincial Animator of the SEPP had to put into action a provincial animation group with the following tasks: engage, enlighten, motivate, indicate methodologies, facilitate, that is, to help those who do not know how to proceed, formulate conclusions and send them back to the confreres to enhance the learning process.[74] With a healthy realism the Handout proposes a project that has only provisional formulations and which evolves dynamically, not following a regulation mindset, but seeing the aim of "helping the groups to operate consciously, carefully, with a shared responsibility".[75]

---

[72] See DICASTERO PER LA PASTORALE GIOVANILE, *Progetto Educativo Pastorale. Metodologia*, Sussidio 1, [s.e.], Roma 1978, p. 3.
[73] See J.E. VECCHI, *Per riattualizzare il Sistema Preventivo*, in ISPETTORIA SALESIANA LOMBARDO-EMILIANA [ILE], *Convegno sul Sistema Preventivo*, Milano-Bologna 3-4 novembre 1978, [s.e.], [s.l.] [s.d.] and *Le principali difficoltà emerse dal dibattito sulla relazione di don J.E. Vecchi*, in ILE, *Convegno sul Sistema Preventivo*, 1978. See also the conclusion of the conference about the project logic, "not from a superior position of power (authority) neither from a superior professional position (experts)", in A. VIGANÒ, *Alcuni punti fondamentali riaffermati dal convegno sul Sistema Preventivo* in ILE, *Convegno sul Sistema Preventivo*, 1978.
[74] See DICASTERO PER LA PG, *Metodologia*, Sussidio 1, p. 6.
[75] *Idem*, p. 8.

The second part of the Handout speaks about the elements of the "Salesian memory" that constitute a SEPP framework. It returns to Don Bosco and his educative and pastoral legacy that "configures our identity". In nine points, with references to documents, it offers a practical and brief summary of the Youth Ministry as conceived by the previous two General Chapters:

- Starting point: love for the young and the consciousness of a mission;
- Subject of the action: Educational Community;
- Fundamental attitude: being in tune with young people;
- Educational methodology criterion: prevention;
- Educational understanding: education as a total service;
- Unifying focus: holistic salvation of the young in Christ;
- Proposal: itinerary towards Christian maturity;
- Constant dimension in the educational process: vocational discernment;
- Some shared options for the educational praxis: educational environment, personal relationship, appeal to the inner forces of the young, groups and associations, assistance.[76]

The third part of the Handout offers some practical methodological suggestions for the process of project development. The methodology proposes a set of stimulating questions for reflection dividing the SEPP into three stages: situation analysis; operational planning; and assessment of the project.

The *analysis of the situation* stage starts the planning process from the understanding of the situation of the youth. It is not just a statistic and an objectifying description of the context, but it must also include the experience of young people, trends, opinions, aspirations and, as a counterpart, the answers that the Educative and Pastoral Community gives to these challenges. The situation has to be interpreted from a faith-based

---

[76] *Idem*, pp. 10-13.

point of view: "We must therefore assess the facts according to their ability to make it easier or more difficult for the young to grow in both the humanity and the faith".[77] In this way the GC21 guidelines were implemented linking education with evangelization in the interpretation phase of the planning. Yet, in this model, a fundamental dimension which characterizes the situation was not considered. It is the resource analysis of the EPC, of the young and of the institution. Paradoxically, in a time of the Salesian demographic crisis, the possibility of failure to provide the necessary resources was not considered. This omission could be interpreted within a typical anthropology of the '70s that emphasized the future and did not look to the past or to the present. As we will see in the next chapter, only a few decades later the project management scholars gave more importance to the "human resources management" aspiring to obtain balance between "production" and "production capacity".

The second step consists in *operational planning*. It proposes the first objective of the formation and the development of the Educative and Pastoral Community. The next objectives should be the main educational and pastoral choices. To express the objectives with sufficient clarity, the EPC should: give a description of the desired results at the end of the process; determine the priority of the objectives based on fundamental values and on the situation's needs; formulate specific, clear and communicable secondary objectives. It seems that the objectives set in this way tend to accentuate the clarity and measurability of the typical Management by Objectives (MBO) of the '70s. In the Handout No.1, the attention to the "educational style", the "spirit of the project", the educator's attitudes (virtues) and characteristics of the environment have been put aside although these themes occupy an important part of the GC21 document. Handout No.2 later tried to repeat a study on educational style, but it was only an additional patch that did not fit into the linear

---

[77] *Idem*, p. 14. See also GC21 (1978), n. 13 that refers to PAULUS VI, *Evangelii Nuntiandi* (1975), n. 19.

logic of analysis-planning-assessment.[78] In this way, we can see why these themes were not included in the planning mindset.

The third and final step of the project cycle consists in *assessment*. The project must be checked according to two perspectives that are mutually enriching. The first one is the evaluation of all parts of the project with the Salesian tradition. The second perspective examines the obtained results according to the planned objectives, thus assessing the operational efficiency of the project.

Handout No. 1 was to accompany the first steps of the Salesian Educational and Pastoral Project in the communities. Despite its thinness, different omissions and a very simple appearance, it is a little gem of Vecchi's first synthesis on this topic. The methodology of the project cycle in the analysis-planning-assessment logic has remained unchanged, with small additions, until now. The logic of the animation process at the provincial level maintained the balance between investment in people and the tasks of planning, between the role of the animation group and the involvement of the communities. What is also interesting is the integration of the systemic logic in the paragraph on the EPC seeing it as a whole and thus as a community. Vecchi had put it this way: "Often when we speak of the Preventive System, we do not go beyond the individual perspective: it is easy to think of one educator [...] It is more difficult to grasp and implement what the word SYSTEM means, i.e., convergence and mutual reference, the organic nature of many elements".[79] He expressed the systemic-circular relationship between the project and the community with two slogan-titles: "The Educational Community produces a Project" and "A Project creates Community".[80] It seems that in Vecchi's mindset the systemic-holistic logic balanced the linear-operational logic of the project management. However, as we shall

---

[78] See DICASTERO PER LA PASTORALE GIOVANILE, *Elementi e linee per un progetto educativo pastorale Salesiano*, Sussidio 2, [s.e.], Roma 1979, pp. 13-14.
[79] VECCHI, *Per riattualizzare il Sistema Preventivo*, in ILE, *Convegno sul Sistema Preventivo*, p. 1.
[80] *Idem*, pp. 5 and 7.

see in the following paragraphs, the history of the SEPP did not go in the direction of this equilibrium and the authors focused more on the linear operational objectives logic pressed by needs of concrete situations or, following a different mindset, they lost themselves in exuberant logorrheic copy-paste projects in order to be legally in line with the newest Salesian Magisterium.

Handout No.2: Elements and Guidelines for the SEPP (1979)

The second Handout, entitled "Elements and Guidelines", was produced by the Youth Ministry Department in October 1979, just ten months after the publication of the first one. Of course the time was too short for an evaluation of the educational and pastoral impact of the projects in the field. In that sense, the feedback from the provinces was based mainly on reading the written provincial projects or drafts. Given the heterogeneity of the SEPPs examined in the Department and the diversity of interpretations on what should be an educational project, Handout No.2 focused on the organization of the written text, and it paid attention to the technical precision of the steps of the project cycle.[81] The nucleus is defined as follows: "The Handout will be used to organize the raw material of a project, to give an idea of the areas of the main concern for our project".[82] Attention to the "content" or the "final product" tends to marginalize attention to the "process" of planning and to the systemic dynamics within the local Educative and Pastoral Community and the Provincial Animation Team.[83]

In many points Handout No.2 clarified the issues in continuity with the previous one: "Having made its fortune, the word [educational project] is likely to be wrought in multiple and generic sense and, therefore,

---

[81] See the presentation in DICASTERO PER LA PG, *Elementi e linee*, Sussidio 2, pp. 5-7.
[82] *Idem*, p. 5
[83] As we will describe in the second chapter, there are three fundamental project management paradigms: 1. Project is a "product", 2. Project is a "process", 3. Project is an "identity".

not to serve as clarification on one issue. For this reason, we would like to illuminate the technical sense and the different scope of the three terms that indicate different levels of realization":[84]

1. *The frame of reference*, understood as a set of ideal guiding principles on anthropology, theory of education, objectives and methods that can be integrated into the project in the form of "guidelines".

2. *The educational project* as a general plan of action that indicates the operational objectives, proposes specific implementing courses of action with their means and creates the roles and functions.

3. *The programming* defined as the moment of task management in terms of personnel, time and place.

The central part of Handout No.2 describes five areas of intervention: Educative and Pastoral Community; education and culture; evangelization and catechesis; vocational guidance; and social experience. For each area, the guidelines describe the overall objective and specific objectives, criteria[85] and intervention choices. The roles and functions of the personnel were developed in the next Handouts because of their dependence on a particular educational structure (school, parish, oratory).

The division into five areas introduced a real risk of losing contact with the overall Salesian priorities and criteria. As some studies suggest,

---

[84] DICASTERO PER LA PG, *Elementi e linee*, Sussidio 2, p. 6.

[85] Handout No.2 introduces a new methodological category, called "criterion", defining it in a very generic sense: "The criteria [...] help us to achieve the goals and to put into practice the guidelines in a given situation". This definition differs from the common sense of the term criterion that stands for "a principle for evaluating, judging or discerning". As the Provincial SEPPs of the '90s are demonstrating, the criteria were not a methodological principle that guides the design, the discernment and the assessment. They became one of the many so-called "operational elements" such as "educational intervention", "activities", "educational experience", "action line", "intervention choice" or "concrete line of work". The high number of criteria combined with the semantic ambiguity often created a big confusion at the text level that could induce an operational paralysis. See DICASTERO PER LA PG, *Elementi e linee*, Sussidio 2, pp. 5; 20-22; 28-30; 35-39; 46-48; 53-55 and DICASTERO PER LA PASTORALE GIOVANILE, *Il Progetto Educativo-Pastorale Salesiano. Raccolta antologica di testi*, Dossier PG 9, SDB, Roma 1995.

the division of interventions and activities into distinct areas can lead to fragmentation of the educational and pastoral mission.[86] The division of the project areas, moreover, multiplies the content of the project, which makes it too long at the level of the text and too problematic to be put into practice. If we count the guidelines, objectives, criteria and intervention choices for the five areas, we can get to 250 elements interconnected at various levels. This high number of elements could also grow as the authors expected that "the individual elements will be further elaborated by the provincial communities".[87]

Summarizing, we can state that Handout No.2 increased the attention of the Salesians to the correct wording, to the compositional linguistic ability and introduced the division into five areas of intervention. It lost the attention to the processual variables (e.g. the Provincial Animation Team is not mentioned); to the execution of a project; and to the convergence among areas, or dimensions.

Handouts No. 3a, 3b, 3c: Parishes, Oratories, Schools

The third series of Handouts, published in November 1980, were explicitly "more a series of tips than of mandatory requirements",[88] though they were referring to the Constitutions, the Regulations and different General Chapter conclusions. The Handouts, therefore, combined some compulsory elements and some practical suggestions. Every Handout of this series had its own structure that tried to adapt to the specific type of

---

[86] See e.g. G. ANGELINI, *Il vincolo ecclesiastico, la pratica religiosa, la fede cristiana*, in G. AMBROSIO et al., *Progetto pastorale e cura della fede*, Glossa, Milano 1996, pp. 38-39. For a more organizational approach see P.M. SENGE, *The Fifth Discipline. The art and practice of the learning organization*, Doubleday, New York [2]2006.

[87] DICASTERO PER LA PG, *Elementi e linee*, Sussidio 2, p. 5.

[88] DICASTERO PER LA PASTORALE GIOVANILE, *Elementi e linee per un Progetto Educativo-Pastorale nelle parrocchie affidate ai Salesiani*, Sussidio 3a, [s.e.], Roma 1980, pp. 3-4.

activity. A common point was the discussion about the definition of objectives and lines of action; an another point was the omission of both
evaluation and the "criteria".

Handout 3a is addressed to the parishes entrusted to the Salesians.
After a description of the Church model and of the Salesian parish characteristics, it is divided into three parts: the parish as a community; the
parish for youth; and the parish as a centre of evangelization and education. The SEPP design in the Salesian oratories is the aim of Handout 3b
which describes the typical oratorian aspects of education and youth ministry linked with the Educative and Pastoral Community model. Handout
3c, speaking about the ministry in schools, is divided into three parts,
namely, the EPC, the educational and cultural dimension, and the dimension of evangelization and catechesis.

We can note a quite heterogeneous presence of the SEPP's five areas
in the third series of Handouts. A common characteristic is to describe
the EPC in a separate chapter. The areas of education, evangelization and
social experience are sometimes explicit as a chapter, other times they
are implicit in small allusions scattered in different parts of the text. The
area of vocational discernment is reduced to a few sentences and in this
way virtually neglected. The next Handout No.4, released in September
1981, proposed an essential outline for a Provincial Plan for Vocations
to bridge this gap, but it was presented as a separate category designed
and organized centrally by the Province, not by the local communities.[89]

1.4 Collaboration between the Youth Ministry Department and the UPS (1980-88)

The joint effort between the Department for YM and the Faculty of
Education of the Salesian Pontifical University began with a series of
meetings in January 1979, in which the common interest in the study of

---

[89] See DICASTERO PER LA PASTORALE GIOVANILE, *Lineamenti essenziali per un Piano Ispettoriale di Pastorale Vocazionale*, Sussidio 4, [s.e.], Roma 1981.

certain points of the Preventive System in connection with the SEPP emerged. This collaborative effort began with a series of conferences and publications. The most significant ones on the themes of educative and pastoral project management and leadership were: the Seminar on "Planning Education Today with Don Bosco" held in 1980,[90] the publication of *Modular Elements of the Salesian Educational Project*[91] in 1984, and the Conference on "Educative and Pastoral Practice and the Sciences of Education" organized on the eve of Don Bosco Centenary celebrations, in 1987.[92]

1.4.1 Seminar on "Planning Education Today with Don Bosco"

The first workshop, held in Rome with the participation of 35 scholars and pastoral agents from Europe, faced some problematic aspects of the SEPP. The primary difficulty was the ambiguity of the concept and the practice of the "project". Vecchi states in the presentation of the Acts: "It is, at times, a small treatise, a declaration of principles, a lecture on an educational problem with some practical advice, an exhortation to put certain guidelines into practice".[93] The second perceived problem stemmed from an "inadequate cultural preparation [...] We face difficulties in the understanding of the historical components in which the core of the Preventive System is offered".[94] The path to be walked in order to find a solution was the systematic and scientific study of the Preventive System seen as a guarantee of pastoral creativity and fidelity. The seminar moved in advancing the line of thought and offering insights on the

---

[90] See R. GIANATELLI (Ed.), *Progettare l'educazione oggi con Don Bosco*, Seminario promosso dal Dicastero per la Pastorale Giovanile della Direzione Generale "Opere Don Bosco" in collaborazione con la Facoltà di Scienze dell'Educazione dell'Università Pontificia Salesiana Roma 1-7 giugno 1980, LAS, Roma 1981.

[91] See J.E. VECCHI – J.M. PRELLEZO (Eds.), *Progetto Educativo Pastorale. Elementi modulari*, LAS, Roma 1984.

[92] See J.E. VECCHI – J.M. PRELLEZO (Eds.), *Prassi educativa pastorale e scienze dell'educazione*, SDB, Roma 1988.

[93] J.E. VECCHI, *Presentazione*, in GIANATELLI (Ed.), *Progettare l'educazione oggi*, p.14.

[94] *Ibidem.*

following topics: loving kindness in the educational relationship; Educative and Pastoral community management; education for freedom; sexuality; social and political commitment; evangelization; liturgy; sense of the Church; and vocational orientation. The third mentioned difficulty to be faced was practical in nature: the confreres' preference for individual educational interventions without seeking the convergence with the community.

The different lectures, although declaring ta goal to target practical applications, were general and theoretical in nature proposing theoretical models of interpretation, documents to be taken into account and structures to be implemented. We can note lack of an organic linkage of different lectures and the absence of a concrete methodological application. An important theme was the Educative and Pastoral Community prepared by Riccardo Tonelli that focused more on principles than on their procedural and methodological translation. Tonelli's synthesis gives us different insights into the mindset of the '80s: "Each community creates its own structures for discussion and dialogue. Once affirmed the necessity, we can offer only examples from a fairly widespread educational tradition: councils at different levels, assemblies, planning methods, goal setting and assessment methodologies, decision making and coordination structures... It is convenient to recall that the proper exercise of these participatory structures requires technical expertise, to be acquired through the study of specialized disciplines (e.g. group dynamics, or the socio-cultural animation). The respect and trust in these technical tools are a precise requirement for all Salesians, as it is a logical consequence of the close relationship between education (and related sciences of education) and evangelization".[95] As a result, methodological issues are considered a question of technical expertise and confidence in the "technical apparatus" is required in the name of an epistemological axiom. As it was usual for pastoral theorists, Tonelli did not discuss the

---

[95] R. TONELLI, *Impostazione della comunità educativa in un contesto pluralista*, in GIANATELLI (Ed.), *Progettare l'educazione oggi*, p. 83.

differences between various models of participative group management. The "participative" label was given importance because it differed from the old "hierarchical" leadership model. In the other lectures of the seminar, there were parts dedicated to meeting some operational requirements, but they were either ad hoc interventions facing the old collegial mentality or an intelligent copy of the Salesian or Ecclesial operational guidelines.

The "Planning Education with Don Bosco" seminar showed the Salesian adaptation of the "leadership through management" paradigm of the organizational sciences of the '70s and early '80s.[96] It brought the feeling of touch with the modern world, although it widened the gap between the content and the method of the Salesian education. The content about loving kindness, proximity in the educative relationship and the importance of group animation should have been carried out through technical skills of a project management team. The last trend to be noted in this seminar is the rise of the experts, seen as scholars or technicians, thus breaking away with the tradition of "educational practitioners" that dated back to Don Bosco.

1.4.2 Publication of "Modular Elements of the Salesian Educational Project"

The volume tried to answer the difficulty of the educative and pastoral projects, expressed by Vecchi as follows: "Once you understand the dynamics and learn the techniques, you realize that the real difficulties are at the roots. They originate in the fundamental understanding of some key points concerning education and the youth ministry".[97] Instead of understanding the Youth Ministry as a whole, we think that the academic

---

[96] See M. WITZEL, *A History of Management Thought*, Routledge, Abingdon 2012, pp. 198-218 and G.P. QUAGLINO (Ed.), *Leadership. Nuovi profili di leader per nuovi scenari organizzativi,* Raffaello Cortina, Milano 2005.
[97] J.E. VECCHI, *Presentazione*, in VECCHI – PRELLEZO, *Elementi modulari*, p. 5.

approach strengthened the division into different dimensions. The volume of *Educative and Pastoral Project: Modular Elements* published in 1984 is a fine example of scholarly compartmentation.

The publication constitutes a mini-encyclopedia of the Salesian education and Youth Ministry divided in 34 themes that followed the same structure: the definition of the term with conceptual or historical references; the importance of the theme; the essential contents; and bibliography. The goal of the volume was not to present practical strategies, but to broaden the sensitivity and form a mentality by offering "a safe and substantially complete framework"[98] on the key issues of the SEPP. Experts in the theological, philosophical, psychological, sociological and educational field cover the development of the themes following the basic elements of a project: general issues, objectives, methods, subjects of action and environments. Specific aspects of project methodology are treated in the modules connected to the area of school education, leaving aside the fields of the oratory, parish, vocation discernment or missionary activities. The link between the project and the school pedagogy was again confirmed by Vecchi: "The terms project and plan did not enter in the pedagogical language until recently [...] This seems due especially to the developments in the sciences of education area, in which the need emerged more clearly of an organic connection between the different requirements of the complex process of the personality development. The decisive push was given by the didactics that introduced the concept of the curriculum".[99]

Another intent of Vecchi was to harmonize various elements of the project, reflecting the fragmented situation of the young and of the society. In this sense the SEPP should propose: a single coherent framework

---

[98] *Idem*, p. 8.
[99] J.E. VECCHI, *Progetto educativo pastorale*, in VECCHI – PRELLEZO, *Elementi modulari*, p. 15.

of values, an organic vision of convergent interventions, and a convergence of roles and execution.[100] The rhetoric highlights interdisciplinary approaches, convergence of instruments and interventions, but the meta-message of the volume seems to be the division into separated modules in fragmentation of themes, instruments, theories and vocabulary of the different sciences. Also the module about the "integral promotion" written by Giuseppe Groppo, which could be unitary *par excellence*, is made up of too many distinctions and subsections. It seems that this disjointedness has to be linked to the nature of science that tends to be specialized in a particular area and is necessarily fragmented. The question arises, therefore, whether the scientific-technical approach is the best tool for achieving holistic education.

The authors' attention to recent developments in the field of education and the youth ministry gives an overall broad vision. The widening of perspectives comes at the cost of losing the specificity of the Salesian tradition. The Salesian identity of the SEPP is present only in one module redacted by Vecchi which links the historical development of the Preventive System with the current experiences of education and youth ministry. His module is an excellent summary of the Salesian education but it is a stand-alone unit that does not permeate, as an underlying paradigm, the rest of the publication.

Among the potentially interesting theoretical references on the planning methodology and project management, we can list the theories of catechesis developed by Emilio Alberich and Giuseppe Groppo; the animation theory developed by Mario Pollo, Riccardo Tonelli and Aldo Ellena; the value education proposed by Pietro Gianola and theories of leadership cited by Pio Scilligo. We will attempt a deeper analysis of the positions of these authors in the second chapter of this study in order to grasp the theoretical background of the SEPP.

---

[100] *Idem*, pp. 16-19.

1.4.3   Conference on "Educative and Pastoral Practice and the Sciences of Education"

The Conference was held on the occasion of the Don Bosco's centenary celebrations in 1988 and addressed two fundamental issues: the fragmentation of different educative approaches and the widening gap between the scientific and practical approaches to the youth ministry. Unlike the previous initiatives, the conference promoted the "dialectic convergence between theory and practice",[101] between scholars and the educative sensitivity of the operators. The seminar involved a hundred SDBs and FMAs from thirty different contexts. The reports were structured in four parts: the historical perspective, the current situation, new questions, and finally proposals and guidelines.

In an interesting contribution, the sociologist Giancarlo Milanesi analyses the use of educational sciences in three significant Salesian pedagogical experiences: the shoeshine boys of Rome, the reeducation home in Arese (Milan), and the experience of Bosconia-la Florida in Colombia. He noted an essentially eclectic and functional use of educational sciences. The Salesians in the selected experiences juxtaposed the originality of the Salesian approach with an exclusive psychological one, selecting only some techniques or methods, while remaining critical of the anthropological assumptions of the individual sciences. As for educational and pastoral planning, in the first two experiments, Milanesi observed a lesser influence of the science education in the formulation of the project. If it was used, it was only *ex post* to justify the already established educational choices. The design work of Bosconia-la Florida, which is considered as the most explicitly connected with a theoretical framework, is described as focused on the people involved in the programme, the theory, the objectives, strategies and assessment.

---

[101] J.E. VECCHI – J.M. PRELLEZO, *Introduzione*, in VECCHI – PRELLEZO, *Prassi educativa pastorale e scienze dell'educazione*, p. 6.

Eclecticism was present also in Bosconia, but unlike the other works, there it was presented as intended and justified.[102]

The theme of the educational and pastoral projects is only treated directly in Vecchi's reflection. He saw planning as an educational tool in the age of complexity. Provinces that use the SEPP are characterized by the first fruits: greater convergence between evangelization and education; educative environment management; attention to the needs of the young and; last but not least, innovation of the contents and of the methodology. Vecchi analyzed the data of the Provincial visits and the *Report on the State of the Congregation* and concluded that the Provinces had only arrived at an early stage of progress in the area of the educative and pastoral projects. For the most part, he noted, the SEPPs were almost absent in local communities.

Other interventions address the issues of epistemological diversity; the need for an operational synthesis that would involve clear choices; the need for a new ministry for the secularized young people; the rethinking of the Salesian associations in the light of the cultural changes; the promotion of teaching and educational skills; the lifelong learning attitude, etc. The proposals resembled more a set of desires or a brainstorming list than a systematic plan. The SEPP was seen as a concrete application of the sciences of education at the practical level. Similar to other proposals, there were only some generic cues, like "enhance and deepen the SEPP [...]; support the validity and centrality of education assessment at all levels; apply a model of institutional analysis to our context".[103]

The conference, which ended a decade of close collaboration between the UPS and the YM Department, noted the existence of two existential and mental "worlds". The first was composed mainly of scholars, who

---

[102] See G. MILANESI, *L'utilizzo delle scienze dell'educazione nell'impegno dei Salesiani per i giovani "poveri, abbandonati, pericolanti"*, in VECCHI – PRELLEZO, *Prassi educativa pastorale e scienze dell'educazione*, pp. 89-115.

[103] *Sintesi dei lavori e conclusioni*, in VECCHI – PRELLEZO, *Prassi educativa pastorale e scienze dell'educazione*, p. 326.

were fairly critical of the educational and pastoral practices, expressing their point of view by highlighting "the need for qualifying the Salesian educational action at all levels".[104] The second "world" was broader and more connected with the daily life of the Salesian works. Viganò stated: "In the present moment of expansion and acceleration of the educational changes, we see the lack of the ability to take on the renewal of content, structures and know-how determined by the cultural evolution in order to make with competence the right choices".[105] The future development of the 1990s seems to indicate a gradual consolidation of the gap between these two "worlds".

1.4.4 Evaluation of the SEPP implementation in the '80s

In the '80s the Salesians of Don Bosco invested many efforts and energies in the educative and pastoral projects development. Progress has been made with the SEPP tool, but unfortunately some shadows were present from the beginning, especially on the practical or operational level. Juan E. Vecchi described the final image as a "gap between the amount of proposals and the ability to implement them".[106] There are different aspects of the little operational translation of the SEPP to be pointed out:
- Stages of implementation were too short. A continuous succession of new proposals has blocked a real assimilation of the SEPP mindset in provinces and rendered impossible the translation into everyday practice. Viganò's motto "to move from paper to life"[107] pointed to the

---

[104] *Idem*, p. 327.
[105] E. VIGANÒ, *La Società di S. Francesco di Sales nel sessennio 1978-83*, in VECCHI, *Pastorale, educazione, pedagogia nella prassi Salesiana*, in VECCHI – PRELLEZO, *Prassi educativa pastorale e scienze dell'educazione*, p. 148.
[106] See VECCHI, *Verso una nuova tappa di PG*, in *Il cammino e la prospettiva 2000*, p. 88.
[107] VIGANÒ, *Opening address*, in GC22 (1984), n. 19.

necessary (but missing) internalization, the danger of the spiritual mediocrity and the weakening of Salesian identity;[108]

- In some regions the SEPP planning has produced only a change of a few terms leaving untouched the previous pastoral mindset;[109]
- Educational and pastoral planning "involves in the first place the SEPP animators at provincial level, while local communities are struggling to adopt it";[110]
- The variety of proposals to be carried out created a dispersion in too many commitments obstructing the desired integration and unity of the Educative and Pastoral Community;
- Suggestions in the field of the Youth Ministry were only "general encouragements, not innovative decisive and operational structural pressures, which would apply to persons, resources and mandatory guidelines [...] The Ministry is considered only an object of 'animation' and not a field of government decisions";[111]
- The communities had to accelerate learning processes in an era that required stable and deep convictions and operational mindset;[112]
- The work of the YM Department in the General Headquarters, the regional YM centres and provincial teams was not coordinated. The teams were more concerned for the presence of their publications on the market, than for the implementation of the directions. Problematic

---

[108] See *La società di san Francesco di Sales nel sessennio 1984-1990*, pp. 151-159. See also VECCHI, *Verso una nuova tappa di PG*, in *Il cammino e la prospettiva 2000*, p. 88 and A. GIRAUDO, *Interrogativi e spinte della Chiesa del postconcilio sulla spiritualità Salesiana*, in SEMERARO (Ed.), *La spiritualità Salesiana*, pp. 142-143.

[109] See CHÁVEZ, *Salesian Youth Ministry*, pp. 9-10.

[110] VECCHI, *Pastorale, educazione, pedagogia nella prassi Salesiana*, in *Il cammino e la prospettiva 2000*, p. 2.

[111] *La società di san Francesco di Sales nel sessennio 1984-1990*, pp. 155-157.

[112] See VECCHI, *Verso una nuova tappa di PG*, in *Il cammino e la prospettiva 2000*, p. 88 and *La società di san Francesco di Sales nel sessennio 1984-1990*, p. 156.

communication channels and also the lack of personnel in the structures of animation have to be noted;[113]

- The ambiguity and multiplicity of directions was increased by the differences of the contexts and in this way an unidirectional proposal was impossible;[114]

- The Youth Ministry proposals were separated from and neglected the vocational dimension, as can be seen in the GC21 document structure and in the YM Handouts' theme structuration.[115]

There were also some paradoxical or unwanted effects. The excessive amount of the Youth Ministry proposals combined with the fruitful cooperation between the YM Department and the UPS, has led to an undesired side effect: a widening gap between the "world of the experts" that does not care about the slowness of mentality change, and the "world of practitioners" immersed in the everyday practical problems.

A loss in the integrality or wholeness of the SEPP can be noted in the division into five areas within the SEPP in Handout No. 2 (1979) and in the thirty modules of the Pastoral Educational Project (1984) that reflected the different specializations of experts. Salesian historian Aldo Giraudo notices a separation between ministry and spirituality, observing a "prayer that moves in between intellectualism and emotionalism, often unable to move the life of the young". The educative and pastoral experiences often tend "to resolve or close on themselves, have a gratifying and anesthetic character, without a real consistency and inner quality. If it were really so [...] the educational and pastoral projects are in danger of becoming a wasted effort, moving on without a soul and a backbone".[116]

---

[113] See *La società di san Francesco di Sales nel sessennio 1984-1990*, pp. 156-157 and VECCHI, *Verso una nuova tappa di PG*, in *Il cammino e la prospettiva 2000*, pp. 88-89.
[114] See *Ibidem*.
[115] See also GC23 (1990), nn. 251-253 and TONELLI, *Ripensando quarant'anni*, pp. 48-49.
[116] GIRAUDO, *Interrogativi e spinte della Chiesa del postconcilio sulla spiritualità Salesiana*, in SEMERARO (Ed.), *La spiritualità Salesiana*, p. 154.

A reaction to the division between evangelization and education is clearly expressed in the 1991 Viganò's letter *The new education*. His insistence on the grace of unity suggests that the tendency to separate the two areas is not only virtually possible, but it is a real problem in the Salesian Youth Ministry. Tonelli confirms the intuition speaking about the YM: "One of the limits of the work of these years has been ... the game of 'before' and 'after'. Someone said: first education and then the announcement. Some other preferred to reverse the moments".[117] Sabino Frigato in his analysis of the relationship between education and evangelization in the Congregation noted that "despite the multiplicity of definitions, the role of faith is revealed substantially 'extrinsic' to the educational process. Faith and education are considered 'distinct', 'mutually independent' and 'polarized' dimensions".[118]

Meanwhile, the only way to make a synthesis in the Salesian Youth Ministry seemed to be the 1990 volume of *Salesian Youth Ministry*, which collected the various issues in the form of symbolic illustrations, gave a brief explanation and listed a more extensive bibliography on the subject. The "symbolic" way of presenting the contents with a picture evaded the problem of the interrelations between the elements and gave the impression of unity. The volume could be considered as the icon of the content and aspirations of Youth Ministry between 1978 and 1990.[119]

1.5 Consolidation of the SEPP (1990-2002)

In the '80s the Congregation invested heavily in the development of the Salesian Educative and Pastoral Project, which expressed with greater clarity the ultimate goals of education and facilitated the setting

---

[117] R. TONELLI, *Ripensando quarant'anni di servizio alla pastorale giovanile*, intervista a cura di Giancarlo De Nicolò, in «Note di Pastorale Giovanile» 43 (2009) 5, 41-42.
[118] S. FRIGATO, *Educazione ed evangelizzazione. La riflessione della Congregazione Salesiana nel Postconcilio*, in BOZZOLO A. – CARELLI R. (Eds.), *Evangelizzazione e educazione*, LAS, Roma 2011, p. 89.
[119] See DICASTERO PER LA PASTORALE GIOVANILE, *Pastorale giovanile Salesiana*, SDB, Roma 1990.

of some standards for different environments, such as schools, oratories or parishes. The formation of Delegates for the Youth Ministry should be also mentioned as part of the process.[120] In some Regions, like Latin America, the effort to develop the SEPP was stronger and the project mentality had more influence on the everyday life of the provinces. Besides the achievements there were, however, some more or less defined shadows, especially in the area of the operational translation of the projects. Based on the Rector Major's assessments we could describe the final image, along with Juan E. Vecchi, as a "gap between the amount of proposals and the ability to implement them".[121]

1.5.1 GC23 and the Programmes of Education to the Faith

The GC23 was purposely designed as an ordinary General Chapter, since the post-Vatican II review of the Salesian Identity was essentially completed. For the convocation of the GC23, the Rector Major Egidio Viganò wrote: "Now the Chapter that is being prepared can be said to be "ordinary" […] It means, in fact, to focus the attention of the confreres on a specific operational topic".[122] In fact, the GC23, which lasted "only" two months, from March until May 1990, set a duration standard for the future GCs. The Chapter accepted the pre-chapter document as a good basis but wanted the final document to be a pastoral document, very practical, operational and addressed to the Salesians seen as educators in the faith for different situations and contexts.[123] Egidio Viganò was re-

---

[120] See e.g the course for Provincial Youth Ministry Delegates in the Pisana General Headquarters from November 1986 until January 1987 or the formation manuals used in the hispanic world: CENTRO INTERNACIONAL SALESIANO DE PASTORAL JUVENIL/ROMA, *Comunidad educativa en formación. Guiones para educadores*, 5 vols., CCS, Madrid 1985-86.

[121] See VECCHI, *Verso una nuova tappa di PG*, in *Il cammino e la prospettiva 2000*, p. 88.

[122] E. VIGANÒ, *Convocazione del Capitolo Generale 23°*, in ACG 69 (1988) 327, 6.

[123] See *Chronicle of the GC23*, in GC23 (1990), n. 370.

elected Rector Major for a third six-year term, Vecchi became his vicar and Luc Van Looy was elected Councillor for the Youth Ministry.

The Programmes of Education to the Faith had to be the operational element of the GCs for it was a translation of the theory into practical programmes of structured learning, in gradual stages, suited to the condition of the young people who are to implement them (objectives, attitudes, knowledge, concrete commitments and experiences) with some clearly defined content. These Programmes had to be structured in four areas, in line with the dimensions of the SEPP, but with the omission of the "Educative and Pastoral Community Area", which, at that time, was the fifth area of the projects.[124]

At this moment, a natural question can arise: What is the difference between a project and a programme? Riccardo Tonelli, a key figure in the preparation of the GC23 pre-chapter document expressed himself in these words: "There is no big difference between the terms project and programme. The two formulas are often used interchangeably".[125] After the Chapter, Tonelli explained the difference with a theoretical and ambiguous definition stating that "a programme is a dynamic synthesis of the project".[126] It seems that the introduction of the new term "programme" should have been the solution for the lack of operative translation of the "old" projects. The tendency of the General Chapters to introduce new terms to solve old and structural issues appears to be a defined trait of the post-Vatican II Salesian mindset.

Although there are not many differences between a project and a programme at the definition level, there have been two practical shifts of

---

[124] See GC23 (1990), nn. 116-118. The four areas are: human growth, meeting with Jesus Christ, insertion in the community of believers, commitment and vocation for the transformation of the world.

[125] R. TONELLI, *Un itinerario di educazione dei giovani alla fede*, in «Note di Pastorale Giovanile» 18 (1984) 8, 62.

[126] R. TONELLI, *Progetto Educativo-Pastorale*, in ISTITUTO DI TEOLOGIA PASTORALE UNIVERSITÀ PONTIFICIA SALESIANA, *Dizionario di Pastorale Giovanile*, a cura di Mario Midali e Riccardo Tonelli, LDC, Leumann (TO) ²1992, p. 906.

attention. The first concerns the application field of a programme. Generally, a programme should be carried out in a group or by a single young person. In this sense a programme is more specific than a project and the introduction of the "programmes" brought the project management method and mentality to a more concrete level.[127] The second shift enforced the already present linear logic of project management. Van Looy adopted a clear linear thinking: "The progressive logic of achieving the objectives in each area specifies a logical order of intermediate milestones. Starting from the point where the young people are, we proceed step by step to reach the objective, you go from X to Y, and again from the arrival point you reach the next grade, from Y to Z".[128] A more systemic and nonlinear logic of the educative programmes proposed by Michele Pellerey in the publication on Modular Elements of the SEPP seems to be neglected and a linear Management by Objectives logic is reinforced.[129]

The GC23 did not only offer the reflection on the Programmes. In connection with the theme of the education to the faith, the Chapter developed the concept of Salesian Youth Spirituality, which expressed a new way of being a disciple in the world. It integrates the insights of the faith, choices of values and lived attitudes. It is a spirituality for young people and therefore it is an educational spirituality developed in five basic dimensions: daily life, joy and optimism, friendship with the Lord Jesus, ecclesial communion and responsible service.[130] Another new element in the area of the Youth Ministry structures is the Salesian Youth

---

[127] See GC23 (1990), n. 280. The accent on the specificity and concreteness of the programmes is confirmed later by Ruta, Sigallini and Domènech in *Itinerari di educazione alla fede. Un confronto interdisciplinare: orizzonti e linguaggi*, Intervista a C. Bissoli, A. Domènech, G. Ruta, D. Sigalini, R. Tonelli, G. Venturi a cura di G. De Nicolò, in «Note di Pastorale Giovanile» 39 (2005) 8, 5-6.

[128] L. VAN LOOY, *Mentalità di itinerario*, in ACG 74 (1993) 345, 55.

[129] See M. PELLEREY, *Itinerario*, in VECCHI – PRELLEZO, *Elementi modulari*, pp. 191-195.

[130] See GC23 (1990), nn. 158-161.

Movement (SYM) formed by all groups who identify with the Salesian spirituality and education.[131]

1.5.2 Revision of the Provincial SEPPs in the early '90s

In the letter of convocation of the General Chapter 23, Viganò spoke of the need to "verify the effectiveness of the Salesian education seen in relation to the life of faith of the young people we work with, and then review with more operational approach the SEPPs of each Province and of the individual houses".[132] The GC23 formulated clearly the need to review the Provincial Educative and Pastoral Projects[133] in order to give an operational answer to the failed resizing of the Salesian institutions proposed in the '60s. Vecchi expressed a realistic estimate of this effort in 1991: "The resizing problem is now taken over with the theme of the 'significance' of the Salesian presence. There are some attempts to relocate or to entrust the institutions to others through shareholding forms of management. There are also some presences in new contexts. But the new projects require additional use of resources, they simply add tasks to existing commitments, weakening the consistency of communities and overloading the confreres with new responsibilities".[134]

Evaluations of the Youth Ministry Provincial Teams

Despite the emphasis of the Chapter on the operational concreteness, the review launched by Luc van Looy wanted "to examine the quality of the written provincial projects; for now, it has not entered in the verification of the actual implementation of these projects in the

---

[131] See GC23 (1990), nn. 275-277.
[132] VIGANÒ, *Convocazione del Capitolo Generale 23°*, 1988, 7.
[133] See GC23 (1990), n. 230.
[134] J.E. VECCHI, *Verso una nuova tappa di Pastorale Giovanile Salesiana, in Il cammino e la prospettiva 2000*, Documenti PG 13, SDB, Roma 1991, p. 79.

institutions".[135] The review gave a "great attention to the written principles"[136] and the completeness of the issues addressed in the projects,
emphasizing again the choice of not wanting to get into the problematic
field of projects' execution or that of the impact on reality. In the area of
the complete formulation of the project, the review has revealed a substantial satisfaction. The Provincial SEPPs were generally well written
with updated references to the previous Salesian Documents. There is an
interesting remark on the integration of the multiple dimensions of the
project. The answers regarding the relationship between the various dimensions of the project were interpreted and reported as follows: "there
is no real relationship of integration" and "the relationship with the other
dimensions is a bit uncertain".[137]

Among the 45 items of the questionnaire, only three deal with the
operational phase of the project. The survey results concerning these
three questions were formulated in a very brief and generic way: "We
can see a slow movement in the educational commitment which translates itself into the formulation of the project and begins to involve the
laity".[138] The fairly generic findings of the review can be specified with
some statistical data taken from van Looy's 1994 letter about the SEPP
in the Provinces. The Councillor for the Youth Ministry highlighted the
following issues:
- *Lack of project methodology*: 38% of the houses do not have a written
  project. 17% of the provinces do not have a SEPP approved by the Provincial Chapter. Of those provinces that have the project, in 76% of

---

[135] L. VAN LOOY, *Il Progetto Educativo Pastorale nelle Ispettorie*, in ACG 75 (1994)
349, 36.
[136] DICASTERO PER LA PASTORALE GIOVANILE, *Il Progetto Educativo-pastorale Salesiano*.
Rilettura dei progetti ispettoriali. Risultati dell'inchiesta ai delegati ispettoriali di PG e
loro équipes sul "Progetto educativo-pastorale", Dossier PG 8, SDB, Roma 1995, p. 6.
See also VAN LOOY, *Il Progetto Educativo Pastorale nelle Ispettorie*, 34-38.
[137] See DICASTERO PER LA PG, *Rilettura dei progetti ispettoriali*, pp. 20-24.
[138] *Idem*, p. 28.

cases it was written only by some Salesians without a co-responsible involvement of others.

- *Deficiency of co-responsibility with the laity in the Educative and Pastoral Community*: In 36% of the houses there is no EPC. 78% of the responses show no knowledge of the EPC being the guarantor of the Salesian charism, and 67% say they do not understand very well how to share responsibility with the laity. 78% are not really clear of the Salesian community's task to form the laity.

- *Failed insertion in the social and ecclesial context*. Only 3% consider the relationship with the social and political organizations important and only 4% value positively the relations with cultural organizations. The insertion in the local church is considered important for 19% of respondents; relationships with the families of the young people are important for 11%, and 14% want to build relations with other educational organizations.[139]

Some results, especially the co-responsibility with the laity and in the territory insertion, were quite alarming. Three quarters of the Salesian communities did not know how to apply it or did not consider teamwork with the laity as important and, of course, the same percentage of the projects was written only by the Salesians. The communion and sharing between Salesians and lay people in the EPC was, therefore, chosen as the guiding theme for the next General Chapter in 1996.

Provincial SEPPs Text Analysis

Another source of analysis of the Salesian project management mindset of the '90s is the *SEPP: Anthology of the Texts* published by the Youth Ministry Department in 1995.[140] The texts that are found in it were selected in order to serve as an inspiration to other provinces or local

---

[139] See VAN LOOY, *Il Progetto Educativo Pastorale nelle Ispettorie*, 36-40.
[140] See DICASTERO PER LA PASTORALE GIOVANILE, *Il Progetto Educativo-pastorale Salesiano. Raccolta antologica di testi*, Dossier PG 9, SDB, Roma 1995.

communities.[141] In that sense it is a good source of "the best material" that represents the shared mindset of these years. Reading the texts, we can summarize a simplified typical scheme of an educative and pastoral project composition in three steps:

1. *Describe the contextual challenges* seen as an absence of quality (A, B, C...) or as a negative phenomenon (X, Y, Z...) and divide them into four dimensions. This operation could be possibly inspired by the documents of the previous General Chapter;

2. *Choose an objective* from the following ones: promote (educate, enhance, improve, endorse, encourage, sponsor, support, boost, develop, form attitudes of) A, B, C or non-X, non-Y, non-Z;

3. *Decide a guideline* and formulate it as a gerund: promoting (educating, enhancing, improving, endorsing, encouraging, sponsoring, supporting, boosting, developing, forming attitudes of, taking steps to get to) a_1, a_2, a_3..., b_1, b_2, b_3..., c_1, c_2, c_3... or non-x_1, non-x_2, non-x_3..., non-y_1, non-y_2, non-y_3..., non-z_1, non-z_2, non-z_3... etc.

Some typical examples could be the following: Example 1: In response to the lack of sufficiently prepared lay teachers (*situation*), the province decides to enhance their formation (*objective*), by sponsoring specific Salesian formation programmes, by improving their teaching skills and by developing a long-life formation attitude (*guideline*). Example 2: The rising number of dropouts challenges our pastoral ministry (*situation*), therefore, we choose the *objective* to enhance the existing services for disadvantaged families by improving those specific programmes that deal explicitly with the dropout risk, by sponsoring responsible parenting formation course and by developing major awareness to the phenomenon (*guideline*).

As one can see, this project methodology has two main risks. The first is to engage only in linguistic issues with little attention to the execution.

---

[141] See *Idem*, p. 7.

Some Provinces preferred to play it in a safe way: make the project become a reformulation of the Preventive System. In those projects, the theoretical aspects prevail and practical guidelines are generally absent.[142] In fact, the assessment of the project's results was treated only by two provinces that have used the tool of a questionnaire. They planned to ask the provincial team about the achievement of the objectives, although no sets of indicators were specified.[143]

The second risk of this planning mentality was the proliferating of objectives that generally follow the exhortations of the last General Chapters. In many projects, the number is so large that their achievement is highly improbable.[144] However, some provinces tended towards certain operational concreteness. There were provinces that embraced a realistic number of objectives.[145] Some SEPPs specified a programme for animators' formation; others presented concrete action steps for the local EPC formation.[146] A realistic approach can be found in those provinces that decided on a brief set of criteria for the recruitment of teachers or for the significance of their institutions.[147] Some projects integrated short and synthetic parts of the mission statement and mission criteria, as part of the SEPP framework.[148]

---

[142] In an emblematic case of a philosophical-theoretical approach, a nine-page description of the world situation from the perspective of the poor introduces the project. See *Idem*, pp. 317-325.

[143] See *Idem*, pp. 247-249.

[144] In Chapter 2 we will address more specifically the limits and paradoxes of Management by Objectives. For a critical view on too many objectives see e.g. J.Y. SHAH – R. FRIEDMAN – A.W. KRUGLANSKI, *Forgetting all else: on the antecedents and consequences of goal shielding*, in «Journal of Personality and Social Psychology» 83 (2002) 6, 1261-1280.

[145] See DICASTERO PER LA PG, *Raccolta antologica di testi*, pp. 231-232; 233-235 and 292-293.

[146] See *Idem*, pp. 94-98; 119-122; 102-110 and 189.

[147] See *Idem*, pp. 237-238 e 243-246.

[148] See *Idem*, pp. 253-256.

1.5.3 Synthesis of the First Two Editions of the "Frame of Reference" (1998, 2000)

The review of the provincial projects of the first half of the '90s carried out by Luc van Looy was followed by two six-year periods (1996-2008) of Antonio Domènech's animation. His influence can be summarized as an effort to diffuse and to synthetize the Salesian Youth Ministry mindset. These two lines of action have not been interrupted since the two *Frame of Reference* editions reflected the feedback from the provincial YM teams received during regional meetings that have served, in turn, as an occasion to form a shared mentality.

Pascual Chávez Villanueva characterizes this effort by stating: "There was an extraordinarily rich and sound heritage of reflection and practice of the Salesian pastoral action, and the need was felt to have a complete overall view, and to bring together, in a structured and shared synthesis, the fundamental guidelines so as to facilitate their personal assimilation and provide directives for the praxis. The Youth Ministry Department tried to respond to this need by offering the Provinces and the communities a guidance manual, and providing a systematic process of pastoral formation in these years, in particular for those confreres with responsibilities for animation and the government, insisting on certain key issues to be borne in mind".[149] In the following paragraphs we will briefly examine two chapters of the first edition of the *Frame of Reference* (1998), which are linked to the content and to the methodology of the SEPP. The third paragraph will describe some improvements of the second edition (2000).

Wholeness and Dimensions of the SEPP

The second chapter of the volume focuses on the fundamentals of the SEPP, dividing it into four parts following the logic of the "dimensions".

---

[149] CHÁVEZ VILLANUEVA, *Salesian Youth Ministry*, 2010, 20.

The dimensions follow the division into five areas of *Handout No. 2* (1979) removing the so called "community area", which becomes a separate chapter on the identity and the animation of the Educative and Pastoral Community. The four dimensions (education-culture, evangelization-catechesis, social experience, vocation) are present in every previous document linked to the SEPP.[150] The decision to deal with the EPC in a separate chapter brings with it advantages and disadvantages at the same time. The benefit is the emphasis on the community subject, which is understandable after the GC24 (1996) that deepened and intensified the theme of communion and mission between the Salesians and lay people. However, there is a collateral risk of the mental separation between the SEPP and EPC, with the practical consequence of not paying attention to the construction and formation of the community within an educative-pastoral project.

The division of the project into dimensions comes together with highlighting the integral growth and the organic unity of all the elements of the SEPP. The text of the first edition expresses that, "The SEPP as a mediation of the SYM, has to express the organic unity in different objectives, measures and actions that are mutually intertwined with one another and all are guided to the same purpose, expressing their concrete complementarity and forming a global unity. This organic unity is expressed in the four dimensions of the SEPP".[151] Unfortunately, the call to organic unity is not accompanied by methodological suggestions that might answer the question of how to arrive at unity out of the different

---

[150] See the following documents in a chronological order: Const, 40; Reg, 5-10; DICASTERO PER LA PG, *Elementi e linee*, Sussidio 2, p. 15; DICASTERO PER LA PASTORALE GIOVANILE, *Pastorale giovanile Salesiana*, SDB, Roma 1990, pp. 63-73; GC23 (1990), nn. 116-118 and 158-161; DICASTERI PER LA PASTORALE GIOVANILE FMA-SDB, *Spiritualità Giovanile Salesiana. Un dono dello Spirito alla Famiglia Salesiana per la vita e la speranza di tutti*, [s.e.], Roma 1996.

[151] DICASTERO PER LA PG, *Quadro di riferimento*, ¹1998, p. 26.

dimensions.[152] Even trans-dimensional themes, such as: prevention, animation, Salesian Youth Spirituality and Salesian Youth Movement are placed inside the respective dimensions neutralizing their potential for a multidimensional synergistic integration. The text, on the one hand, expresses a strong need for integration, and on the other, is dominated by the dimension logic.

Unchanged Methodology after Twenty Years of Practice

The sixth chapter on methodological lines on processing and assessment of the Salesian Educational and Pastoral Project is located at the end of the volume and takes up a little more than five pages of the text. The title does not seek to explain an entire project management methodology; it only states some principles. The fact of entering only into a few basic methodological issues is confirmed in the last page of the *Frame of Reference* that recommends creating a methodology that encourages participation of all groups and organizations of the EPC according to their responsibilities and possibilities. This broad approach gives one the freedom to choose a methodology, but on the other side it leaves unresolved some real methodological dilemmas without offering a unifying method harmonized with the theoretical framework. In this sense a community risks to be playing the role of a "secretary" that prepares all requested documents without raising questions about execution, implementation, feasibility, interrelations, sustainability, resources, group dynamics, roles, etc.

---

[152] There are only some rhetorical suggestions, e.g.: "raise positive development of the cultural reality of the human group towards a synthesis of faith and life"; "A unified personality"; "Educating socializing"; "The prospect of education that evangelizes and evangelization which educates the ultimate goal of the process is the synthesis of faith and life in a particular culture"; "Vocational choice is an ever-present dimension at all times, activities and stages of our educational and pastoral action"; "The youth group has to look at the social and ecclesial insertion outlet according to its vocational choice." See DICASTERO PER LA PG, *Quadro di riferimento*, [1]1998, pp. 27-38.

The content of this chapter summarizes the methodology as it was presented in the two first *Handouts* in 1978 and 1979. In summary it describes:

- *levels* of the design (frame of reference, educative and pastoral project, annual plan, planning programme, timetable);
- *steps* of planning (situation analysis, operational planning, assessment);
- design *criteria* (involvement and participation of all, clarifying the points of reference, clarity about the different levels of participation, continuous assessment);
- Educative and Pastoral Community seen as the *subject* of the whole process.[153]

Methodological Improvements of the Second Edition

Antonio Domènech and his team[154] took concrete steps to promote the organic unity of the Salesian Youth Ministry, to translate the *Frame of Reference* into different languages, and in organizing regional courses for the Provincial Youth Ministry Teams. The YM Department collected the fruits of the regional courses' experience and decided to revisit the text and make it clearer and more precise. The result of their work was the publication of the *Frame of Reference* in 2000 (Italian version) and in 2001 (English version).[155]

The first change of a considerable importance was shifting the EPC chapter from the "working model" to the "fundamental elements" part of the publication. Following the editors' intentions, the Community had to be considered a fundamental reality of the Youth Ministry model, not only a pragmatic or operational structure.

---

[153] N.B. There are improvements in the proper use of the term "criterion" and in the introduction of the term "continual evaluation".

[154] In Domènech's Youth Ministry team there were: Jerome Vallabaraj, a Salesian scholar and practitioner in the area of catechetics from India, and José Raúl Rojas, a Salesian expert in cooperative learning in the Latin-American context.

[155] See SALESIAN YOUTH MINISTRY DEPARTMENT, *Salesian Youth Ministry. A Basic Frame of Reference*, Direzione Generale Opere Don Bosco, Rome ²2001, p. 5.

The second interesting shift concerns the concept of the frame of reference that not only declares "principles that define a philosophy of education",[156] but rather the fundamental answers "to the question, Who are we and what are we doing? What do we want to achieve and where do we want to get to?".[157] In this way the frame of reference is connected with the concepts of "mission", "vision" or *propuesta educativa*" which did not appear in the first edition.[158]

The third interesting common line of thought of the second edition is a more precise use of project management terms such as criterion, objective, assessment, evaluation, etc. (for example, the term "educational-pastoral decisions" was changed to a more appropriate and common term "objectives"). In the assessment section, the list of ten instructions of the first edition was simplified and an important "holistic" attention recalled: assess "whether a genuine educative process has evolved through the different activities (continuity, interaction, new possibilities and resources, involvement of the people concerned)".[159]

The paradigmatic concluding task of the EPC, recommended on the last page of the publication, to "think of a method of encouraging the participation of all" remains the same also in the second edition. We intend it as an open ending, confirmed by the authors' initial statements: "This document remains open to revision and enrichment brought on by reflection, experience and life itself".[160] The need of a new methodology, a new type of presence and a unified organic vision was confirmed in 2010 by Rector Major Pascual Chávez Villanueva: "All this effort in rethinking the educational practice necessarily implies openness to new schemes and new practices, a new way of thinking and a new way of

---

[156] See DICASTERO PER LA PG, *Quadro di riferimento*, ¹1998, p. 117.

[157] YM DEPARTMENT, *Salesian Youth Ministry*, ²2001, p. 166

[158] See DICASTERO PER LA PG, *Quadro di riferimento*, ²2000, p. 129. N.B. we are quoting the Italian version because the concepts of "mission", "vision" and *propuesta educativa*" were omitted in the English translation.

[159] YM DEPARTMENT, *Salesian Youth Ministry*, ²2001, p. 172.

[160] See DICASTERO PER LA PG, *Quadro di riferimento*, ²2000, p. 5. N.B. The whole presentation section is missing in the English version.

organising those elements which are part of the educational process, a new methodology and a new way of being present among the young [...] It is important to adopt a unified and organic vision of a ministry, centered on the individual young person and not so much on works or services, overcoming a compartmentalization still present in everyday practice".[161] As we will see in the following paragraphs, some of his exhortations were followed in the revision and the integrations of the third edition in 2014.

1.5.4 "Planning Mentality" that Implies an Unsustainable Number of Projects (2002)

A legacy of the General Chapter 25 held in 2002, besides deepening the understanding of the Salesian community today, accentuated the so called "planning mentality". An immediate operative translation of it was the introduction of three new types of projects: Personal Plan of Salesian life,[162] Plan of Salesian Community Life,[163] and the Organic Provincial Plan.[164] These projects are an addition to an already complex web of various projects and plans designed at different levels (provincial, local, personal), with different perspectives (education, pastoral, economy, formation of Salesians, formation of lay people, etc.) and in different times with different teams coordinated by different facilitators-animators. Counting all projects and plans one could arrive at 24 units.

An optimist could read this situation as a ubiquitous application of the "planning mentality" to the whole life of a Salesian. These three new projects should, as the GC document wishes, become an asset of integral coordination and unification of intent at the personal, communitarian and provincial level. But a more realistic approach could also see several

---

[161] CHÁVEZ VILLANUEVA, *Salesian Youth Ministry*, 2010, 48.
[162] See GC25 (2002), nn. 14 and 56.
[163] See GC25 (2002), nn. 15; 46; 61; 64; 72-74.
[164] See GC25 (2002), nn. 82-84.

problems of the current rather complex project management model that could lead to an organizational paralysis or to a formal planning model:
- *Priority*: Which project is given top priority? Is there always a top-down mindset? If so, are we only implementing the newest directions from the centre (Rome) that imply a re-active (not pro-active) mindset?
- *Heterogeneity*: How to solve different proposals of different design teams? Does the Organic Provincial Plan override the Provincial SEPP? Which project has the priority in my personal life: Personal or Communitarian Project?
- *Synchronization*: Which is the right synchronization sequence of projects? Is the newer project more valid only because it is more "updated" to the current situation?
- *Continuity*: If the team that designed the current project has changed, is the project still valid? Is the schematic language of a project sufficient to guide a community through the change of key players?
- *Method*: Which model of planning is the "right" one for the creation of a mentality (Vecchi's educative-pastoral approach, Domènech's OPP logic, Cereda's formation logic)?

1.6 New Youth Ministry Challenges and Perspectives (2002-2014)

Some of the questions posted above combined with new challenges of the third millennium have introduced some new perspectives or ideas concerning planning and project management. Some of them found their way also in the texts of the General Chapters or in other manuals. We shall synthetize some lines of development in the following chapters.

The different evaluations underline the following: in some Provinces the SEPPs are in the hands of individual Salesians and do not direct the pastoral ministry of the communities;[165] there is only a small portion of provinces that accompany the processes in order to achieve the objectives and to verify the processes in due time;[166] favouring the organizational aspect over the pastoral one;[167] SEPPs designed and EPCs built by the planning mentality are not easily assumed;[168] a practical reduction of the whole ministry to pastoral actions, which implies little attention to processes;[169] little assimilation and practical implementation of the operational model of the Salesian Youth Ministry;[170] and finally, the predominance of a rigid organizational mindset in the setting of pastoral activities pays little attention to the rhythm of young people's life and does not promote cooperation.[171]

1.6.1 "Planning Mentality" as a Broader Holistic Concept

From GC25 (2002) to GC27 (2014) the planning mentality was not only about planning more and increasing the number of projects, plans and programmes. The concept evolved and tried to become a new project management mentality linked with the category of the "new presences". It is useful to remember that in the '70s and '80s the expression "new presence" was often interpreted in reference to new forms of service to the poorest or it was intended as a "small community" and therefore the

---

[165] See *La Società di san Francesco di Sales nel sessennio 1996-2002*. Relazione del Vicario del Rettor Maggiore don Luc Van Looy, SDB, Roma 2002, n. 110.

[166] See *La Società di san Francesco di Sales nel sessennio 1990-1995*, n. 137.

[167] See GC25 (2002), n. 194 and CHÁVEZ VILLANUEVA, *Salesian Youth Ministry*, 2010, 56-57.

[168] See *La Società di san Francesco di Sales nel sessennio 1996-2002*, n. 118.

[169] See *La Società di san Francesco di Sales nel sessennio 2002-2008*. Relazione del Rettor Maggiore don Pascual Chávez Villanueva, SDB, Roma 2008, p. 45 and GC25 (2002), nn. 44-47.

[170] See *La Società di san Francesco di Sales nel sessennio 2002-2008*, pp. 41 and CHÁVEZ VILLANUEVA, *Salesian Youth Ministry*, 2010, 20-22.

[171] See GC26 (2008), n. 103.

newness did not apply to all houses of the Congregation.[172] In the third millennium, the attention shifts from a "new type of structures" to a "new type of presence" in all educational and pastoral works or structures. The ninth successor of Don Bosco Pascual Chávez Villanueva insists: "To make the traditional works that we have, Schools, Vocational Training Centres, Parishes, Oratories and Youth Centres, University hostels etc. new requires that we concentrate the role of the Salesian community not so much on the management and organization of the work as on the accompaniment and on the formation of the educators and of the young people".[173] We can summarize some traits of this "new presence" mindset in the following way:

- Change focus from work management to *accompaniment* and *formation* together between the Salesians and lay people;
- Move from a mentality that favours roles of direct management to a mentality that favours *evangelizing presence* among young people;
- Cultivate *co-responsibility* through planning together with the Salesian Family and creating collaborative networks;
- Have apostolic courage to rethink the works for young people and to promote more *flexible forms* of presence;
- Ensure the quantitative and qualitative *consistency of the communities*, which is coordinated by a director available for its primary role.[174]

---

[172] See SGC (1972), nn. 510, 619 and GC21 (1978), n. 159. This type of interpretation was criticized for example in *Relazione Generale del Rettor Maggiore sullo stato della Congregazione*, in GC21 (1978), n. 157.

[173] CHÁVEZ VILLANUEVA, *Salesian Youth Ministry*, 2010, 56-57.

[174] Cfr. GC (2002), nn. 26; 46; 50; 60; 138; 157; GC26 (2008), nn. 10-11; 20; 31; 38; 100; 103; 112; 113. Note that GC27 (2014) sometimes omits the term "planning mentality" and speaks about the "Salesian culture" of communion and co-responsibility in the Salesian community and the Educative and Pastoral Community, in GC27 (2014), n. 71.

1.6.2 Cereda and Domènech's Method of Discernment

In the formal structure of the last three General Chapters (2002-2014) we can find a new line of a project design methodology.[175] It has been called the "discernment method" and it is also intended for the designing process of the three new "projects" introduced by the GC25: Personal Plan of Salesian life, Plan of Salesian Community Life, and the Organic Provincial Plan. The methodological approach is linked to the proposals of Francesco Cereda and Antonio Domènech which differ from the SEPP methodology in different points.[176]

1. Firstly, the discernment process begins with recognizing the *"God's call"*, which allows to capture urgent calls and priorities. The focal point is to distinguish what is essential from what is secondary so choices can be made around priority issues. The stage of the "call" is similar to the SEPP operational planning phase, but in this method it comes as the first step.

2. The second step is the *analysis of the situation* that identifies resources, foundation of hope, limitations and challenges, but always seen in relation to the fundamental choices identified in the previous phase of God's call.

---

[175] See e.g. P. CHÁVEZ VILLANUEVA, *Presentation*, in GC26 (2008), pp. 11-12 and ÁNGEL FERNÁNDEZ ARTIME, *Presentation*, in GC27 (2014), pp. 10-11.

[176] ANTONIO DOMÈNECH, *The Organic Provincial Plan*, in ACG 84 (2003) 381, 35-42 and FRANCESCO CEREDA, *The Salesian Community Plan. A process of discernment and of sharing*. Letter of 13 December 2002 addressed to Provincials, Provincial Councils, Provincial Delegates for formation and Provincial Commissions for formation, in sdb.org/images/en/Formazione/Documenti/zip/Salesian_community_plan.zip; ID., *The Personal Plan of Life. Initial Formation*. Letter of 5 July 2003 addressed to Rectors and Members of Formation Communities, Provincials and Provincial Formation Delegates, in sdb.org/images/en/Formazione/Documenti/zip/Personal_plan_Initial.zip; ID., *The Personal Plan of Life. Ongoing Formation. A process of creative faithfulness towards holiness*. Letter of 21 June 2003 addressed to Provincials, Provincial Councils, Provincial Formation Delegates and Provincial Formation Commissions, in sdb.org/images/en/Formazione/Documenti/zip/Personal_plan_ongoing.zip.

3. *Guidelines* are set in the third moment, following this succession: first come the processes to be activated in order to move from challenges to a new mentality and structures. Only in the second moment concrete actions, events or decisions are made, planned and scheduled.

Cereda synthetizes the method in his letter: "The three moments of the process of discernment could be expressed in the form of expectations, invitations or desires as a first step describing God's call; in the form of resources, difficulties and above all challenges as a second step describing the situation of the community; and in the form of objectives, strategies or processes and interventions as a third step, spelling out the lines of action".[177]

Compared to the traditional logic of the SEPP, some methodological improvements have been added. The horizon of the change of mentality broadens the model and it could become less linear and mechanistic. There are measurable and concrete objectives to be pursued, but their achievement is not the only purpose. The fundamental aim is to follow a call and that is a more holistic concept compared to measurable improvements of concrete educational and pastoral challenges divided into four dimensions. The method of discernment could promise therefore a shorter project with a more integrated vision of God's call valuing the spiritual and motivational resources of the individual and of the community.[178]

The main difficulty of the discernment method was the placement of the moment of the "God's call" at the beginning of the process, leading implicitly to considering the vocation as a disembodied reality without significant relations to the context in which it takes place. In this sense, the second step of the analysis of the situation that followed the call was

---

[177] CEREDA, *The Salesian Community Plan.*
[178] See *Address of the Rector Major Fr Pascual Chávez Villanueva at the conclusion of the GC25*, in GC25 (2002), n. 185; PASCUAL CHÁVEZ VILLANUEVA, *Presentation*, in GC25 (2002), pp. 15-16; GC25 (2002), nn. 73, 81; CEREDA, *The Salesian Community Plan.*

only functional to the operative and executive logic. It is interesting to see how the GC27 in 2014 reverses the order and goes back to the old SEPP order of the three steps: listening, interpretation and way forward (i.e. situation analysis, interpretation and operational planning).[179] Another limit of the discernment method is the lack of assessment although, paradoxically, it requires measurable objectives. This fact confirms the shift towards a more motivational and less operational type of projects which is understandable because formation is the area where it was developed. The dilemma between concreteness of the objectives and the integral vision is one of many theoretical and epistemological core issues to be addressed in the following chapters.

1.6.3 Changed Perspectives in the Third Edition of the "Frame of Reference"

The Councillor for the Youth Ministry Fabio Attard received from the GC26 a mandate for an update of the *Salesian Youth Ministry Frame of Reference*. He, together with his team, has coordinated a wide consultation on the required "deeper understanding of the relationship between evangelization and education in order to put the Preventive System into practice, and adapt the frame of reference for youth ministry to changing cultural circumstances".[180] The third edition wants to be in continuity with the previous editions enriching them with theological, spiritual and more consciously charismatic reflection developed in the last 15 years. Some themes are emerging with more strength bringing a valuable contribution to the pastoral-education balance: need to open up to the life and culture of today's young people (Chapter 1); importance of inspiration in Christ the Good Shepherd and inclusion in the evangelizing Church (Chapter 2); accentuation of the relationship between education and evangelization (Chapter 3); the methodological importance of the

---

[179] See FERNÁNDEZ ARTIME, *Presentation*, in GC27 (2014), pp. 10-11.
[180] See GC26 (2008), n. 45.

process of discernment; and finally, the Preventive System of Don Bosco, "a project of holistic education, [that] comprises essentially two aspects. It is a project of Christian life (Salesian Youth Spirituality) and a practical pedagogical method".[181]

The concept of the SEPP is explained in the last chapter of the *Frame of Reference*. It does not seem to have been substantially affected by the theological foundation perspective of the first three chapters. The Manual emphasizes the role of discernment understood as being the transverse attitude of listening to God's plan,[182] but the phases of planning (situation analysis, operational planning, assessment) are retained in their Management by Objectives logic. Discernment is conceived as global attention that accompanies the whole process to prevent extremism of commercial, economic, political projects on the one hand, and a spiritualistic vagueness on the other. Discernment is the criterion that should maintain the educative and pastoral spirit of the SEPP and its evangelical nature in offering salvation in Christ to the young and overcome the risk of a static, rigid and anonymous project.[183]

The introduction of discernment, the call to the simplicity of the projects, the known risk of the technical project management mindset, the danger of the one-man-made project made at the desk, the organizational complexity that can overshadow the educational and pastoral spirit, could be considered as the Congregation's distress signal about a dysfunctional project management model. One can add that, according to the text, the Salesians do not even have a unique design methodology. Compared to the second edition that suggested "thinking of a method of encouraging the participation of all", in the third edition three methods of discernment (1. see, judge, act; 2. God's call, situations, action plans;

---

[181] YM DEPARTMENT, *Frame of Reference*, ³2014, p. 85. See also F. ATTARD, *Ripensare la pastorale giovanile*, LAS, Roma 2013
[182] See YM DEPARTMENT, *Frame of Reference*, ³2014, pp. 35-36.
[183] See YM DEPARTMENT, *Frame of Reference*, ³2014, p. 300.

3. review of life) are mentioned. The *Frame of Reference* gives the operators freedom to choose a methodology depending on circumstances and contexts.[184] The same methodological freedom, with a different set of criteria, concerns the methodology of the "programmes" introduced by the GC23.[185]

The hypothesis of this study, as we will see in the second chapter, is that the SEPP has already had a method since 1978 and it is inspired by the Management by Objectives theory. Of course its use in the educational and pastoral settings seems too technical, thus the Salesians have been adjusting it with different "criteria" without touching the problematic core of the theory. So it happens that the different documents emphasize, on the one hand, the concreteness and measurability of the objectives, and, on the other, give the operators the right to choose whatever methodology. In the next chapters we would like to propose a methodology inspired by Don Bosco's experience in the Oratory of Valdocco following this principle: "The pedagogical approach of the method, closely linked to the content and dynamics, is important. [...] There are some very important 'points of no return', based on reality. [...] Youth Ministry is authentic if it is characterised by flexibility and creativity. In this sense, the method is also the message".[186]

---

[184] See YM DEPARTMENT, *Frame of Reference*, ³2014, pp. 289-290.
[185] The chapter on the Preventive System states: "We need to translate the theory into practical programmes of structured learning, in gradual stages, suited to the condition of the young people who are to implement them (objectives, attitudes, knowledge, concrete commitments and experiences) with some clearly defined content." Then it indicates four areas of human and Christian maturity (not aligned to the four dimensions of the SEPP); a set of four practical and seven methodological criteria. See YM DEPARTMENT, *Frame of Reference*, ³2014, pp. 107-111.
[186] YM DEPARTMENT, *Frame of Reference*, ³2014, p. 109.

2. Theoretical backgrounds of Salesian Leadership and Project Management

In the previous chapter we covered the main turning points of the Salesian Youth Ministry that had an impact on educative and pastoral project management. After the preludes of the General Chapter 19 in 1965, the crucial period came of Juan Edmundo Vecchi's systematical and methodological approach to the Youth Ministry (YM) from 1978 to 1990. We have seen the fundamental evolution of the Salesian Educative and Pastoral Community (EPC) being the active subject of the Salesian Educative and Pastoral Project (SEPP) developed in four dimensions and planned through a three-step methodology (situation analysis, operational planning, assessment). From the mid-1980s the evolution has been terminated and the YM Department consolidated the model through the idea of "planning mentality". In the third millennium we could find indicators of some limits of the post-Vatican II Salesian project management model on the one hand and proposals for improvement on the other.

In this chapter, in the first place, we will analyze the theoretical background of the Salesian project management methodology, its strong points and blind spots. The second step will lead us to the recent but already consolidated developments of the organizational sciences in order to find a more balanced theoretical model.[1] The third part of this chapter will summarize the different approaches to management and leadership in the area of consecrated life in order to see its uniqueness. These three steps should lead us to adopting a more integrated organizational model that builds on tradition, to dialogue with the organizational sciences and with its recent practical improvements, to respect the specific traits of Christian and consecrated life's organizational needs, and lead us in the

---

[1] In this study we understand the "organizational sciences" as the area of scientific management, leadership theory and reflective organizational practice.

reshaping of the Salesian Leadership and Project Management method-ology.

The Salesian Educative and Pastoral Project methodology developed by the Youth Ministry Department from 1978 to 1984 under the guidance of Juan Edmundo Vecchi was not created as a *tabula rasa*. It was not inspired only by the "Salesian memory", but also and especially by pro-ject management theories popular during the years around Vatican II. Vecchi describes the situation of the '60s and '70s and its implications for education emphasizing these aspects: "There were new levels of ed-ucational needs and a new way of putting educational issues in a basically urban society with post-material needs dominated by the spirit of science and technology. In this way the changed mindset gives more importance to becoming than to persevering, to existence rather than to being, to a man-as-project more than to a man-as-subject".[2] The new way of looking at human beings, society and education influenced the thinking of Sale-sian educators and education theorists. The main, but not exclusive, source of study of the theoretical background of the SEPP is the ency-clopedic publication on the Educative and Pastoral Project edited in 1984 by Juan Edmundo Vecchi (from the YM Department) and José Manuel Prellezo (from the Faculty of Educational Sciences of the Salesian Pon-tifical University).[3]

Vecchi made some explicit references to the sciences of education in the very first paragraph of the module on the Educative and Pastoral Pro-ject: "The terms project and project design have only entered the pedagogic language recently [...] This seems mostly due to the develop-ments in the educational sciences area. The organic connection among different needs of the complex personality evolution emerged more clearly. The decisive push was given by the didactics that introduced the

---

[2] See J.E. VECCHI, *Pastorale, educazione, pedagogia nella prassi Salesiana*, in *Il cam-mino e la prospettiva 2000*, p. 20.
[3] See J.E. VECCHI – J.M. PRELLEZO (Eds.), *Progetto educativo pastorale. Elementi mo-dulari*, LAS, Roma 1984.

concept of the curriculum".[4] Vecchi then uses the definition of curriculum given by the educationist Lawrence Stenhouse that influenced most his concept of the educational and pastoral project: the curriculum is "an attempt to communicate the essential principles and features of an educational proposal in such a form that it is open to critical scrutiny and capable of effective translation into practice".[5]

Scholars that have studied the theory and practice of educational and/or pastoral projects, the educational community, the objectives, programmes and curriculum design can be divided into three groups. The first consists of the Salesian scholars in the area of didactics or curriculum design, authors of the articles in the 1984 "encyclopedic" publication of *Progetto Educativo Pastorale*: Juan E. Vecchi, Youth Ministry Councillor and editor of the publication together with two professors at the UPS; Michele Pellerey, an expert in curriculum design;[6] and Silvano Sarti, a specialist in statistics and in the education assessment field.[7]

The second group of scholars is linked to the field of didactics and curriculum design and consists of explicitly quoted authors in the methodological aspects of the educative and pastoral project. There is an American group consisting of students and collaborators of Ralph W. Tyler: Benjamin S. Bloom, Robert M. Gagné, and Leslie J. Briggs. Influential European authors are Belgians Erik de Corte, Gilbert L. de Landsheere and the aforementioned British scholar Lawrence Stenhouse.[8]

---

[4] J.E. VECCHI, *Progetto educativo pastorale*, in VECCHI – PRELLEZO, *Progetto educativo pastorale*, p. 15. See also VECCHI, *Per riattualizzare il Sistema Preventivo*, ILE, Convegno sul Sistema Preventivo, p. 4.

[5] L. STENHOUSE, *An Introduction to Curriculum Research and Development*, Heinemann, London 1975, p. 4.

[6] See M. PELLEREY, *Progettazione didattica*, SEI, Torino 1979; ID. (Ed.), *Progettare l'educazione nella scuola cattolica*, LAS, Roma 1981.

[7] See S. SARTI, *Valutazione*, in VECCHI – PRELLEZO, *Progetto educativo pastorale*, pp. 310-321.

[8] See e.g. VECCHI – PRELLEZO, *Progetto educativo pastorale*, pp. 100; 196; 312 and 321.

The third group of scholars is distinguished by their main reference to the animation theory developed in the 1970s and '80s. The leading influential author is the Salesian Riccardo Tonelli, the author of an article on the educational community, followed by the Salesian Aldo Ellena and Mario Pollo who develop a more specific reflection on forms of animation.[9]

In this section we will describe the theories and main ideas of these authors in order to understand the model and methodology of the SEPP. We will begin with the development of the curriculum design theories until 1984, the year when *Progetto Educativo Pastorale* was published that concluded the building of the SEPP methodology. Afterwards we will analyze the animation theory that influenced significantly the Salesian leadership model. The animation theorists only adopted some diluted principles from the field of didactics for the project management methodology.[10]

2.1 Curriculum Design Influences from Bobbitt through Tyler to Stenhouse

Pellerey describes the educational projects of the '60s and '70s as a movement that wanted to "overcome both the risk of bureaucracy and the inefficiency of the spontaneous wishful thinking model. And so the field of pedagogy was invaded by the curricular design theories and the educators were following the educational technology directions".[11] The beginning and the background of this impressive movement of those years originated in the early twentieth century.

---

[9] See *Idem*, pp. 285-309; 355-363; 399-417 and R. TONELLI, *Per fare un progetto educativo*, in «Note di Pastorale Giovanile» 14 (1980) 6, 57-66 mentioned by Vecchi in VECCHI – PRELLEZO, *Progetto educativo pastorale*, p. 25.

[10] Tonelli acknowledges that the inspiration for the projects in the animation area came from curriculum design in TONELLI, *Per fare un progetto educativo*, 3-13.

[11] PELLEREY, *Progettazione didattica*, p. 10.

The origin of the innovative curricular theories can be traced back to John Dewey. In his 1902 book, *The Child and the Curriculum*, he traces an innovative and flexible theory of curriculum seen as both "the child's present experience" and "the subject-matter of studies".[12] But in the beginning of the 20th century efficiency was prized more. Strongly influenced by time and motion studies in industry, scientific curriculum designers applied an industrial design to schools: a systematically designed programme, including tracking and testing, would efficiently sort students by aptitude and achievement.

In the first years of the century, a pioneer curriculum maker Franklin Bobbitt surveyed the knowledge, skills, and values possessed by successful adults in Los Angeles and designed curricula in the Philippines. He gave precedence to subjects he believed to have a major utility in daily life, such as spelling and arithmetic. His theory is summarised in his publication of *The Curriculum*: "Human life, however varied, consists in the performance of specific activities. Education that prepares for life is one that prepares definitely and adequately for these specific activities. However numerous and diverse they may be for any social class, they can be discovered. This requires only that one go out into the world of affairs and discover the particulars of which these affairs consist. These will show the abilities, attitudes, habits, appreciations, and forms of knowledge that men need. These will be the objectives of the curriculum. They will be numerous, definite, and particularized. The curriculum will then be that series of experiences which children and youth must have by way of attaining those objectives".[13]

Bobbitt's way of conceiving education was strongly influenced by the rise of scientific management. In 1911, Frederick W. Taylor, in his most important work on scientific management, proposes three elements to

---

[12] J. DEWEY, *The Child and the Curriculum*, in D.J. SIMPSON – M.J.B. JACKSON, *John Dewey's View of the Curriculum in The Child and the Curriculum*, in «Education and Culture» 20 (2003) 2, 25. See also C. KRIDEL (Ed.), *Encyclopedia of Curriculum*, Sage, Thousand Oaks CA 2010, pp. 199-200.

[13] J.F. BOBBITT, *The Curriculum*, Houghton Mifflin, Boston 1918, p. 42.

raise substantially the efficiency of any process: 1. scientific study of the tasks; 2. detailed description and breakdown of activities; and 3. extension of managerial control and the scientific study of all the elements of space and time in which the activities take place. The educational process would be, according to this rationalist and voluntarist model, similar to a production line in industry.[14]

Bobbitt's theory and practice did not win a big acclaim in the '20s and '30s due to the popularity of Dewey's "progressive education" which focused more on experiential learning and the personality of the pupil. In the changed context of the late '40s there was a possibility of new developments of curricular theories. Although there is no direct influence of Bobbitt's theory to the methodology of the SEPP, we can perceive his influence through the link he introduced between organizational thinking and curriculum design. In the post-World War II period there were different educational needs that fostered the exchange between project management and curriculum design. We could divide the most influential schools according to three major paradigms: curriculum as a product; curriculum as a process; and curriculum as an inquiry.

2.1.1 Product Model

The leading figure of educational curriculum design of the 1950s was Ralph W. Tyler. A key reference is his 1949 book entitled *Basic Principles of Curriculum and Instruction*, a bestseller with 36 editions and a

---

[14] See J.F. BOBBITT, *Some general principles of management applied to the problems of city-school systems*, National Society for the Study of Education, Bloomington 1913; R. CALLAHAN, *Education and the Cult of Efficiency*, University of Chicago Press, Chicago 1962; C.H. EDSON, *Curriculum Change During the Progressive Era*, in «Educational Leadership» 36 (1978) 64; T. BUSH, *Leadership and management development in education*, Sage, London [4]2011, p. 10; R. BATES, *History of Educational Leadership/Management*, in P. PETERSON – E. BAKER – B. McGAW (Eds.), *International Encyclopedia Of Education*, vol. 4, Academic Press, Oxford [3]2010, p. 724.

considerable influence on educative practice.[15] The publication, among other things, intended to reaffirm the importance of the education and instruction against the invasion of psychometrics and the statistical thinking. Tyler begins his book with four questions that determine, together with their answers, the rational framework that encompasses the issues relating to the curriculum and education. The questions are:

1. "What educational purposes should the school seek to attain?
2. What educational experiences can be provided that are likely to attain these purposes?
3. How can these educational experiences be effectively organized?
4. How can we determine whether these purposes are being attained?".[16]

In the first part of his book, he introduces the concept of an educational objective. In the concept of the "objective" he connects interdisciplinary contributions of philosophy and psychology with the learner's needs, with his relationships to the physical and social environment and with values, skills and abilities to promote. There is a clear emphasis on the concept of the "objectives" with a sketch of a taxonomy of educational objectives for a social studies curriculum.[17] The linearity of his scheme starts with stating the objectives, continues with the selection of learning experiences, and ends with the evaluation of the objectives' achievement. The key to design a curriculum is the set of objectives to be reached. In this sense this model is based on the final "product" and organizes all activities looking to the "output". Other

---

[15] See R.W. TYLER, *Basic Principles of Curriculum and Instruction,* The University of Chicago Press, Chicago 1949. N.B. "Instruction" and "Education" have different nuances in American and British English. Here we perceive "Education" as a holistic integrated process of personality development and we see "Instruction" as the process of acquiring specific knowledge and competencies.

[16] TYLER, *Basic Principles of Curriculum,* p. 1.

[17] *Idem*, pp. 3-62 e 89-94.

names given to this paradigm are "Outcome-Based Education" or "Organizing for Results" model.[18]

Tyler also tries to formulate the concept of continuity of different learning experiences threads. "It is also essential to identify the organizing principles by which these threads shall be woven together".[19] Unfortunately, an integrating "organizing principle" remains a concept without wider developments and the author focuses almost exclusively on the organizational structures of the curriculum such as lessons, units, and topics. Also the examples he uses in the curriculum design are linked to the contents of the school subjects and there are very few values, skills or attitudes to be acquired.[20]

Some of Tyler's students and colleagues integrated his model with some instances of programmed learning theories of Burrhus F. Skinner and Norman A. Crowder. There is a clear technological accent on the programming of sequences that consist in: a clear design; the project implementation process; the systematic monitoring of both the product (quality control) and the process (evaluation).[21] Education technology and teaching machines experimentation were combined with some outcomes of radical behaviourism and with the popular Management by Objectives (MBO) theory. The "Decade of education" in the United States (1957-68) that followed the impression of being left behind by the Soviets in the "Space race" had created a context for the development of a massive curriculum design movement of the '60s and '70s.[22]

---

[18] See J. MCKERNAN, *Curriculum and Imagination. Process theory, pedagogy and action research*, Routledge, London 2008.

[19] TYLER, *Basic Principles of Curriculum*, p. 95.

[20] *Idem*, pp. 95-100.

[21] R. GLASER – A.A. LUMSDAINE (Eds.), *Teaching Machines and Programmed Learning. A Source Book*, National Education Association, Washington DC 1961 and J. HARTLEY, *Programmed Instruction 1954-1974. A Review*, in «Innovations in Education & Training International» 11 (1974) 6, 278-291.

[22] J.I. GOODLAD, *Improving Schooling in the 1980s: Toward the Non-Replication of Non-Events*. We have learned some painful lessons about how not to achieve change, in «Educational Leadership» 40 (1983) 4; P.M. SENGE, *The Industrial Age System of Education*, in P.M. SENGE et al., *Schools That Learn. A Fifth Discipline Fieldbook for*

Hilda Taba, a curriculum design scholar, after collaboration with Dewey, Tyler and Bloom, develops her own curriculum theory. She introduces the concept of "needs", upgrading Tyler's curriculum development steps by diagnosing the needs at first point and only then formulating the objectives.[23] Her theory distinguishes between the general aims of education and the more specific educational objectives. The aims are general intentions so as to transmit culture or to pass on a style of democratic life. The objectives are more specific and related to a desired behaviour. The aims are defined, but the importance is attached to the objectives – the effectiveness of the educational process is seen in proportion to the concreteness of the objectives because it guides the choices in the creation and the assessment stage of the curriculum.[24]

The problem of the correct formulation of educative objectives drew attention of a large portion of scholars who often focused on clear wording and precise formulation of the objectives. Ralph Tyler has dedicated half of the *Basic Principles of Curriculum* to this theme. The attempt to produce a taxonomy of educational objectives arose in the United States in the late '40s and had its highest development in Benjamin S. Bloom's publications. Bloom published two of the three planned volumes in which the taxonomy of cognitive and affective objectives was described. The third volume, published after some years, describes the areas of psychomotor development. Bloom's taxonomy describes human growth in

---

Educators, Parents, and Everyone Who Cares About Education, Doubleday, New York 2000, pp. 27-49 and J.L. MILLER, *Curriculum and Poststructuralist Theory*, in PETERSON - BAKER - MCGAW (Eds.), International Encyclopedia Of Education, vol. 1, ³2010, pp. 499-500.

[23] See H. TABA, *Curriculum development: theory and practice*, Burlingham: Harcourt, Brace & World, New York 1962, pp. 12; 284-289.

[24] See *Idem*, pp. 196-199 and W.J. POPHAM – E.L. BAKER, *Systematic instruction*, Prentice-Hall, Englewood Cliffs NJ 1970, p. 19. The influence of the aim-objective distinction is to be noted in M. PELLEREY, *Obiettivi*, in VECCHI - PRELLEZO, *Progetto Educativo Pastorale*, pp. 94-95; 99-100.

three areas, eleven sub-areas, with a total of 54 items that need to be further specified with curricular objectives.[25]

Later, tools were prepared to facilitate the formulation of educational objectives using Bloom's taxonomy. As an example we can mention the publication by Newton S. Metfessel, William B. Michael and Donald A. Kirsner that offers an instrument arranged in three columns: the first contains the original classification of Bloom's; the second presents examples of verbs that express the related action; and the third column provides examples of an object that can further specify the described action.[26] The same linguistic formulation issues, as we have already seen, emerged in the analysis of the Provincial SEPPs of the early '90s. There is a similar logic also to be seen in other applications: the Instructional Objectives Exchange bank of educational objectives developed for teachers in the '70s could be compared with the anthology of the SEPPs published by the YM Department intended to be an inspiration for the project designs of the Provinces and Salesian houses.[27]

There are other authors who can help us understand the overstated number of objectives of the SEPP. Following Bloom's logic, they prefer a complete rationalistic description of education to a realistic number of objectives. One of these authors, quoted by Pellerey, is Louis D'Hainaut, a chemistry researcher turned education theorist, who has developed a

---

[25] See B.S. BLOOM – D.R. KRATHWOHL et al., *Taxonomy of Educational Objectives. The Classification of Educational Goals*, Handbook 1: *Cognitive domain*, David McKay, New York 1956 e D.R. KRATHWOHL – B.S. BLOOM – B.B. MASIA, *Taxonomy of Educational Objectives. The Classification of Educational Goals*. Handbook 2: *Affective domain*, David McKay, New York 1964 and A.J. HARROW, *A taxonomy of the psychomotor domain. A guide for developing behavioral objectives*, David McKay Company, New York 1972.

[26] See D. BROWN, *Usiamo il cervello*, SEI, Torino 1976, pp. 287-291 that reproduced the quoted instrument and was proposed later in PELLEREY, *Progettazione didattica*, 1979, pp. 240-244.

[27] See W.J. POPHAM, *Instructional Objectives Exchange rationale statement*, UCLA Center for the Study of Evaluation, Los Angeles CA 1970 and DICASTERO PER LA PASTORALE GIOVANILE, *Il Progetto Educativo-pastorale Salesiano. Raccolta antologica di testi*, Dossier PG 9, SDB, Roma 1995.

detailed model of educational objectives based on 20 intellectual operations. These twenty intellectual operations are subdivided into more than
100 objectives, which in turn are further specified in more than 200 sub-
objectives.[28] Pellerey used this model because it was the most complete
one in the late '70s, confirming the rationalistic scientific paradigm of
those years. Based on the model of natural sciences, the authors believed
in the creation of a complete rational model of human growth and the
corresponding educational projects.

Pellerey's model presented in the *Progetto Educativo Pastorale* and
in his previous publications[29] is based on the theories of "Tyler's circle":
Bloom, Gagné – Briggs, Glaser, Mager and Taba. We will only list some
of his proposals which soften the technical approach to educational projects. The first interesting distinction in his theory is between educational
and teaching (didactical) objectives. Following Taba's differentiation between aims and objectives, he defines educational objectives as basic
guidelines, principles of action that create an educational horizon or a
framework of values to be implemented. The teaching objectives are
more specific goals to be achieved in the context of teaching specific
subjects or areas.[30] This distinction is useful when designing an educational project in a less formal or informal structure: family, youth group,
oratory, sport organizations, etc., where the educational objectives
should impact more concretely the designed activities.[31]

---

[28] See L. D'HAINAUT, *Des fins aux objectifs de l'éducation*, Labor, Bruxelles 1977, pp.
106-120.
[29] Pellerey's primary curriculum design experience is in the field of mathematics didactics. See M. PELLEREY, *L'educazione matematica. Problemi e sperimentazioni*, in
PELLEREY, *Progettazione didattica*, p. 245; ID., *Per un insegnamento della matematica
dal volto umano. Contributi per una didattica della matematica per la scuola media*,
SEI, Torino 1983 and ID., *L'insegnamento della matematica*, SEI, Torino 1986.
[30] See PELLEREY, *Progettazione didattica*, pp. 54-55.
[31] See PELLEREY, *Obiettivi*, in VECCHI - PRELLEZO, *Progetto Educativo Pastorale*, pp. 96
and 99. This equilibrium is not found in the article about project assessment which is
seen only in a teaching perspective. See SARTI, *Valutazione*, in VECCHI - PRELLEZO,
Progetto Educativo Pastorale, pp. 310-321.

The second innovative idea is the definition of an educational need, seen as a gap between an existing situation and a desired educational ideal, or between "what should be" and the situation "as it is". The definition was thought to overcome the dilemma of the starting point of the curriculum design: Do we start with the ideal objectives or with the situation analysis? Developing this definition, Pellerey proposes various types of educational needs:

- Need as a variance compared to a norm;
- Need as a desire in a person's soul;
- Need as an expressed demand;
- Need that arises from the confrontation with people who own something more;
- Need as an anticipation of future necessities.[32]

There is a third group of useful concepts put together by Pellerey's intuitions that were not followed in the SEPP model. The notion of "institutional aims" could introduce some specific elements of the Salesian tradition in the objectives formulation process. Different institutions respond differently to the same need.[33] Another useful, but not applied proposal in the Salesian Youth Ministry documents was the introduction of the socio-cultural project model, based on the interaction between people, values and resources present in the community and in the territory. Often a socio-cultural project does not provide a clear linear path of its realization. Also the theory of nonlinear design sequences within the programmes had no following in the future.[34]

---

[32] See PELLEREY, *Progettazione didattica*, pp. 90-93.
[33] See PELLEREY, *Obiettivi*, in VECCHI - PRELLEZO, *Progetto Educativo Pastorale*, pp. 93-94.
[34] See PELLEREY, *Itinerario*, in VECCHI - PRELLEZO, *Progetto Educativo Pastorale*, pp. 191-192 and 194-195.

2.1.2 Process Model

In his proposal, Pellerey is confronting two concepts of the curriculum design: the product model and the process model. His solution, or synthesis, lies in the distinction between educational goals, which are linked more to the whole educative "process", and the teaching objectives, linked to specific didactical units or competences seen more as a "product". This solution of the dilemma remains altogether linked to the product paradigm design model because it only makes a subdivision in a general Management by Objectives logic.

There are authors worth mentioning which have gone further in the processual logic and changed the paradigm of curriculum design. Richard Stanley Peters, professor of education philosophy at the University of London, goes beyond the linear scheme of need-objective-assessment. Knowing that education needs the participation in different activities, the worthwhile activities "can be appraised because of the standards immanent in them rather than because of what they lead on to".[35]

In his theory, Peters distinguishes between "aims" and "principles of procedure", where the former are behavioural objectives and the latter are the criteria for the selection and adaptation of worthwhile activities. As an example, we can consider the intrinsically rewarding process of understanding concepts like tragedy from reading *Macbeth* that goes beyond a simple behavioural objective. Teachers and theorists in the arts and humanities in particular have countered that in these fields the concern is not for students to reach objectives or outcomes once and for all, but rather for them to develop standards of judgment, criticism, and taste. Peters confirms his position in his later publication on philosophy of education, seeing the notion of "being educated" as not arriving at the destination, but travelling between different perspectives. What is needed is not a feverish preparation for something beyond, but to work

---

[35] R.S. PETERS, *Ethics and Education*, George Allen and Unwin, London 1966, p. 155.

with precision, passion and taste in things that are worthy and valid at hand.[36]

James D. Raths, an American expert in curriculum design and teacher formation, offers an interesting list of twelve criteria to identify activities that have an inherent value in themselves regardless of the content or the objectives. A worthwhile activity:

1. helps to make informed choices and to reflect on the consequences;
2. assigns to students active roles rather than passive ones;
3. asks students to engage in inquiry into ideas, applications or current problems;
4. involves children with realia (concrete objects, materials, artifacts, etc.);
5. may be accomplished successfully by children at several different levels of ability;
6. asks students to examine in a previously studied idea, or problem;
7. requires to examine topics that are normally or systematically neglected in the society;
8. involves in taking a risk of failure or success;
9. requires students to rewrite, rehearse, and polish their initial efforts;
10. involves students in the application and mastery of meaningful rules, standards, or disciplines;
11. gives a chance to develop a project, carry it out and share the results with others;
12. is relevant to the expressed purposes of the students.[37]

It seems that the process model is therefore focused on the intrinsic quality of the activities and by its nature it does not tend to have a final exam in order to test the achievement of the designed objectives. This characteristic makes it less applicable in formal education, especially in

---

[36] See R.S. PETERS (Ed.), *The Philosophy of Education*, Oxford University Press, Oxford 1973.

[37] See J.D. RATHS, *Teaching without specific objectives*, in «Educational Leadership» 28 (1971) 714-720.

a complex society setting that requires various standards. It is more natural to adopt the process paradigm in humanities teaching and in non-formal or informal education programmes. Another important difference between the two mentioned curricular paradigms is the different weight given to the uniqueness of each specific setting of class, school or student[38] and the diversification about the view on "results" or "educational success" of the processes that take place in environments and with unique people. The students, according to the paradigm of the process, are not passive objects. They have an important voice in deciding the way in which the lessons and curriculum evolve. The focus of the process is therefore centred on the interactions that shift the accent from teaching to learning.

2.1.3 Research Model

Lawrence Stenhouse is a British education scholar who has developed a framework that wants to go beyond the product-process dilemma. His thinking moved around a central point in curriculum design – the teacher as an active part of the educational research. Overcoming the rigid standardization of the product model and at the same time avoiding the not very applicable vagueness of the procedural model is not an easy task. In a polarized situation between product and process theories, every researcher risked to be understood within these two paradigms and not as an author of an original third model. In fact, Stenhouse's successors John Elliott and Stephen Kemmis identify him as a follower of Peters and call his theory "processual", neglecting the originality of his approach.[39] As

---

[38] See Raths' valorization of educational activities that do not have a specific objective but create a learning environment in RATHS, *Teaching without specific objectives*, 716.
[39] See J. ELLIOTT, *Education in the Shadow of the Education Reform Act*, in J. RUDDUCK, *An Education that Empowers. A collection of Lectures in Memory of Lawrence Stenhouse*, BERA, Clevedon (Avon) 1995, pp. 54-55 and M. JAMES, *An alternative to the objectives model. The process model for the design and development of curriculum*, in J. ELLIOTT – N. NORRIS (Eds.), *Curriculum, Pedagogy and Educational Research. The Work of Lawrence Stenhouse*, Routledge, London 2012, pp. 64-83.

we have seen, Stenhouse was a primary inspiration for Vecchi's SEPP methodology. Both of them put in place a balanced model that is not easy either to understand in all theoretical equilibriums and to apply in practical applications linked with the theory. As it seems, not every scholar has the fortune to be understood by his successors, and so Stenhouse was linked to the process paradigm and Vecchi seems to be interpreted within a linear product model of project management.[40]

Stenhouse turned his attention to the relationship between the theory and practice in education and brought forward a new perspective. He noted that a large-scale research does not necessarily lead to the improvement of local educational practice. In order to arrive at sustainable improvement in the quality of education, there is always a need of every single teacher's research on their specific educational practices. In this sense the author conceives the curriculum as the interaction between the teacher and students in the curriculum construction, understood as a process of research and verification of educational assumptions.[41] His proposal is not easy to implement, as we can see in the first pages of his publication where he defines curriculum. "As a minimum, a curriculum should provide a basis for planning a course, studying it empirically and considering the grounds of its justification. It should offer:

"*A. In planning:*

1. Principle for the selection of content – what is to be learned and taught.
2. Principles for the development of a teaching strategy – how it is to be learned and taught.
3. Principles for the making of decisions about sequence.

---

[40] The interpretation of Vecchi's model has to do mostly with the general scientific context of the '70s that preferred technological linear solutions. The synthetic explanations of his theory are more balanced and his personal facilitation method was very inclusive and functional. In this sense, SEPP's simplified history of effects overrides the balance of his theory and practice.

[41] See L. STENHOUSE, *An Introduction to Curriculum Research and Development*, Heinemann, London 1975, pp. 123-141.

4. Principles on which to diagnose the strengths and weaknesses of individual students and differentiate the general principles 1, 2 and 3 above, to meet individual cases.

B. *In empirical study:*

1. Principles on which to study and evaluate the progress of students.
2. Principles on which to study and evaluate the progress of teachers.
3. Guidance as to the feasibility of implementing the curriculum in varying school contexts, pupil contexts, environments and peer-group situations.
4. Information about the variability of effects in differing contexts and on different pupils and an understanding of the causes of the variation.

C. *In relation to justification:*

A formulation of the intention or aim of the curriculum which is accessible to critical scrutiny".[42]

Stenhouse reaffirms the British tradition of individual schools and of teachers' autonomy, decentralizing both the product and the process of the curriculum creation. His integration of the previous models accepts the curriculum with its objectives, but only as a hypothesis. He also integrates the processual logic, applying it not to the teaching process but to the curriculum design process.

In this way, the teacher becomes a researcher and the curriculum a problem-solving research tool for a classroom or a school.[43] In the product model, school is primarily a workshop where the teacher is a worker and the child is the product. For Stenhouse each class is a laboratory and the teacher is a member of the scientific community. He sees "curriculum as a policy, but to take the Popperian view of policies, asserting that policies evolve and improve continuously and progressively by the study of their shortcomings and their gradual elimination. On such a view the concepts of success and failure become irrelevant. A curriculum without

---

[42] STENHOUSE, *An Introduction to Curriculum*, p. 5.
[43] See *Idem*, pp. 142-165.

shortcomings has no prospect of improvement and has therefore been insufficiently ambitious. [...] Its dilemmas should be important dilemmas. Its shortcomings should reflect real and important difficulties".[44] In addition to Popper's falsification research model, it seems that Stenhouse is not far from Kurt Lewin's model of Action-Research developed in the USA in the late 1940s. In fact, different authors affirm that under the influence of Stenhouse, Action-Research regarding sciences of education was rediscovered in Britain and Australia.[45]

2.1.4 Critical Evaluation of the Models of Curriculum Design

The described models have a deeper underlying philosophical groundings. We want to pinpoint some advantages and limits of each of these conceptions.[46] In this sense, different models can be more suitable for different organizational settings that embody a specific line of thought. Simplifying, we can state that the product model has strong references to natural sciences and technical solutions; the process model is more linked to arts, literature, philosophy or the humanities. Stenhouse's model is not only linked to a set of specific subjects, but to a practitioner's philosophy of action in the field of curriculum design.

It seems that the Salesian context of the post-Vatican II required a simple and clear model for the Salesian Educative and Pastoral Project. Pellerey confirms that the SEPPs should have become an instrument of the central government after the turbulent years. The product model with its concreteness, which was shared by many scholars of the '70s, responded to the technocratic optimism of those years and was practised especially in the Spanish-speaking Salesian countries. On the contrary, the process model was too generic and not suitable for central government purposes. And Stenhouse's (and Vecchi's) research model was

---

44 *Idem*, p. 125.
45 See KEMMIS, *Some Ambiguities in Stenhouse*, in RUDDUCK, *An Education that Empowers*, p. 77.
46 See MCKERNAN, *Curriculum and Imagination*, pp. 3-36.

quite fluid, complicated and required too many roles and qualities from the same person: teacher, researcher, curriculum designer and project manager. It has to be noted that Stenhouse's experimentation with the *Humanities Curriculum Project* took place in a specific "optimistic" setting of the years 1967-72 under the authority of the Schools Council for Curriculum and Examinations in England and Wales.[47] We can conclude that the product model, linked with the Management by Objectives (MBO), had the main influence on the SEPP methodology. We will describe its strengths and limits in the following paragraphs.

The strength and appeal of the product paradigm is mainly the organizational strength and the simple linearity of the model. The concreteness and measurability of results is rooted in the formulation of behavioural objectives, in linking objectives and specific activities, and finally in the assessment of the objectives achievement. Besides these organizational advantages, which can be applied in certain structures and programmes, there are some difficulties inherent to the paradigm itself.

There is the risk of depersonalization or even alienation for both students and teachers. This difficulty is heightened because the curricula are created once for all, outside the concreteness of an educational environment. The curricula tend to be standardized and "teacher proof". Being driven by a prescribed programme, teachers become educational technicians that cannot positively exploit the concrete interaction in the classroom.[48]

Another difficulty was already seen by Joseph J. Schwab consisting in the excessive theorization of curricular studies after Tyler. The core of

---

[47] See STENHOUSE, *The Humanities Curriculum Project*, in «Journal of Curriculum Studies» 1 (1968) 1, 26-33.

[48] See H.M. KLIEBARD, *Curricular Objectives and Evaluation. A reassessment*, in «The High School Journal» 51 (1968) 246; STENHOUSE, *An Introduction to Curriculum*, pp. 98-106; J. FORESTER, *Planning in the Face of Power*, University of California Press, Berkeley CA 1989; M. GALTON, *Big change questions: Should pedagogical change be mandated? Dumbing down on classroom standards. The perils of a technician's approach to pedagogy*, in «Journal of Educational Change» 1 (2000) 2, 199-204.

his criticism attacks the process of the formulation of objectives, which are often equivocal and ambiguous and therefore not suitable for practical educational decisions. A group of teachers will willingly agree on the objectives and, right after that, each one will follow a different path of concrete educational decisions.[49] It should be noted that the use of auxiliary instruments for the formulation of objectives, like the *Instructional Objectives Exchange* database or the Metfessel's model, reinforces the ambiguity of the theoretical objectives that could remain empty concepts without contextual semantic concreteness.

The third difficulty concerns the measurability and concreteness of educational objectives. In education there is always uncertainty and doubt about the method and the object of measurement. In continuity with Taylor's scientific management and Management by Objectives, the objectives are split in different levels of sub-objectives. Thus we come to endless lists of skills often more trivial than significant, losing the whole picture and reducing education to a repetition of gestures or content.[50] Pellerey also criticizes the taxonomy logic that cannot take into account the diversity of situations, and according to him, if the taxonomy becomes more specific and detailed it becomes also too bulky and impracticable.[51] We could see this tension between concreteness and extension in the development of the SEPP Handouts. The model proposed by the Handouts has become increasingly extended and less applicable.

A fourth risk of this outcome-based education is that it should guarantee passing the exams, but does not take into account the long-term outcomes considered in its entirety as a whole. The product paradigm adopts an analytical look at the educational reality and prefers a linear

---

[49] See J.J. SCHWAB, *Science, curriculum and liberal education*, The University of Chicago Press, Chicago 1978.
[50] See M.J. PICKARD, *The New Bloom's Taxonomy: An Overview for Family and Consumer Sciences*, in «Journal of Family and Consumer Sciences Education» 25 (2007) 1, 52.
[51] See. PELLEREY, *Progettazione didattica*, pp. 109-110.

causality project management. It puts aside the non-linear causality, unanticipated consequences, delayed effects, complexity of the interactions and other implications of the general theory of systems applied to the educational reality.[52] Stenhouse states: "Knowledge is primarily concerned with synthesis. The analytic approach implied in objectives model readily trivializes it".[53] In this sense, we think that the Salesian Documents constantly reminding of an integral or organic oneness of the SEPP's dimensions could be perceived as an expression of the lack of systemic approach, inherent in Management by Objectives.

A final difficulty comes from the field of educational praxis. After a period of initial enthusiasm scholars that have adopted the curriculum based on objectives have noted the lack of real impact on concrete educational practices. It seems that the product paradigm is more suitable for a theoretical model of human behaviour and education than for a concrete educational methodology. In the Salesian environments the mentioned practical difficulty becomes stronger because of the solid presence of general educational objectives, like ability to love, generosity, active citizenship, etc. The difficulty persists if we consider the application in less structured Salesian educative environments like the traditional oratory or the newer ones like youth centres, groups and movements.

Stenhouse, as a practitioner, notes a negative aspect of the MBO that can be referred to the development of the SEPP in the '90s: "I believe there is a tendency, recurrent enough to suggest that it may be endemic in the approach, for academics in education to use the objectives model as a stick with which to beat the teachers. 'What are your objectives?' is more often asked in a tone of challenge than one of interested and helpful inquiry. The demand for objectives is a demand for justification rather

---

[52] Cfr. A.L. WILSON – R.M. CERVERO, *Program Planning*, in PETERSON - BAKER - MCGAW (Eds.), *International Encyclopedia of Education*, vol. 1, ³2010, pp. 53-54 e Z. DENG, *Curriculum Planning and Systems Change*, in PETERSON - BAKER - MCGAW (Eds.), *International Encyclopedia of Education*, vol. 1, ³2010, pp. 384-389.

[53] STENHOUSE, *An Introduction to Curriculum*, p. 83.

than description of ends. As such it is part of a political dialogue rather than an educative one".[54]

2.2 Animation as a Theoretical Leadership Model

The term "animation" has been successful especially in the neo-Latin language contexts such as Italy, Spain, France, Canada and Latin America. In every setting it had a different focus ranging from a praxis of community development through programmes of informal education to a holistic education methodology. In Italy, animation started as a trend of theatrical experimentations in state schools and as new participative techniques of community development. 1968 and the succeeding years are the take-off period of animation that embodied a good part of the political tension of that time. In the '80s animation moved to a more educational horizon promoting collaboration with education and socialization agencies. Especially in France and Canada, animation was perceived as a continuation of educational methodologies used in informal settings of summer camps, free time activities, youth centres, etc., dating back to the last decades of the 19th century.[55]

In the Italian context, which is fundamental for Salesian animation, we can distinguish three major types of animation theory and practice. In two of them there was a key presence of the Salesians of Don Bosco. The first type refers to theatrical animation and we have authors such as Gianni Rodari, Giuliano Scabia and Franco Passatore, supporting it. This type of theatre was developed as a means for liberation of expressiveness and imagination. The second category is called cultural animation and its main authors are Riccardo Tonelli and Mario Pollo, both professors at the Salesian Pontifical University and contributors to the Italian Youth

---

[54] *Idem*, p. 77.
[55] See M. POLLO, *L'animazione culturale: teoria e metodo*, LAS, Roma 2002, pp. 13-15; J.P. AUGUSTIN – J.C. GILLET, *L'animation professionnelle. Histoire, acteurs, enjeux*, Harmattan, Paris Montréal 2000, pp. 23-40 and H. CAMPFENS (Ed.), *Community Development Around the World*, University of Toronto Press, Toronto 1997.

Ministry Journal *Note di Pastorale Giovanile*. The third line of animation is built around the activity of the Salesian Aldo Ellena in the northern Italy and the journal *Animazione Sociale*. We will analyze the cultural and social animation in their references to the SEPP through Tonelli, Pollo and Ellena's publications and articles in the compendium *Progetto Educativo Pastorale*.[56]

2.2.1 Cultural Animation

The fundamental publication for this type of animation is Mario Pollo's *L'animazione culturale: teoria e metodo. Una proposta* that offers a theoretical scheme of cultural animation. In his concept, "cultural animation is an overall education methodology that aims at the growth and harmonious development of the individual considered as an indivisible unity and not as a sum of parts or functions. The individual and social groups develop through the awareness about the inhabitance of a symbolic world. Then, as a first and foremost task, they must develop their ability to learn, use and create symbolic systems".[57] This definition provides us with the elements that guide Pollo's thought through the entire publication: wholeness of the person inserted in a symbolic world; animation as a holistic education methodology; the interaction between individuals in social groups; communication as creation and use of symbolic systems; and finally, research methodology.

Pollo's animation puts together different pieces of theories that were popular among scholars of the '70s and the '80s. Man, the subject and object of animation, is seen through the lenses of Ernst Cassirer's theory as an *animal symbolicum*. The concept of Cassirer is upgraded with Bernard Kaplan's communication theory, Ludwig von Bertalanffy's systems

---

[56] See VECCHI – PRELLEZO (Eds.), *Progetto Educativo Pastorale*, pp. 285-309; 355-363; 399-417 and POLLO, *L'animazione culturale*, p. 12.

[57] M. POLLO, *L'animazione culturale: teoria e metodo. Una proposta*, LDC, Leumann (TO) 1980, p. 33.

theory, and James G. Miller's living systems model. From this anthropology Pollo expects some meaningful results: "It is the belief of many
social science scholars that the only real passage to get out of the banality
of the numerous results is to approach the study of homo symbolicus".[58]
The cultural animation offers, according to the author, a comprehensive
approach to the education methodology: "It is undoubtedly a rather tough
approach to see in man an area of emotional, intellectual and finally social life [...] The cultural animation tends to exceed this whole series of
dichotomies that have long characterized human choices, like rationality-
emotions, mind-body, thought-instinct".[59] For him, the unity of man "is
guaranteed by the fact that he builds and inhabits symbolic worlds".[60]
High hopes to overcome the dichotomies of reality in the creation of
symbolic worlds are combined with systems theory, which exceeds the
linearity of Newton's world, and with Fromm's idea of social ethics that
goes beyond the alienating power of conformity.

This theoretical framework, in order to be linked with the Salesian
Educative and Pastoral Project, has to be seen in two important aspects:
the place of religious or spiritual dimension in the educative process and
the methodological implications of animation. Pollo's position about religion is between mysticism and science, and he starts his thoughts on
the matter with Ludwig Wittgenstein's quotation about the limits of
knowledge: "There are, indeed, things that cannot be put into words.
They make themselves manifest. They are what is mystical. [...] What
one cannot speak about, one must remain silent".[61] With this starting
point he cannot move forward and sees the religious dimension only as
the inexpressible, as a non-linguistic symbolism, and postulates that animation is an existential communication, a tool that succeeds in this
difficult, impossible task of expressing the inexpressible. We can see

---

[58] *Idem*, p. 13.
[59] *Idem*, p. 34.
[60] *Idem*, p. 35.
[61] L. WITTGENSTEIN, *Tractatus logico-philosophicus*, in POLLO, *L'animazione culturale.
Una proposta*, p. 67.

how Pollo practically accepts Wittgenstein's invitation to silence and does not develop applications about spirituality or religion. In fact, the chapter about the religious dimension is the shortest one, occupying only seven pages. Without significant connections to the rest of the theory, religion and spirituality remain at the margin of his interests.

There are some methodological implications of Pollo's animation theory. He suggests three so-called "instruments", but two of them are supporting theories and only one is a practical method to make animation more real – it is called "the primary group". Pollo describes seven evolutionary stages of the life of a group and introduces some elements of the animation applied to group dynamics: interactions, psychological unity of the group, norms, common purposes, informal-formal structure, collective subconscious, equilibria for stability, climate, stereotypes, standards and compliance.

In the animation theory, group dynamics became an almost "magical formula" that should solve many organizational issues in a paradigm centred at co-responsibility, collegial democratic decision making and civil rights logic. The author confirms the necessity of educational planning: "Within a given social system, the link between any educational theory and its translation into a concrete activity is carried out by an educational project".[62]

Educational project design within the animation theory was influenced mostly by the collegial egalitarian decision making. For Pollo it is difficult not to contradict a real practice of liberation within the practice of educational projects. Liberation is achieved when a project is not written at the desk or only by animators, but is designed by the group that is the subject of animation. Pollo tries to go beyond the mechanistic and linear model of planning speaking about systemic models of project management. However, he gives no indication of authors and does not provide procedures, models or concrete methodologies. The definition of

---

[62] POLLO, *L'animazione culturale*, p. 51.

objectives is seen as the "creation of a conceptual system", the activities or means to achieve the objective are called "moral and cultural coordinates", and finally, assessment should be realized as the "creation of feedback systems".[63] It seems he remains in his preferred domain – liberation participative theory at the level of principles.

Some methodological indications come from the Salesian Riccardo Tonelli, who has written about pastoral projects in youth ministry since 1968.[64] The author focuses mainly on the general approach to the youth ministry and not on the methodology, which is considered by him as a rather technical issue, that "requires a technical skill to be acquired through the study of specialized disciplines [...] This trust and respect of technical equipment is an accurate Salesian need, as a logical consequence of the realization that there is a close relationship between education (and related sciences of education) and evangelization".[65]

Despite the emphasis on the technical aspect of the projects, Tonelli offers interesting methodological steps of the pastoral planning.[66] As a beginning, he presents two already mentioned schemes of planning from Pellerey's publication: one begins with the objectives, the other with the situation analysis (See Scheme A). Tonelli rejects the two schemes for epistemological reasons: the first is too objective and the second too subjective. His proposal is therefore a further "hermeneutic model". The objectives and the questions that arise from the analysis of the situation must be read in the light of the so-called "event of God". Tonelli states: "We must use faith as a key. It cannot replace the descriptive sciences. When these sciences want to research deep existential human needs, they

---

[63] POLLO, L'animazione culturale, p. 66.

[64] See the monographic issue of «Note di Pastorale Giovanile» 2 (1968) 8-9, 4-84. Particularly important are the articles: R. TONELLI, Riunioni di verifica, in «Note di Pastorale Giovanile» 2 (1968) 8-9, 60-65 e ID., Punti fermi per una programmazione valida, in «Note di Pastorale Giovanile» 3 (1969) 8-9, 43-59.

[65] R. TONELLI, Impostazione della comunità educativa in un contesto pluralista, in GIANATELLI (Ed.), Progettare l'educazione oggi con Don Bosco, p. 83.

[66] See R. TONELLI, Per fare un progetto educativo, in «Note di Pastorale Giovanile» 14 (1980) 6, 57-66.

cannot proceed without faith".[67] The interpretation in the light of "event of God", in the light of faith, is important both for reading of the youth situation and for the formulation of objectives. The interpretation of the situation in the light of faith has already been present in the SEPP methodology since 1978, but the link between objectives and faith is not accentuated. Tonelli affirms that objectives have to be in a close relationship with the truths of faith, "to prevent that the re-invention of the objectives would empty and reduce the event of God to an anthropological level only".[68] Tonelli's interesting remarks remain at the level of theoretical principles without applying it to the methodological level. The question of how to interpret the situation in the light of the "event of God" remains unanswered.

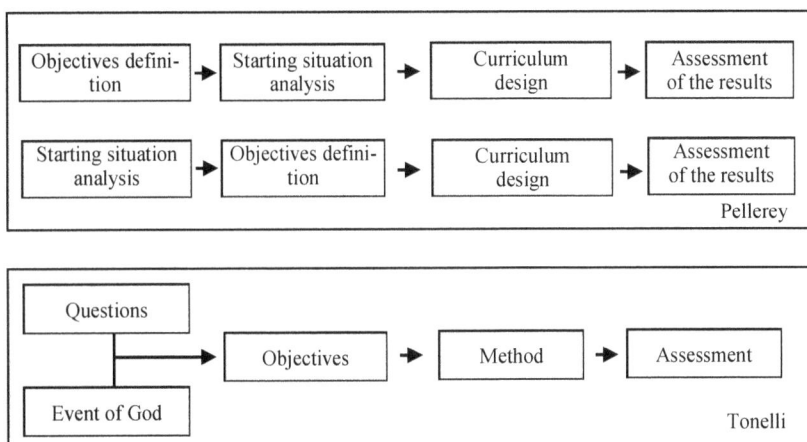

Scheme A: Tonelli's and Pellerey's Project Methodology

2.2.2 Social Animation

A different type of animation was structured around the activities of the Salesian Aldo Ellena, the founder of the journal *Animazione sociale*

---

[67] *Idem*, p. 61.
[68] *Ibidem*.

in 1971. His reflections are closely connected with the activities carried out in the '70s and '80s that consisted mainly in leader formation and in community development activities.[69] Ellena's theoretical interests were wide-ranging from the translation of *Psychology of the Leaders* by H. Harroux and J. Praet, through publishing an Encyclopedia of Social Studies to editing two volumes on educational presence.[70]

Looking more closely at his first publication on animation, one can understand his interest in animation as a social practice that "aims to raise awareness and to develop the latent potential of an individual, a group or a community that was suppressed or removed".[71] Animation is not seen as a new specific profession and neither as a technical method of social practice, but as a "new way to adapt a professional profile in a changing society". The animation activities are described in the areas of physical and social well-being, expressiveness, creativity, volunteering, free-time activities, group dynamics, values education, commitment to the territory or active citizenship.

Interesting is his set of criteria applied to a formation project for young animators, published in the already mentioned Vecchi and Prellezo's volume of *Progetto Educativo Pastorale*. We reproduce it here because this list is a good synthesis of the shared anthropological paradigms on the animation theory. According to Ellena, the application of these instances should make a qualitative difference between a technical use of animation activities and a genuine approach to life and people:

[69] See e.g. G. CONTESSA – A. ELLENA – R. SALVI, *Animatori del tempo libero*, Società Editrice Napoletana, Napoli 1979; G. CONTESSA – A. ELLENA, *Animatori di quartiere*, Società Editrice Napoletana, Napoli 1980 and P.G. BRANCA – G. CONTESSA – A. ELLENA, *Animare la città*, Istituto di Scienze Amministrative e di promozione sociale, Milano 1982.
[70] See H. HARROUX – J. PRAET, *Psicologia dei leaders*, SEI, Torino 1957; A. ELLENA (Ed.), *Enciclopedia sociale*, vol. 1: *Introduzione ai problemi sociali*, Paoline, Roma 1958; F. DEMARCHI – A. ELLENA (Eds.), *Dizionario di Sociologia*, Paoline, Roma 1976 and A. ELLENA (Ed.), *Presenza educativa*, 2 volumes, LDC, Leumann (TO) 1976-77.
[71] CONTESSA – ELLENA – SALVI, *Animatori del tempo libero*, p. 132.

- keep in mind some fundamental values:
  - priority of concrete human persons;
  - freedom of conscience;
  - secular state;
  - social pluralism as an assurance of freedom of individuals and groups;
  - not a depository or adaptive education, but a critical and evolutionary approach (see Paulo Freire), realized through a process of ongoing formation.
- think of the animator as:
  - a person who knows how to deal with the strategy of freedom rather than the strategies of non-freedom: fear, waiting, prudence, regulation, tradition, ambivalent compromise, anonymity;
  - a person with some basic "meanings" of life that match the usual typology of an adult: openness to the truth, loyalty, responsibility, respect, fidelity, sense of reality and of its limits, sense of gradual experimentation, priorities, historical awareness, sense of the particular, sense of the collective, sense of risk, capacity for dialogue, sensibility to poverty;
  - a unified personality opened to the universality of values;
  - a person of hope and utopia.
- in consistency with the values and fundamental directions indicated, the animator has to follow with wise flexibility some operating principles:
  - do not persist in an identity crisis with masochistic attitudes seen as an excuse and a compensation of own limits;
  - do not live animation as a compensatory dynamic to unsettled personal psychological situations;
  - animate according to the practice-theory-practice concept, which can be expressed also in the trio see-judge-act;

- live according to the situation and at the same time follow a direction;
- constantly perform self-questioning through a reasonable review
of life model;
- develop imagination: invent new activities; catch up and to antic-
ipate the future;
- overcome the social worker technical role (specific, vertical with
defensive and corporate function) by a functional role (shared,
horizontal, unifying all social workers) for the needs of the community;
- act according to the principle of mediation *et-et*, and not according
to the principle of exclusion *aut-aut* (embraced with determination
by pseudo-revolutionists).[72]

2.2.3 Animation Theories Critical Evaluation

Animation theory seems to provide an anthropological point of view
with some applied methodological principles. From the analysis of some
principal writings we can conclude that animation, especially in Pollo's
and Ellena's view, is linked with selected "civil rights movement" views
on persons and society choosing group dynamics and critical pedagogy
as methods of education. Cultural animation has a high aspiration of being "a method that does not only allow the educational activities to be
organized in a certain way, but also redefining and selecting objectives
they pursue".[73] As we have seen, this operation was done partially on a
principles level. Animation mixes the conception of *homo symbolicus*,
systems theory, democratic philosophical principles and communication
theory, and rejects a mechanic and deterministic conception of human

---

[72] CONTESSA – ELLENA, *Animatori di quartiere*, pp. 92-94 and A. ELLENA, *Animatori*, in
VECCHI – PRELLEZO, *Progetto Educativo Pastorale*, pp. 359-360.
[73] POLLO – TONELLI, *Animazione*, in VECCHI – PRELLEZO, *Progetto Educativo Pastorale*,
p. 288.

beings linked to a hierarchical organization model.[74] In this sense, animation could be considered more as a shared or community leadership theory than as an innovative project management theory.

On a more practical and methodological level, animation does not offer a different project management methodology. The Management by Objectives that comes from the curriculum design theories is accepted with some generic advice of unification, participation, co-responsibility, etc. Interesting is the way Pollo defends his theoretic position: "To provide a detailed programme of animation is an overly technical operation, based on a mechanistic model of animation".[75] He does neglect the existence of a methodology that exists between a pure theory and a "to-do list" technical type of management. This axiom leads the authors to adopt a dual approach: they either remain in the general theory or they adopt the product model of the curricular theories.[76]

Despite the stated limitations, we can perceive some marked methodological innovations typical for animation. The first and most significant is project building through group dynamics, which balances the implicit individualism of Stenhouse's proposal, focused on a single teacher and not the educational community. The second innovation is Tonelli's accent on the hermeneutic moment in the project design process. The interpretation of the situation and of the objectives with the eyes of faith is an integration with curricular theories demanded by the complementary relation between education and evangelization within the SEPP.

---

[74] Although Tonelli made different adjustments and applied animation in the field of Salesian Youth Ministry, animation theory does not require *in se* the religious and spiritual dimension of educational or pastoral action. This limit of its anthropology summed with the position of disregarding the hierarchical model, makes animation in the Salesian EPC setting problematic if it is the only model. It requires other elements in order to balance the theoretical and practical framework.

[75] POLLO, *L'animazione culturale*, p. 75.

[76] This approach is present in different master degree theses guided by Pollo at the UPS.

2.3 Management by Objectives and Beyond

Previous analysis allowed us to cast a glance on the theories quoted directly in the formulation and articulation of the SEPP methodology, especially in the 1984 publication on Educative and Pastoral Project. Curricular and animation theories were presented in their interdisciplinary interaction with management and organizational sciences. From the 1970s to the present day, the Salesian project management methodology has been substantially influenced by the Management by Objectives model (MBO) which was inspiring the curriculum design theories of the sixties. Among the education theorists who have had the greatest impact upon the formulation of the SEPP we find Ralph Tyler, Leslie Briggs, Robert Gagné, Robert Mager, Hilda Taba and, above all, Lawrence Stenhouse, who influenced Juan Edmundo Vecchi the most. It is to Vecchi, who was the Councilor for the Youth Ministry in the Congregation from 1978 to 1990, that we owe the main ideas around the SEPP. The different difficulties with the objectives logic present from the first evaluations of the '70s to the provincial projects of the '90s could be understood if we study the objectives model for itself. Often the Salesians were correcting the model with external theological principles and criteria but the model logic remained unchanged. Let us see the development of the MBO model and the attempts to overcome its flaws by contemporary organizational models.

2.3.1 Management by Objectives

The political, economic and social post-war situation favoured the development of project management as a specific branch of studies. The increasing economic collaboration of the '50s, the military strategy of the Cold War and the Space Race gave chance of managing projects on a scale incomparable with the past. The denomination Management by Objectives (MBO) was made famous by Peter Drucker's 1954 bestseller *The Practice of Management* and was successfully developed further in his later publications.[77] The MBO was trying to involve managers in a team decision-making process around the formulation of goals, overcoming the traditional loyalty to the defined tasks and the loyalty to the hierarchy. According to Drucker, the MBO is not only a management tool, used in many profit and nonprofit organizations, but is a philosophy of action that transforms real needs into objectives. A person is conceived as a free being who decides to implement an objective that is not imposed by others but reflects a real need. The subsequent implementation of the objective in actions and events is carried out mainly through self-control.[78]

Some particular aspects of Drucker's theory were examined by various scholars and were integrated with the help of psychology. As an important example, we could mention the pioneering studies of Edwin A. Locke and Gary P. Latham formulated as *Goal Setting Theory* that correlates motivation and effectiveness of action with specific and challenging objectives.[79] Other theorists and practitioners develop the MBO of the '80s suggesting SMART objectives with five characteristics: Specific, Measurable, Assignable, Realistic and Time-related.[80]

---

[77] See P.F. DRUCKER, *The Practice of Management*, Harper & Row, New York 1954; ID., *Management. Tasks, Responsibilities, Practices*, Truman Talley Books, New York 1986; J. DAVIDSON FRAME, *The New Project Management. Tools for an Age of Rapid Change, Complexity, and Other Business Realities*, Jossey-Bass, San Francisco CA ²2002, pp. 1-6 and M. WITZEL, *A History of Management Thought*, Routledge, Abingdon 2012, pp. 162-164.

[78] See DRUCKER, *Management*, pp. 10-11 and 303-304.

[79] See E.A. LOCKE – G.P. LATHAM, *Goal setting: A motivational technique that works*, Prentice Hall, Englewood Cliffs NJ 1984; ID., *A theory of goal setting and task performance*, Prentice Hall, Englewood Cliffs NJ 1990; ID., *Building a practically useful theory of goal setting and task motivation. A 35-year odyssey*, in «American Psychologist» 57 (2002) 9, 705-717 e ID., *New Directions in Goal-Setting Theory*, in «Current Directions in Psychological Science» 15 (2006) 5, 265-268.

[80] See G.T. DORAN, *There's a S.M.A.R.T. way to write management's goals and objectives*, in «Management Review » 70 (1981) 11, 35-36 and K. BLANCHARD – P. ZIGARMI – D. ZIGARMI , *Leadership and the one minute manager : Increasing effectiveness through situational leadership*, William Morrow and Company, New York 1985

Although MBO is still widely used in different organizations, especially in the industrial sector where the concreteness and measurability
of the objectives are easier to apply, the model's validity has been questioned. Already in the '80s and '90s, researchers suggested different
factors as contributors to the failure of MBO: problems in MBO's implementation process, lack of appropriate incentive systems, inadequate top
management support, inadequate staff training, etc.[81] And yet, it seems
that giving up on MBO is uneasy to digest and so different scholars are
trying to make it work. As a recent example of many similar attempts,
Sharon Gotteiner asks himself the main question: "If goal setting alone
works, why doesn't the whole MBO system work?" Then he searches for
answers trying to fix MBO by proposing an "Optimal MBO" model.[82] In
the following pages we will see the inherent flaws of MBO and then we
will summarize the development of alternative models.

2.3.2 Critics of Management by Objectives

After years of practice, the founding father of the objectives approach
Peter Drucker remarks: "MBO is just another tool. It is not the great cure
for management inefficiency. [...] Management by Objectives works if
you know the objectives: 90% of the time you don't".[83] Locke and Latham, for their part, recognize the pitfalls of their objectives theory but
only propose some symptomatic adjustments remaining at the same level

---

[81] See J.N. KONDRASUK, *Studies in MBO Effectiveness*, in «The Academy of Management Review» 6 (1981) 3, 419-430; J.P. MUCZYK – B.C. REIMANN, *MBO as a
Complement to Effective Leadership*, in «The Academy of Management Executive» 3
(1989) 2, 131-138; M.F. DUFFY, *ZBB, MBO, PPB and their Effectiveness within the
Planning/Marketing Process*, in «Strategic Management Journal» 10 (1989) 2, 163-
173 and R. RODGERS – J.E. HUNTER, *Impact of Management by Objectives on Organizational Productivity*, in «Journal of Applied Psychology» 76 (1991) 2, 322-336.
[82] S. GOTTEINER, *The Optimal MBO. A Model for Effective Management-by-Objectives
Implementation*, in «European Accounting and Management Review» 2 (2016) 2, 43-
56.
[83] T. HINDLE, *Guide to Management Ideas and Gurus*, The Economist, London 2008, p.
122.

of thinking, that is, using primarily the logic of the objectives. A symptomatic solution is the proposal of an additional layer of intermediate objectives to rediscover the lost link between the specific objectives and the long term aims.[84]

Having in mind the historical evolution of the Salesian project management methodology, it is important to point out various limits of the MBO viewed from different perspectives. Many of the mentioned difficulties were also present in the Salesian educative and pastoral setting.

- According to William Edwards Deming, MBO causes the organization to focus on the fulfillment of the objectives and to neglect quality. In his famous 14 points of quality management he insists to abandon the MBO and substitute it with leadership.[85]

- Aaron Wildavsky, one of the first critics, was showing deficiencies inherent in MBO. Wildavsky argues that "the planner has become the victim of planning; his own creation has overwhelmed him. Planning has become so large that the planner cannot encompass its dimensions. Planning has become so complex planners cannot keep up with it. Planning protrudes in so many directions, the planner can no longer discern its shape. He may be economist, political scientist, sociologist, architect

---

[84] See LOCKE – LATHAM, *Has Goal Setting Gone Wild*, p. 21 e G.P. LATHAM, *Work motivation: History, theory, and practice*, Sage, Thousand Oaks CA 2007, p. 183. See also an interesting dispute between Locke-Latham and Ordóñez-Schweitzer-Galinsky-Bazerman in L.D. ORDÓÑEZ – M.E. SCHWEITZER – A.D. GALINSKY – M.H. BAZERMAN, *Goals Gone Wild: How goals systematically harm individuals and organizations*, in «Academy of Management Perspectives» 23 (2009) 1, 6-16; E.A. LOCKE – G.P. LATHAM, *Has Goal Setting Gone Wild, or Have Its Attackers Abandoned Good Scholarship?*, in «Academy of Management Perspectives» 23 (2009) 1, 17-23 and L.D. ORDÓÑEZ – M.E. SCHWEITZER – A.D. GALINSKY – M.H. BAZERMAN, *On Good Scholarship, Goal Setting, and Scholars Gone Wild*, in «Academy of Management Perspectives» 23 (2009) 3, 82-87.

[85] See W.E. DEMING, *Out of the Crisis*, MIT Press, Boston 1986 and WITZEL, *A History of Management Thought*, pp. 196; 202-204.

or scientist. Yet the essence of his calling-planning escapes him. He finds it everywhere in general and nowhere in particular".[86]

- MBO does not consider reliance on human and material resources. The number of objectives should be scaled up or down to the resources. In organizations there are various paralyzing dynamics linked with the disproportion between resources and objectives.[87]

- MBO overlooks the fact that objectives are interconnected, dependent on cognitive and contextual variables. The objectives also have an impact at the subconscious level and they can counteract each other. It is normal that different means, tools or activities lead to the accomplishment of an objective but, at the same time, they bring many side effects that can paralyze the accomplishment of other objectives. There is also an associative transfer between objectives and means (or vice versa) that affects the motivation.[88]

- The anthropology of the MBO, linked to the conception of Drucker, is incomplete and flawed. The mechanism of a rational decision to pursue an objective and the subsequent implementation through conscious self-control is pretty simple and convincing. But in recent years it has faced a strong criticism, not only from a philosophical or theological point of view, but also from an evidence- based organizational one. We

---

[86] A. WILDAVSKY, *If Planning Is Everything, Maybe It's Nothing*, in «Policy Sciences» 14 (1983) 4, 127.

[87] See B. WERNERFELDT, *A Resource-Based View of the Firm*, in «Strategic Management Journal» 5 (1984) 2, 171-180; R.M. GRANT, *The Resource-Based Theory of Competitive Advantage: Implications for Strategy Formulation*, in «California Management Review» 33 (1991) 3, 114-135 and G. HAMEL – C.K. PRAHALAD, *Competing For the Future*, Harvard Business School Press, Boston 1994.

[88] See A.W. KRUGLANSKI et al., *A Theory of Goal Systems*, in M.P. ZANNA (Ed.), *Advances in Experimental Social Psychology*, vol. 34, Academic Press, San Diego CA 2002, pp. 331-378.

mention especially Daniel Kahneman's line of thought on the interrelations between intuitive and rational components in human action for which he received Nobel Prize in the field of economy.[89]

- MBO often inhibits organizational learning especially in complex situations by turning all the attention to specific objectives and neglecting the study of the complexities and interrelations in the organization.[90]

- MBO promotes competition rather than cooperation and tends to neglect community building because it is not related to specific roles that have responsibilities for achieving concrete objectives.[91]

- An overly specific set of objectives causes a narrowing of the field of perception. It is a dangerous condition causing wrong and ineffective decisions especially in unstable situations with many variables.[92]

- Too specific objectives can cause lower long-term results because all the energy is spent on the achievement of specific objectives, and the more important general objective or aim is neglected.[93]

---

[89] See the synthesis in D. KAHNEMAN, *Thinking Fast and Slow*, Farrar Straus and Giroux, New York 2011 and other research together with Amos Tversky: ID. – A. TVERSKY, *Prospect Theory: An Analysis of Decision Under Risk*, in «Econometrica» 47 (1979) 2, 263-291; ID. – P. SLOVIC – A. TVERSKY (Eds.), *Judgment under uncertainty: Heuristics and biases*, Cambridge University Press, Cambridge 1982 and A. TVERSKY – ID., *Extensional versus intuitive reasoning: The conjunction fallacy in probabilistic reasoning*, in «Psychological Review» 90 (1983) 293-315.

[90] See D. CERVONE – N. JIWANI – R. WOOD, *Goal setting and the differential influence of self-regulatory processes on complex decision-making performance*, in «Journal of Personality and Social Psychology» 61 (1991) 2, 257-266 and LOCKE – LATHAM, *Building a practically useful theory of goal setting*, 2002.

[91] See T.R. MITCHELL – W.S. SILVER, *Individual and group goals when workers are interdependent: Effects on task strategies and performance*, in «Journal of Applied Psychology» 75 (1990) 2, 185-193 and P.M. WRIGHT – J.M. GEORGE – S.R. FARNSWORTH – G.C. MCMAHAN, *Productivity and extra-role behavior: The effects of goals and incentives on spontaneous helping*, in «Journal of Applied Psychology» 78 (1993) 3, 374-381.

[92] See M.H. BAZERMAN – D. CHUGH, *Decisions without blinders*, in «Harvard Business Review» 84 (2006) 1, 88-97.

[93] See B.M. STAW – R.D. BOETTGER, Task revision. A neglected form of work performance, in «The Academy of Management Journal» 33 (1990) 3, 534-559 e A.E.

- In the case of too many objectives, people tend to prefer one goal and consider the others as secondary.[94] In the situation of multiple objectives they favour a quantitative rather than qualitative objective[95] and a short-term rather than a long-term one.[96]
- People tend to perceive objectives as the top limit of their performance. After their achievement they tend to relax diminishing commitment to the whole project.[97]
- It is true that challenging objectives tend to mobilize more energy. But there is evidence suggesting that challenging objectives are also linked to riskier or morally questionable strategies. Also they induce exaggerated expectations of the people working in the project, a situation that can get the organization to a paralyzing stalemate in relation with the real context.[98]
- MBO can lead to unethical behaviour in extreme cases, but it also affects the ethical dimension indirectly through its effect on the

TENBRUNSEL et al., Understanding the Influence of Environmental Standards on Judgments and Choices, in «The Academy of Management Journal» 43 (2000) 5, 854-866.
[94] See J.Y. SHAH – R. FRIEDMAN – A.W. KRUGLANSKI, *Forgetting all else: on the antecedents and consequences of goal shielding*, in «Journal of Personality and Social Psychology» 83 (2002) 6, 1261-1280.
[95] See S.W. GILLILAND – R.S. LANDIS, *Quality and quantity goals in a complex decision task: Strategies and outcomes*, in «Journal of Applied Psychology» 77 (1992) 5, 672-681.
[96] See M. CHENG – K.R. SUBRAMANYAM – Y. ZHANG, *Earnings Guidance and Managerial Myopia*, in kellogg.northwestern.edu/accounting/papers/k.r%20subramanyam.pdf. (accessed 1. 1. 2017)
[97] See ORDÓÑEZ – SCHWEITZER – GALINSKY – BAZERMAN, *Goals Gone Wild*.
[98] NEALE – BAZERMAN, *The Effect of Externally Set Goals*, 1985, pp. 19-32; D. KNIGHT – C.C. DURHAM – E.A. LOCKE, *The Relationship of Team Goals, Incentives, and Efficacy to Strategic Risk, Tactical Implementation, and Performance*, in «The Academy of Management Journal» 44 (2001) 2, 326-338; A.D. GALINSKY – T. MUSSWEILER – V.H. MEDVEC, *Disconnecting outcomes and evaluations: The role of negotiator focus*, in «Journal of Personality and Social Psychology» 83 (2002) 5, 1131-1140; M.E. SCHWEITZER – L. ORDÓÑEZ – B. DOUMA, *Goal Setting as a Motivator of Unethical Behavior*, in «Academy of Management Journal» 47 (2004) 3, 422-432 and B. HOFMEISTER, *Werte im Management*, VDM Verlag, Saarbrücken 2006.

organizational culture. Objectives draw the attention rather to the accomplishment of results than to the ethical questions around the means. An aggressive MBO blurs the awareness of ethical issues and endorses the rationalization of unethical behaviour.[99]

- Challenging objectives have a counterproductive side effect: they decrease the satisfaction with the achieved results and lead people to perceiving themselves as less effective. It obviously has consequences for their actions and performance in the future.[100]

- If the purpose of an activity is to achieve an objective, we work on a level of controllable external motivations. It decreases the internal motivations connected with the essence or the typical dynamics of the activity.[101]

- A specific objective is not related to the environmental variables and does not respect the idiosyncrasies of a personal action.[102]

2.3.3 Change of Organizational Paradigm

It is important not only to criticize the MBO, but to see in which direction it moved the researchers and practitioners in the organizational

---

[99] See A. BARSKY, *Understanding the ethical cost of organizational goal-setting: A review and theory development*, in «Journal of Business Ethics» 81 (2008) 1, 63-81 and P. FLEMING – S.C. ZYGLIDOPOULOS, *The Escalation of Deception in Organizations*, in «Journal of Business Ethics» 81 (2008) 4, 837-850.

[100] H. GARLAND, *Influence of ability, assigned goals, and normative information on personal goals and performance: A challenge to the goal attainability assumption*, in «Journal of Applied Psychology» 68 (1983) 1, 20-30; T. MUSSWEILER – F. STRACK, *The "relative self": Informational and judgmental consequences of comparative self-evaluation*, in «Journal of Personality and Social Psychology» 79 (2000) 1, 23-38 and GALINSKY – MUSSWEILER – MEDVEC, *Disconnecting outcomes and evaluations*, 1131-1140.

[101] See A.J. ELLIOT – J.M. HARACKIEWICZ, *Approach and avoidance achievement goals and intrinsic motivation: A mediational analysis*, in «Journal of Personality and Social Psychology» 70 (1996) 3, 461-475 and L.J. RAWSTHORNE – A.J. ELLIOT, *Achievement Goals and Intrinsic Motivation: A Meta-Analytic Review*, in «Personality and Social Psychology Review» 3 (1999) 4, 326-344.

[102] See ORDÓÑEZ – SCHWEITZER – GALINSKY – BAZERMAN, *Goals Gone Wild*, pp. 15-16.

field. Halfway through the '80s different management theorists began to detect the social, political and economic changes and they started to design the passage from the *management* paradigm of the industrial society to the shared *leadership* paradigm related to the interconnectedness of the information society. The transition is well noticeable in the extensive documentation of the 1990 edition of Bass and Stogdill's *Handbook of Leadership*.[103] It must be noted that this paradigmatic shift is in no way meant to indicate that leadership is superior to management; rather it speaks of their differences and of how they are a complementary dual concept. This is the understanding of John P. Kotter and Warren Bennis, two of the foremost scholars in the area of management and leadership during those years.[104]

The change of paradigm has many facets present in the various theories. Similar to what we have seen in the Salesian area, there are organizational studies scholars who keep the MBO logic and add a few principles or tools that help manage a further element of turbulence or uncertainty. But we are interested in leadership theories that go beyond the MBO in order to see the core dynamics of projects and planning. Having the SEPP history in mind, it is useful to recall some aspects of the paradigm shift as it developed with some key concepts of its methodology.

As the first aspect of change there is an appreciable integration of the linear objectives-activities-assessment logic with a *systemic approach* to organization, introduced by William E. Deming. Through his well-known publication named *Out of the Crisis* he inspired a vast movement

---

[103] See B.M. BASS, *Bass and Stogdill's Handbook of Leadership. Theory, Research and Managerial Applications*, Free Press, New York 1990.

[104] See J.P. KOTTER, *A Force for Change: How Leadership Differs from Management*, Free Press, New York 1990; W. BENNIS, *An Invented Life. Reflections on Leadership and Change*, Addison-Wesley, Reading MA 1993; W. BENNIS – J. GOLDSMITH, *Learning to Lead. A workbook on Becoming a Leader*, Addison-Wesley, Reading MA 1997, pp. 9-10.

of Total Quality Management.[105] His systemic concept is a profound knowledge that understands the organization as a whole and recognizes the overall processes. The study of interactions and feedbacks between the elements of a system can make the system behave as a single organism that automatically seeks a steady state. The systemic vision also inspires applications in the education area. Among many authors, we will study more in depth the theory of Peter M. Senge, Deming's successor at the Massachusetts Institute of Technology in Boston.[106]

The second aspect of the paradigm shift was the passage from *transactional change* to **transformational change**. The transactional change is the use of planning, command and centralized control; the transformational change on the other hand requires the involvement of a group, a shared vision, a personalized communication and has the potential to change models of thought and action. This distinction between the two styles of leadership comes from James MacGregor Burns, who analyzed the political leaders in the '70s, but it became well-known by the 1985 Bernard M. Bass' book *Leadership and Performance*.[107] A year later, the transformational concept was further reinforced by Noel M. Tichy and Mary A. Devanna in their publication of *Transformational Leader*.[108] The ideas of transformation and the importance of the perspective change

---

[105] See the bestselling edition: W.E. DEMING, *Out of the Crisis*, MIT Press, Boston 1986. Deming's explicit distances from the Total Quality Movement have to be noted. According to him, it has only become a set of tools and techniques leaving aside the profound systemic knowledge linked with anthropology and epistemology of its own. See SENGE, *Fifth Discipline*, pp. XI-XV.

[106] See P.M. SENGE et al., *Schools That Learn. A Fifth Discipline Fieldbook for Educators, Parents, and Everyone Who Cares About Education*, Doubleday, New York 2000.

[107] See J.M. BURNS, *Leadership*, Harper&Row, New York 1978; B.M. BASS, *Leadership and Performance*, Free Press, New York 1985 and MULFORD, *Leadership and Management Overview*, in PETERSON - BAKER - MCGAW (Eds.), *International Encyclopedia Of Education*, vol. 4, p. 698.

[108] See N.M. TICHY – M.A. DEVANNA, *Transformational Leader*, Wiley, New York 1986.

are further developed in education, especially in Jack Mezirow's transformative learning.[109]

The third change of perspective, in connection with the previous one,
is the importance of *participation* and *complementarity* in leadership. It
was promoted by Edgar H. Schein with the learning organization concept
and by Arie de Geus with the idea of planning as learning.[110] These ideas
found an application in the theory of organizational learning developed
later by Senge. In this perspective, the leadership is shared in a complementary manner among all active participants, eliminating the
identification of leadership with the formal hierarchical role. Senge defines leadership as "the ability of a human community to shape their own
future".[111] The idea to integrate empowerment in organizational settings
goes beyond the polarization between the leader and the followers, present in the traditional leadership theories and helps to expand a more
genuine educational type of approach. Here we can collocate Robert
Greenleaf's Servant Leadership model.[112] Significant is also the contribution of Etienne Wenger and his community of practice concept that
focused on the dynamics existing between the relationships within a
community and practical sharing of knowledge. In this sense we change
from a project team to a community of practice.[113]

---

[109] See J. MEZIROW et al., *Fostering Critical reflection in adulthood. A Guide to Transformative and Emancipatory Learning*, Jossey-Bass, San Francisco 1990 e ID.,
Transformative Dimensions of Adult Learning, Jossey-Bass, San Francisco 1991.
[110] See E.H. SCHEIN, *Organizational Culture and Leadership*, Jossey-Bass, San Francisco
1985; A. DE GEUS, *Planning as Learning*, in «Harvard Business Review» 66 (1988) 2,
70-74 and W.R. KING (Ed.), *Knowledge Management and Organizational Learning*,
Springer, New York 2009, pp. 301-384.
[111] P.M. SENGE et al., *The Dance of Change. The Challenges of Sustaining Momentum in
Learning Organizations*, Doubleday, New York 1999, p. 16.
[112] See R.K. GREENLEAF, *Servant Leadership. A Journey into the Nature of Legitimate
Power and Greatness*. 25th Anniversary Edition, Paulist press, New York 2002.
[113] See E. WENGER, *Communities of Practice. Learning, Meaning, and Identity*, Cam-
bridge University Press, Cambridge 1998; E. WENGER – R. MCDERMOTT – W.M.
SNYDER, *Cultivating Communities of Practice*, Harvard Business School Press, Boston
MA 2002.

The fourth aspect of the paradigm shift is given by the transition from effectiveness in a managerial setting to the *greatness* of a leader in all sectors and the roles of the life of persons and groups. The change goes in an educational direction as there is a real need to develop competences in different areas: communication, decision-making, strategic planning and even ethical qualities of leaders going beyond successful "results" according to "objectives". The publications of Max de Pree, Warren Bennis and John W. Gardner go in this direction.[114] This type of organizational thinking accepts the importance of values. The related ethical commitment was further developed by Stephen R. Covey. He was a bestselling author of the '90s and developed a character ethics within a Principle-Centered Leadership model.[115] The ethical dimension of leadership and management is generally accepted in the theories developed after the paradigm change of the late '80s.

The fifth input comes from the school of *Resource-based Management*, that became popular with the publications by Coimbatore K. Prahalad and Gary Hamel. Their theory brings the necessary consideration of limited available resources to the objectives logic. The organization should not imitate the success and objectives of other organizations regardless of its own resources. Instead, it is more realistic to focus on its strengths and develop further its own "core competence", which consists in the ability to do a particular activity better.[116]

---

[114] See M. DE PREE, *Leadership is an Art*, Michigan State University Press, East Lansing MI 1987; W. BENNIS, *On Becoming a Leader*, Perseus Books, Reading MA 1989; J.W. GARDNER, *On Leadership*, Macmillan, New York 1990 and J. COLLINS, *Good to great. Why Some Companies Make the Leap... and Others Don't*, HarperCollins Publishers, New York 2001.

[115] S.R. COVEY, *The 7 Habits of Highly Effective People. Restoring the Character Ethic*, Simon & Schuster, New York 1989; ID., *Principle – Centered Leadership*, Free Press, New York 1992; ID., *The 8th Habit. From Effectiveness to Greatness*, Free Press, New York 2004.

[116] See B. WERNERFELDT, *A Resource-Based View of the Firm*, in «Strategic Management Journal» 5 (1984) 2, 171-180; C.K. PRAHALAD – G. HAMEL, *The core competence of the corporation*, in «Harvard Business Review» 68 (1990) 3, 79-91; ID., *Competing for*

The sixth element is the *spiritual dimension* seen in organizational settings that is also called transcendent leadership. Various theories consider spirituality as an innate and integral dimension of all persons that involves deep levels of meaning, direction, motivation, understanding, inner completeness and deep connection with others. Spirituality is not perceived as sectarian or confessional and the authors try to find common features in spiritual experiences of different religious traditions. We can see the importance of spirituality in the leadership theories of Covey and Senge, as well as in Claus Otto Scharmer's "Theory U".[117]

The seventh deepening of organizational studies is linked to the question of the method, seeking a research methodology that could guarantee the scientific proceeding and simultaneously would be significant in the leaders' daily applications. The pioneering studies of the '70s of Chris Argyris were resumed in the '80s by Dian Marie Hosking and Ian Morley, noting that practitioners saw managerial studies on leadership as confused, disorganized, and poorly integrated with many discrepancies.[118] The new paradigm of the *management scholar-consultant* is located in an intermediate position between an academic and a practitioner. The dilemma between rigour and relevance suggests that an organizational theory is either evidence-based but too reductionist, and thus too trivial to have a practical significance, or relevant in a holistic

---

the Future, Harvard Business School Press, Boston MA 1994; DAVIDSON FRAME, *The New Project Management*, pp. 2-5 and 252-273.

[117] See especially the third millennium publications of the "second" Covey and Senge: COVEY, *The 8th Habit*; C.O. SCHARMER – P. SENGE – J. JAWORSKI – B.S. FLOWERS, *Presence. Exploring Profound Change in People, Organizations, and Society*, Currency Doubleday, New York 2004 and for Scharmer see C.O. SCHARMER, *Theory U. Leading From the Future as it Emerges. The Social Technology of Presencing*, SoL, Cambridge MA 2007.

[118] See C. ARGYRIS, *How normal science methodology makes leadership research less additive and less applicable*, in J.G. HUNT – L.L. LARSON (Eds.), *Crosscurrents in leadership*, Southern Illinois University Press, Carbondale IL 1979, pp. 47-63; D.M. HOSKING – I.E. MORLEY, *The skills of leadership*, in J.G. HUNT – B.R. BALIGA – H.P. DACHLER – C.A. SCHRIESHEIM (Eds.), *Emerging leadership vistas*, Lexington Books, Lexington MA 1988, pp. 89-106.

practice but lacking sufficient rigorous validation.[119] Not without ambiguity and risks, the consultants and management gurus try to join the two concepts of organizational theories entering, in some cases, into the philosophical and metaphysical field that was abandoned by organizational scholars long ago.[120]

LEADERSHIP	MANAGEMENT
people oriented	task oriented
spontaneity and serendipity	structure and formality
empowerment	control
principles and purposes	techniques and practices
transformation	transaction
discernment	measurement
process – do right things	procedure – do things right
process – direction and effectiveness	procedure – speed and efficiency
act upon the systems	operate within the systems

Scheme B: Leadership and Management Binomials

---

[119] J.M. BEYER – H.M. TRICE, *The Utilization Process: a Conceptual Framework and Synthesis of Empirical Findings*, in «Administrative Science Quarterly» 27 (1982) 591-622; D.A. SCHÖN, *The Reflective Professional. How Professionals Think in Action*, Basic Books, New York 1983, pp. 3-69; J.B. MINER, *The Validity and Usefulness of Theories in an Emerging Organizational Science*, in «Academy of Management Review» 9 (1984) 296-306; J.E. VAN AKEN, *Management Research Based on the Paradigm of the Design Sciences: The Quest for Field-Tested and Grounded Technological Rules*, in «Journal of Management Studies» 41 (2004) 2, 221.

[120] See R. WHITLEY, *The Management Sciences and Managerial Skills*, in «Organization Studies» 9 (1988) 1, 47-68; G. BURRELL, *The Absent Centre. The Neglect of Philosophy in Anglo-American Management Theory*, in «Human Systems Management» 8 (1989) 307-312.

Scheme B presents a series of binomials (interrelated coupled contrasts) inspired by the synthesis of Stephen R. Covey.[121] They illustrate the change of paradigm in several interdependent aspects between leadership and management. Organizational studies have passed from a "leadership as management" paradigm to one which understands "leadership as interdependent with management". Leadership and management are seen as two poles in the world of organization, because of which there exists an equilibrium between concern for the persons and concern for the systems and tasks. Even though the distinction between leadership and management as interdependent aspects can run the risk of becoming a mere *cliché* presuming to resolve all organizational problems, it still remains a valid theory which can exert influence on the area of organizational studies.[122]

This paradigm shift was not explicitly perceived in the Salesian Educative and Pastoral Project methodology that still refers to the '80s MBO logic. It seems also that the Salesian post-Vatican II leadership model finds itself trapped between two models. The first is the classical ecclesiastical hierarchy model that tends to micromanage the everyday life. The second is the animation model of a leader as an animator-facilitator of the community. The latter model incorporates a "leadership by project management" logic of the '80s and it comprehends the director more as a project team facilitator than as a real leader.

We will try to implement the organizational paradigm shift within the SEPP core logic in order to balance the importance of planning effectiveness (management reasoning) with the importance of government, discernment and motivation (leadership reasoning). We suppose that

---

[121] See S.R. COVEY, *The 8th Habit. From Effectiveness to Greatness*, Free Press, New York 2004, p. 364.
[122] See. J.P. KOTTER, *Accelerate. Building Strategic Agility for a Faster Moving World*, Harvard Business Review Press, Boston 2014 and G. EDWARDS et al., *Exploring power assumption in the leadership and management debate*, in «Leadership & Organization Development Journal» 36 (2015) 3, 328-343.

there must be equilibrium between the need for clear and shared objectives (management), and working side by side with the others and appreciating their insights (leadership). Without leadership, accompaniment and communal discernment one would most likely arrive at lists of insignificant objectives neither shared by all nor with any value for the day's activity. The consolidated practice and organizational theories of the past two decades confirm the inadequacy of Management by Objectives model which aims toward realizing goals merely through self-control. There is a clear need of deep spiritual motivation along with the dynamics of communal co-responsibility not only as criteria but also as methodology.

3. Don Bosco in the Oratory: Permanent Renewal Criterion

In the first chapter we have seen the development of the Salesian Youth Ministry with a focus on Educational and Pastoral Project (SEPP) as a main tool for management and leadership of the Educative and Pastoral Communities (EPC). In the second chapter we have analyzed the theoretical background of the Salesian project management and leadership model. In the final section we have moved forward some critical remarks on behalf of the SEPP model that reflects a basic Management by Objectives (MBO) mindset, popular in the years of the SEPP definition and major development. We have also seen that the Salesian planning and project management model has remained without substantial updates in the recent 30 years.

In order to update the SEPP model, we could simply integrate some of the recent popular organizational theories and practices. But it would only be a "running late" strategy that tries to catch up with the latest models and does not have an internal criterion for sorting out theories and practices. We want to learn some lessons from the past and in order to do so, we would like to maintain some lines of continuity with the post-Vatican II thought and organizational models. If we look closely enough, the Special General Chapter (SGC) already defined an "enduring criterion for the renewal of Salesian action" and called it "Don Bosco in the Oratory".[1] The SGC states that the criterion for any authentic renewal has to go back to the first moments the of Salesian history – to the person of Don Bosco in the developments of the Oratory of Valdocco. As it often happens, the criterion was defined but was applied only to some "hot issues" of that time and was neglected in other areas. In the area of organizational and project management models, the Handouts of

---

[1] See SGC (1972), p. 150.

the Youth Ministry Department and other publications did not refer to Don Bosco at all or if some authors did, it was only in a generic way.

This chapter will describe, in the first section, the "Don Bosco in the Oratory" criterion and its (limited) application and use in the '70s and '80s. The second section will prepare the ground for the criterion's application in the organizational area by examining organizational studies of consecrated life that refer to the legacy of their founders. The last, and more substantial analysis section, will put forward some leadership and management traits of Don Bosco with the purpose of giving organizational concreteness to the "Don Bosco in the Oratory" criterion. To do so we will draw on historical studies that see Don Bosco in his time and in the context of the development of his works.

3.1 Criterion for Vatican II Renewal Needed and Found

The Special General Chapter document uses clear argumentation of the theme and here we will summarize its highlights. There are two essential parts of an authentic renewal, in accordance with the Council: a return (reditus) to the sources, and an adjustment (aptatio) to the new and changed conditions of our times and context.[2] The Chapter proposes a fundamental concept of dynamic fidelity. Fidelity to the spirit of the founder is "one of the principles of renewal, and one of the surest criteria of what any institute should eventually undertake".[3]

A suitable criterion must be found which can separate the authentic formulae of renewal from their eventual imitations that go from mechanical repetition to relativism. For a criterion to be ideal, it must be certain in its function as a distinctive sign; specific in the concrete information, and universal, i.e. accessible to everyone, everywhere and at all times. As a result, such a criterion must necessarily be objective and external.

---

[2] See SGC (1972), n. 192 that refers to *Perfectae Caritatis*, n. 2.
[3] PAULUS VI, *Evangelica Testificatio*, as quoted in SGC (1972), p. 151.

It seems that a mere appeal neither to the "spirit" of the founder, nor to his concrete "works" alone meets these requirements. Not only the "spirit", because often enough one's subjective evaluations encroach on the matter, and give rise to a need for further criteria. Not only the "works" alone, because they are not immune from being idealized and even deformed, and therefore need a prior assessment. It is clear then that the criterion of dynamic fidelity in the renewal of our specific field of work demands more a "sign" than an identification with one particular work.[4]

Then follows the central argumentative part stating in a concise and rich manner: "The Don Bosco we see in the Oratory admirably fulfils the requirements of an ideal criterion. We must go back to that figure, alive and at work in the midst of his boys, throughout the period of his apostolic life. We must go back to the Oratory itself, as pictured for us by his biographers and remember the fascination of the early days. We ought not to look upon it however as a concrete piece of work, as distinct from the other works started by Don Bosco, but rather as the matrix, the synthesis, the sum total of all the genial apostolic creations of our Founder, the mature fruit of all his efforts".[5] The first criterion of our Salesian renewal must be found in the person of Don Bosco who in the Oratory gives us an exemplary lesson of dynamic fidelity to his apostolic vocation: "I have always gone ahead as the Lord inspired me, and as circumstances demanded".[6]

---

[4] The SGC's skepticism about the authenticity of the works is to be read in the context of the Salesian boarding schools' crisis and criticism about some "repressive" aspects of the traditional Salesian educational model.

[5] SGC (1972), n. 195.

[6] *Biographical Memoirs*, vol. 18, p. 127 as quoted in SGC (1972), n. 197. This passage is a crucial text in the debate about Don Bosco being only an educator or also an education theorist. From the '30s to the '50s, different interpretations were given by General Councilor for the Schools Fr. Bartolomeo Fascie, Rector Major Fr. Pietro Ricaldone and also by the early scholarly writings of Pietro Braido. In this passage of SGC it is one of the first times to give it a methodological meaning, seeing Don Bosco as an example of a dynamic fidelity method.

3.1.1 SGC's Description of "Don Bosco in the Oratory"

In the following chapter of the document, the SGC recalls the criterion and describes some typical and permanent traits of Don Bosco's action. By Oratory, as Don Bosco created it, we do not mean the institute but rather a spirit that pervades the whole complex of work with youth in need. When this is understood, the Oratory recalls everything Don Bosco did and desired to do, and today it stands out as a constant reminder of what a Salesian should be. The Oratory, in this way, would not be just one among many other Salesian works, but the fundamental formula from which all others derive, different works carried on by a Salesian community on behalf of all the young of a particular area, with widely differing activities. This is precisely what the Oratory was originally. The SGC chooses to reconstruct Don Bosco's line of thought on his work either by starting from his early vocation and passing on to his work as realized in the Oratory, or by starting from his many activities and going back to the motives that inspired them. A simple way of doing this is to recall his dreams about his vocation on the one hand, and to read the Rules of the Oratory on the other.[7]

The narration analysis of Don Bosco's boyhood dream, seen as the origin of his educative and pastoral action, pinpoints some fundamental aspects of his personality and activity. Don Bosco was convinced of a higher vocation to be a shepherd of youth. His favorites were the poorest and most abandoned youth. The style of his action had to be a fusion of kindness and solicitous care. The catechism teaching was the first area of his interventions and of the pedagogical art. Blessed Mary, as a Mistress, was the icon of God's care for young people deprived of the warmth of a family and the love of a mother.[8] The final article of this paragraph makes a synthesis stating: "As desired by God in the dreams,

---

[7] See SGC (1972), nn. 203-204.
[8] See SGC (1972), nn. 206-210.

the Oratory was to become a house for the religious instruction of deprived youth. It was to be especially a training ground where they could obtain an integral formation according to the living truths of the gospel, and where (since the Mistress was also a Mother) they would also find a real family, where poor orphans could discover the saving goodness of the Father, made apparent to them through the pedagogy of the gospel, which is a pedagogy of love".[9]

The Regulations of the Oratory, on the other hand, identify Don Bosco's typical approach in a different way, but coming to similar conclusions. The first is the imitation of Christ in gathering together the sons of God who were scattered. This was to be done in a happy, pleasant and attractive way. But, at the same time, this action is formative, educative, and aimed at the salvation of souls. The catholicity of Don Bosco is interpreted as universal, in so far as it is open to all. The Regulations affirm also the preference for the poor, the abandoned and the backward. Don Bosco's education and youth ministry see the whole young person, considering him as both a human being and a Christian. The method is permeated by intense evangelical charity.[10] The final synthesis recalls the four fundamental elements of the later fortunate formulation of the "oratorian criterion" in the Constitutions: a home for those who have none; a parish for those who do not know where their parish is; a school open to all who might find insuperable difficulty elsewhere; recreation as the first incarnation of evangelical charity, of a happy and serene friendship, of a true family and of loving kindness.[11]

---

[9] SGC (1972), n. 211.
[10] See SGC (1972), nn. 212-218.
[11] See SGC (1972), nn. 216 and 218.

3.1.2 Criterion's Application Contextualized

The "Don Bosco in the Oratory" criterion was further developed in two chapters of the SGC document trying to balance a framework between dynamism and fidelity, speaking about "dynamism backed by loyalty" and "dynamic aspect of fidelity".[12] It seems, nevertheless, that the focus of the applications was typical of the '70s era. The Salesians of that time focused especially on two topics: the possibility (and urgency) of change and the restructuration of the works.

The document speaks about dynamic fidelity, but gives more space to the changing aspect focusing on guaranteeing freedom of action: "No unnecessary limitations need be feared in the true apostolic dynamism already in action".[13] In this sense, Vatican II is perceived by the Salesians as a call for innovation and so "the true Salesian attitude will therefore be one of fidelity to the pastors of the Church so that while retaining our Salesian identity we can even sacrifice some of our cherished family traditions".[14] They see themselves as facing "situations that are entirely new"[15] and exalt the daring courage of Don Bosco in a perspective of expansion. The section about fidelity to Don Bosco's legacy and the grassroots of our works is therefore reduced to 4 from the total 45 articles of the two chapters.

The main argumentation and applications are directed towards resolving the problem of the boarding school crisis that seemed to suffocate the Salesians of the '70s. There are some clear signs of it: Salesian teacher's work is described as hindering or rendering impossible or precarious a specifically pastoral work. There are too many occupations which prevent direct contact with young people. The "works" are seen as a correspondence to the basic ideal and should not be necessarily fixed in

---

[12] See SGC (1972), nn. 228-273.
[13] SGC (1972), n. 246.
[14] SGC (1972), n. 238.
[15] SGC (1972), n. 248.

rigid outmoded structures.[16] The argumentative mindset is synthetized in the central article about fidelity to Don Bosco: "It is necessary to reconsider the traditional works for youth. In this regard there are neither preferences nor limits. What matters is the harmony with the work of Don Bosco. Rather than an enumeration of possible works it is better to concentrate our attention on the point of Salesian action. Three principles will control its legitimate expansion:
- that it tends to the finding and preparation of educators;
- that it is directed towards the human and Christian formation of youth;
- that it serves to facilitate meeting of those involved in the educative process".[17]

We can state that this synthesis of three elements is too poor and can practically be applied to whatever educational work carried out by whatever Christian denomination or charism in any context. Some acute remarks of Pietro Braido can be remembered. He speaks about the SGC within a title about "fidelity and utopia"[18] and criticizes the extreme use of the new terms "pastoral" and "ministry". The argumentation of the SGC often uses them as a universal remedy that renders it almost an empty semantical container. Big plans of expansion were to be carried out in new frontiers such as: secular institutes, collaboration with international organizations as UNO, UNESCO, FAO, etc., immigrants, apprentices, abandoned youth, universities, parishes. All these efforts had to be executed with "absolute dedication" following the path of the biblical, liturgical and pastoral movements of the 20th century.[19] There is only one concrete example for this type of expansion: openness to non-Catholics.[20]

---

[16] See SGC (1972), nn. 231-232 and 242.
[17] SGC (1972), n. 244.
[18] P. BRAIDO, *Le metamorfosi dell'Oratorio Salesiano tra il secondo dopoguerra e il Postconcilio Vaticano II (1944-1984)*, in «Ricerche Storiche Salesiane» 25 (2006) 49, 333.
[19] See SGC (1972), nn. 250-265.
[20] See SGC (1972), nn. 268-269.

1st GC22 draft	2nd GC22 draft	Final GC22 draft	Definitive version
In the concrete realization of our activities and works, we inspire ourselves with dynamic fidelity in the Oratory of Don Bosco, seen as the lasting criterion for discernment and renewal. --- For our Founder, the Oratory is a representative synthesis of his brilliant action and his educational style; it is "a *home* for those who have none, a *parish* for those who do not know where their parish is, a *school* open to all who might find insuperable difficulty elsewhere".[21]	In the concrete realization of *our mission*, we inspire ourselves with dynamic fidelity in the Oratory of Don Bosco, seen as a permanent criterion for discernment and renewal. --- Every work of ours, as the Valdocco, becomes for the youngsters a home that welcomes, a parish that evangelizes, a school that prepares for life, and a playground where friends could meet.	Don Bosco *lived a pastoral experience in the first* Oratory *which serves as a model*; it was for the youngsters a home that welcomed, a parish that evangelized, a school that prepared them for life, and a playground where friends could meet *and enjoy themselves.* --- As we *carry out* our mission *today*, the Valdocco *experience is still* the lasting criterion for discernment and renewal *in all* our activities and works	Don Bosco lived a pastoral experience in *his* first Oratory which serves as a model; it was for the youngsters a home that welcomed, a parish that evangelized, a school that prepared them for life, and a playground where friends could meet and enjoy themselves. --- As we carry out our mission today, the Valdocco experience is still the lasting criterion for discernment and renewal in all our activities and works.

Scheme C: Evolution of the "Don Bosco in the Oratory" Criterion

---

[21] SGC (1972), n. 216.

3.1.3   Further Applications of the Criterion Needed

The "Don Bosco in the Oratory" or the Oratorian criterion had further applications and developments. We focus here on two in particular: the text evolution in the Constitutions and the Rector Major Egidio Viganò's teaching.

As we can see in the Scheme C, the Oratorian criterion was "fortunate" entering the Salesian Constitutions during GC22 (1984).[22] The first draft resembles the Special General Chapter mindset. It uses the dynamic fidelity concept, focuses in the first places on the works and quotes the SGC text explicitly. It also uses a functional three dimensional view: Oratory is a home, parish, school for the needy young people. The second draft moves ahead and gives priority to the mission, the works come only in the second place. It also integrates a less functional dimension of the playground where young people meet as friends ("cortile" in Italian means courtyard a meeting place not only for recreation purposes). The final draft and the definitive version accept the second draft developing further accents. The changed order of the two paragraphs indicate that Don Bosco's lived experience comes first and the problem of carrying out our works follows afterwards.

This evolution was probably influenced by the teachings of Egidio Viganò that values the formula "Oratorian criterion" or another linked concept of "Oratorian heart". In 1978, the newly elected Rector Major suggested the formula "Oratorian heart" in the closing address of the Chapter. Until the end of his life he did not stop to propose it almost like a summary of being and operating of a Salesian educator. Viganò in his teachings links the Oratorian heart to the educative Preventive System as depicted in the *Memoirs of the Oratory*. The Oratorian criterion is not linked to the works and activities, but to a fundamental attitude of Don

---

[22] See the unpublished reconstruction of the Article No. 40, in J.L. PLASCENCIA MONCAYO, *Costituzioni della Società di san Francesco Di Sales. Processo diacronico dell'elaborazione del testo*, vol. 1: Articoli 1-95, Roma-Guadalajara 2007.

Bosco – the pastoral charity. It is not used in the sense of dedicating one-self to a particular kind of works, but in the sense of living and expressing a characteristic pastoral attitude that qualifies every Salesian presence in any work. Practically it was urgent to prioritize the Salesian Youth Ministry, filling the hearts with an "Oratorian longing" and putting the criterion of predilection for the young as the root of all our work. Oratorian heart is often linked by Viganò with the typical Salesian motto *da mihi animas*.[23]

The "Don Bosco in the Oratory" is a fortunate synthesis, an evocative and understandable criterion for the Vatican II renewal. It is present in many documents of the Congregation and it has shaped the Salesian identity. Nonetheless, we have to note that although it is universal as a synthesis, it is not complete. It means that it focuses on some elements and neglects the others. The link to the material aspect of the works is evident (house, parish, school, playground) and so is the ideal thrust of the pastoral charity (*da mihi animas*). There are some aspects that could be neglected:

- The Oratorian criterion misses concrete applications, as was already noted by the SGC;[24]
- At the level of dimensions of the Youth Ministry, evangelization (parish), education (school) and social experience (playground) are present, but the vocational dimension is missing;
- It pinpoints the general educative passion or pastoral charity but it does not describe concretely Don Bosco's attitudes or virtues;
- An actual methodology linked to the criterion is missing, as noted by Egidio Viganò.[25]

---

[23] See GC21 (1978), pp. 328-33; E. VIGANÒ, *Lettera del Rettor Maggiore*, in «Atti del Consiglio Superiore» 64 (1983) 310, 10 and BRAIDO, *Le metamorfosi dell'Oratorio*, 347-350.

[24] See SGC (1972), nn. 270-273.

[25] See E. VIGANÒ, *Lettera del Rettor Maggiore*, in «Atti del Consiglio Superiore» 61 (1980) 297, 28.

In the following pages we would like to fill the gap and describe more concretely Don Bosco in the Oratory. We will focus on his attitudes or permanent principles of his action and also on some elements of his methodology. But first we will see how religious orders describe their Founders and charisms in relation to organizational issues.

3.2 Consecrated Life and Organizational Research

Leadership and management are not unknowns in the world of consecrated life. There are many studies which deal with this topic and the points of view vary. We will recall just some authors who understand that the binomial *leadership – management* as seen within religious orders has much to say to the secular world and that the organization scholars can enlighten some aspects of community life in religious orders as well.

3.2.1 Consecrated Leadership as a Universal Model

In his book *Heroic Leadership: Best Practices from a 450-Year-Old-Company That Changed the World*,[26] Chris Lowney, a former Jesuit, now a consultant and manager, dwells at length particularly on the experience of the first generations of the Company of Jesus and selects four key principles of leadership implicit in the Jesuit "way of proceeding". The author proposes this model as a universally valid method, not restricted to the Company of Jesus. The Jesuit "heroic leadership" is founded on four pillars:

Self-awareness: of one's strengths, weaknesses, values and vision of the future, nurturing the habit of self-examination and of deepening their knowledge through the Spiritual Exercises;[27]

---

[26] See C. LOWNEY, *Heroic Leadership: Best Practices from a 450-Year-Old-Company That Changed the World*, Loyola Press, Chicago 2005.
[27] See *Idem*, pp. 113-126.

Ingenuity: which consists in embracing the world ever in change and in initiating changes. Jesuit leaders "anchored by nonnegotiable principles and values, cultivate the 'indifference' that allows them to adapt confidently".[28]

Love: a concrete loving attitude towards all those involved in the mission. So everyone is disposed to "greater love than fear";[29]

Heroism: nourished by heroic ambitions which pour energy into them and others, leaders "endeavor to conceive grand resolves and elicit equally grand desires".[30]

The author's starting point is John Kotter's concept of leadership[31] and he compares him with other authors of books dealing with managerial sciences.[32] However, he immediately makes it clear that his concept is different, and that he speaks of a shared leadership; of the inner source of leadership, the ongoing formation of leadership and of leadership understood as a way of life, not as a technique or a set of separated actions. The author also describes the quality of Jesuit organization comparing it with the already established traditions of the Benedictines, Dominicans and Franciscans whose managerial structures he considers insufficient.[33]

Craig S. Galbraith, a Benedictine Oblate, student of management and co-founder of several businesses in the area of biotechnology, has a similar approach to Oliver Galbraith III. The latter is a professor emeritus of San Diego State University. Both authors have described the Rule of St. Benedict from the point of view of leadership and have produced a synthesis reducing it to 15 principles: common interest; selection and

---

[28] *Idem*, p. 39.
[29] *The Constitutions of the Company of Jesus*, in LOWNEY, *Heroic Leadership*, p. 32.
[30] *Letters of St. Ignatius of Loyola*, in LOWNEY, *Heroic Leadership*, pp. 33-34.
[31] See J.P. KOTTER, *Leading Change*, in LOWNEY, *Heroic Leadership*, pp. 13-14.
[32] See the references made to leadership authors as Badaracco, Collins, Drucker, Goleman, Herzberg, Heskett, McGregor, and Zaleznik throughout the *Heroic Leadership* by Lowney.
[33] See LOWNEY, *Heroic Leadership*, pp. 137-149.

formation; merit and seniority; focused ventures; innovation; ethics; stability; purposeful ritual; group reliance and respect; discipline; counsel;
grumbling; leader example; humility and moderation; iron resolve.[34]

3.2.2 Comparative Studies between Consecrated and Secular Settings

A second type of approach is offered by Claudius Johannes Eckert,
Benedictine and Theology professor at the Ludwig Maximilian University in Munich, which makes a comparison between the organizational
culture of the Bayerische Motoren Werke (BMW) and of the Bavarian
Benedictine Congregation (BBK).[35] The in-depth analysis, developed in
nearly 500 pages, starts by describing the actual cultural challenges that
question economic management models and at the same time the organizational praxis of the Church. In the second part, the author follows the
path of reflection with a philosophical and theological anthropological
foundation (conscience, socialization, conflictual existence, freedom and
bonds, needs, work and formation of identity, society, community, organization).

From an exhaustive comparison of the two organizational cultures,
that build the centre of the publication, the final message originates: "It
is in our mutual interest that BMW and BBK learn from each other. If
we look over the factory fences and the walls of the monastery, we can
find common areas and on that basis learning opportunities arise".[36] Of
course Eckert sees the differences that consist especially in objectives
setting (creation of material values vs. creating ideal values), function of
the whole (industrial organization vs. life- sharing community) and in the
bottom line mindset (flexibility vs. stability). These do not prevent him

---

[34] See C.S. GALBRAITH – O. GALBRAITH III, *Benedictine Rule of Leadership*, Adams Media Corporation, Avon, MA 2004.
[35] See J.C. ECKERT, *Dienen statt Herrschen. Unternehmenskultur und Ordensspiritualität: Begegnungen, Herausforderungen, Anregungen*, Schäfer Poeschl, Stuttgart 2000.
[36] *Idem*, p. 234.

from seeing an area of mutual learning built on these common principles: continuous renewal awareness; achievement of the objectives through communication (group reflection) and participation (mutual openness), and finally, common guiding principles of formation (co-responsibility and servant leadership).[37] In his next publication the author offers practical leadership advice actualizing Bernard of Clairvaux's sermon to Pope Eugene III. The balanced view combines the contemplative spirit with care and responsibility for ministry in the Church and integrates practical experiences from leadership seminars guided by the author himself.[38]

The Salesian Reinhard Gesing, Director of the Institute for Salesian Spirituality in Benediktbeuern, directs his reflections in the same course, but with a specific focus. He compares the function of the traditional Salesian community rector's monthly talk to the employee-manager interview at RWE (a multinational energy company).[39]

The comparison of the two types of dialogue puts an emphasis on the learning opportunities for both organizations: Salesians may value the monthly talk more and return to its practice also being motivated by recent managerial studies. In this sense, the role of the rector could integrate some functions of the coach (giving and receiving feedback, communication skills training). The dialogue should follow methodological guidelines and could be enlarged also to the lay collaborators in Salesian works as a coordination and ongoing formation tool. For RWE the learning opportunities are: give attention to the dignity of the person as a fundamental guideline of the dialogue; develop a set of guidelines

---

[37] *Idem*, pp. 234-280.
[38] See J.C. ECKERT, *Die Kunst, sich richtig wichtig zu nehmen. Führungskompetenz aus dem Kloster*, Kösel, München 2012.
[39] See R. GESING, *Das Mitbrudergespräch in einer Ordensgemeinschaft und das Mitarbeitergesprach im Unternehmen. Eine vergleichende Darstellung unter besonderer Bezugnahme auf das Mitbrudergespräch bei den SDB und das Mitarbeitergespräch bei RWE*, Manuscript in the series „Benediktbeurer Schriftenreihe zur Lebensgestaltung im Geiste Don Boscos", Benedikbeuern 2004.

for discretion and employee protection; give priority to empowerment, and lastly , increase the ability to learn from mistakes.[40]

3.2.3 Leadership Theories Applied to Consecrated Life

A different approach is taken by the Maltese Jesuit Alfred Darmanin, as professor of psychology and past president of the Conference of European Jesuit Provincials, in his article on Ignatian spirituality and contemporary leadership.[41] He makes a list of the trends in contemporary theories of leadership, and then looks for similarities with the organizational method spelled out by Ignatius of Loyola. In his article he examines the following trends: shared vision-mission (Hesselbein); situational leadership (Hersey-Blanchard); transformational leadership (Burns); organizational culture (Schein); leadership-management (Kotter, Covey); organizational metaphors (Morgan); learning organization (Senge); and servant leadership (Greenleaf). In a subsequent article, Darmanin applies his analysis of managerial research to some of the materials of the 35th General Congregation of the Jesuits. Besides bringing attention to the organizational structure he insists on the need for leadership training within the Company of Jesus.[42]

A fourth study of the relationship between organizational sciences and the life of religious institutes was made by the Vincentian Family which adopted and implemented the systemic change theory in the life of the Institutes of the Daughters of Charity, the Congregation of the Mission and the Vincentian Volunteer Work, the Association Internationale des Charités (AIC).[43] Robert Maloney, the Superior General between 1992 and 2004, summarizes the essence of systemic change in

---

[40] See *Idem*, pp. 45-47.
[41] See A. DARMANIN, *Ignatian Spirituality and Leadership in Organizations Today*, in «Review of Ignatian Spirituality» 36 (2005) 2, 1-14.
[42] See A. DARMANIN, *Governance in the Society of Jesus. What's New?*, in «Review of Ignatian Spirituality» 39 (2008) 3, 75.
[43] See *The Vincentian Family*, in aic-international.org/content.php?m=4&l=en (accessed 1.1. 2017).

the life and the pastoral activity of Vincent de Paul: changing social structures; integral evangelization and witness, preaching and human promotion; holistic service; quality; organization; solid foundations as the basis for sustainability; transparency; education and job-training; networking; and advocacy.[44]

Still another viewpoint is that adopted by Pat Smith, a Franciscan from the United States, who takes up the idea of a leader as proposed by Lowney and compares it with the experience of Francis of Assisi, while drawing from other sources as well.[45] "A leader is one who has a profound experience of and passion (love) for life coupled with a vision of the future. A leader is one who can successfully communicate this vision and who is able to inspire and motivate others to share in it and own it. A leader can assist others to achieve it, despite conflicts and obstacles that might have to be overcome".[46] Franciscan leadership is Gospel-centred and familial, rooted in being (not in doing), it springs from littleness, and requires continuous conversion. Unlike Lowney and the Vincentian Family leadership model, Smith's article and other Franciscan publications are directed as formation texts above all to the religious family and do not aspire to have a global organizational impact.[47]

A particular perspective of study is adopted by the Salesian Ric Fernando Lorenzo in his doctoral thesis in canon law entitled *Management*

---

[44] R. MALONEY, *Ten seeds of systemic change in the life and works of St. Vincent,* in aic-international.org/pdf/publicationions/cahier13en.pdf (accessed 1.1. 2017).

[45] See M. CARNEY – J. CHINNICI, *Implications for Governance from Franciscan Christology. Response to Zachary Hayes' presentation on Christology,* Franciscan Federation, Anaheim, LA 1995; D. JULIEN, *Clare's Model of Leadership,* in «The Cord» 51 (2001) 4, 184-198; P. SMITH, *Franciscan Leadership: Mutual Love Generating a Future. Keynote presentation at the Franciscan Federation Annual Conference 2009,* in franfed.org/Keynote - AFC2009, PatSmithOSF.pdf (accessed 1.1. 2017).

[46] SMITH, *Franciscan Leadership,* p. 1.

[47] See P. O'MARA, *The Franciscan Leader: A Modern Version of the Six Wings of the Seraph. An Anonymous Franciscan Treatise in the Tradition of St. Bonaventure,* Franciscan Institute Publications, St. Bonaventure, NY 2013; D.D. REAM – T.A. REAM (eds.), *Handbook for Secular Franciscan Servant Leadership,* in troubadoursofpeace.org/ Documents/Formation/SFO Formation Resource Manual.pdf (accessed 1.1. 2017).

of Governance structures in Religious Institutes of active life: Applied to the Salesian Society of St. John Bosco.[48] The author analyzes the world-wide organizational structure of the Salesians (general, regional and provincial level) from the point of view of canon law and organizational sciences. Lorenzo proposes some courageous improvements in governance structures through the combination of various theories, unfortunately without a thorough and unitary perspective.[49] Inspired by the Verbites, he suggests strengthening of the Regions as an intermediate structure of government. Another proposal involves a major coordination of the Departments within the Directorate-General through a "Coordination Office".

3.2.4 Other Organizational Studies Written by SDBs or FMAs

Besides Gesing's comparative study and Lorenzo's structural reform proposal, we can find publications of different nature written by the Salesians or the Daughters of Mary Help of Christians. They do not write explicitly about Don Bosco or the Salesian charism and their characteristics vary from academic analysis to self-help or motivational books. An interesting academic publication is presented by the Salesian Giuseppe Tacconi, a researcher and lecturer at the University of Verona. The publication of *Alla ricerca di nuove identità* ("In Search of New Identities") broadens the horizon of ongoing formation of the religious orders of active apostolic life. Tacconi affirms that organizational structures of the religious orders are more ways of thinking rather than mere technical instruments. In this sense, the author proposes Edgar Schein's organizational learning as a tool for lifelong learning. Referring particularly to the

---

[48] See F. RIC LORENZO, *Management of Governance structures in Religious Institutes of active life. Applied to the Salesian Society of St. John Bosco*, Salesian Pontifical University; thesis no. 0810D; director: J.M. Graulich; date of discussion: 3. 4. 2006.
[49] For organizational theories, the author makes references almost exclusively to management textbook: J.M. IVANCEVICH – M.T. MATTESON, *Organizational Behavior and Management*, McGraw Hill/Irwin, New York ⁶2002, pp. 4-32 and RIC LORENZO, *Management of Governance structures*, pp. 217-241.

religious orders in the Italian context, he offers educational tools and methods from psychological, sociological, narrative, autobiographical and clinical areas. He follows the French philosopher and sociologist Edgar Morin in affirming the need to pass from a "simple" paradigm of consecrated life to a "complexity" paradigm. The publication also indirectly offers different stimuli for the formation of the Educative and Pastoral Community that will be taken into account in the next chapters.[50]

There are also some other publications by Salesian authors that are not strictly academic or they focus on leadership in general. The Daughter of Mary Help of Christians Enrica Rosanna, who was the Undersecretary of the Congregation for Institutes of Consecrated Life and Societies of Apostolic Life from 2004 to 2011, wrote together with Notkert Wolf a bestselling book *Die Kunst Menschen zu führen* (Art of Leading People).[51] The authors take cues from organizational ideals of the consecrated life and integrate them with personal experience. In *Leadership Success: The Real Way*, the Salesian Michael Biju, a specialist in moral theology, approaches the theme of leadership from a Christian perspective and from a more general point of view of integrity based on the relationship between the leader and the followers in a quest to achieve the common good.[52] A similar perspective on Christian leadership that mediates between execution of plans and the sense of the hidden presence of God in all events is proposed by David O'Malley.[53]

---

[50] See G. TACCONI, *Alla ricerca di nuove identità. Formazione e organizzazione nelle comunità di vita apostolica attiva nel tempo di crisi*, LDC, Leumann (TO) 2001.

[51] See N. WOLF – E. ROSANNA, *Die Kunst Menschen zu führen*, Rowohlt Taschenbuch, Hamburg 2007.

[52] See M. BIJU – R.J. LOCHRIE, *Integrity. The Core of Leadership*, Tate Publishing, Mustang OK 2009.

[53] See D. O'MALEY, *Christian Leadership in Education*, Don Bosco Publications, Bolton 2007.

3.3 Don Bosco's Leadership and Management

The aforementioned approaches could be categorized with different criteria. All the authors make an analysis of the order's charism and compare it with contemporary organizational theories. If we go beyond extent and quality of analysis, the difference lies mainly in the purpose of the publication:

1. *phenomenological approach* (Lowney, Galbraith, in part Darmanin and Eckert) starts from the founding experience of an order to extract an explicit model of leadership or management;

2. *comparative approach* (Eckert, Gesing) dialogues between the religious order organizational model and a practical business organization model to draw some consequences for the organizational learning of both parties;

3. *applicative approach* (Maloney, Smith, in part Lorenzo and Darmanin) adopts a management - leadership set of theories, reads the charism of the religious order through its lenses and provides operational guidance for the order.

In the presented study, we see a problematic point in the comparative and applicative approaches. The authors following them often apply a specific theory or practice to a religious order without a deeper analysis of the implicit mental frameworks that are often contrary to the founding charism. In the last section of this Chapter we will therefore develop a phenomenological approach to describe Don Bosco in the concreteness of the evolving Oratory. We will take a deeper look on his mental worlds and profound Christian and Salesian organizational attitudes he put in practice in different phases of his life. Afterwards, in the next Chapter, rooted in Don Bosco's anthropological model, we will choose some organizational theories that can help develop the potential of the Salesian Educative and Pastoral leadership and project management.

In the following paragraphs, which will be framed from a phenomenological point of view, we will examine the life of Don Bosco with the help of the universal dual concept *leadership-management*. Our aim is to uncover how he was able to unify these two perspectives in his life. By *leadership* we understand a type of human activity which is directed towards persons, searching for direction and for ultimate goals with the help of principles and criteria. Emphasis is placed on methods of transformation, empowerment, informality and reorganization of systems. *Management*, on the other hand, is a type of human activity focused on things and objects using formal and structured methods, efficient customs and techniques, relying on the strategy of control, measurement and evaluation within existing systems.

3.3.1 The Various "Worlds" in the Life of Don Bosco

Every person exists in a physical, cultural and spiritual setting and carries with himself the paradigms that have been handed on to him during his formative years. These physical, cultural and spiritual systems are the "worlds" in which Don Bosco's personality developed, as well and they constitute the coordinates within which his activity took place. These "worlds" that have now become a part of the person usually carry a tension among various elements as they relate to one another. The tension between "worlds" or their components can stimulate the development of the person or, if handled improperly, it can paralyze any growth. As regards the managerial style in Don Bosco's activity we shall examine above all the aspects related to how he responded to the reality in which he found himself; his leadership style, on the other hand, will appear within the coordinates of a meaningful horizon or the ideal future that gives a purpose to the day-by-day managerial endeavours. In this perspective we intend to sketch Don Bosco's multifaceted relationship with his socio-cultural milieu.

1. The rural world of Piedmont during the post-Napoleonic Restoration period (1815-48) was the first context in which Don Bosco was born. Pietro Braido describes it in relation to his leadership and management style: "In this soil abound the psychological and mental roots of a frugal man and priest in the handling of large amounts of money that would

come his way, being firm and cautious in business, simple and prudent, clever in making himself well-liked and in soliciting funds, resolute and flexible in putting into effect his projects 'for the greater glory of God and the salvation of souls', as he might have heard in sermons and in catechetical and moral instructions".[54]

Don Bosco, true to his roots, managed to combine prudence with a wealth of wisdom, of anecdotes and experiences drawn from his Piedmontese lore, all of which could be summarized as "an austere school of entrepreneurship together with trust in Providence."[55] The binomial *manual work – trust in Providence,* when it is a person's actual way of life, could very well be a suitable description of the binomial management-leadership within a rural setting.[56] This binomial reveals the interdependence between both elements and prevents falling into a form of fatuous reliance upon providence or a kind of practical Pelagianism. Pietro Stella has synthesized, in his own words, this mentality that appears in Don Bosco's writings: "God dominates human events, even though human beings are the actors".[57]

2. The world of the working class and that of the Christian humanism, assimilated during the years of study in Chieri, are another two coordinates of Don Bosco's relation to the reality. The contemporaneity of *craftsmanship* with his *studies* nurtured in him a strong mindset: hard work needed to manage everyday tasks is as necessary as the study that broadens horizons and gives sense to the day. However, both of these "cultures […] would continue to be two distinct worlds in Don Bosco's

---

[54] P. BRAIDO, *Don Bosco prete dei giovani nel secolo delle libertà,* vol. 1, LAS, Roma ²2003, pp. 111-112.

[55] BRAIDO, *Don Bosco prete dei giovani,* vol. 1, p. 118.

[56] Regarding Don Bosco's affinity with rural life and environment, see P. STELLA, *Don Bosco nella storia economica e sociale (1815-1870),* LAS, Roma 1980, pp. 11-27; P. STELLA, *Don Bosco,* Il Mulino, Bologna 2001, pp. 23-26; BRAIDO, *Don Bosco prete dei giovani,* vol. 1, p. 112-121. For the binomial "Providence – human history" in Don Bosco, see P. STELLA, *Don Bosco. Religious Outlook and Spirituality,* Salesiana Publishers, New Rochelle NY 1996, pp. 45-86.

[57] STELLA, *Don Bosco. Religious Outlook,* p. 53.

personal and institutional mindset. Also the youngsters he was educating were from different socio-economic extraction and had different life aspirations, yet they were sharing common life in a brotherly and organized society, each one in the hands of Providence".[58] The joining of these two worlds creates the strong communion of the lay Salesians and clerical Salesians in the Congregation.[59]

3. The formation that Don Bosco received in the Chieri Seminary (1835-41) and at the "Convitto Ecclesiastico" in Turin (1841-43) left him with the imprint of an *austere spirituality* of salvation as well as a *benign spirituality* of love. The years in the seminary were marked by insistence on saving one's soul; the theology taught at that time was abstract but left some theological notions in young John Bosco that stayed with him throughout his life: examining all things in the light of eternity, being accountable before the Divine Judge, awaiting either eternal life or eternal death; and also the relationship between Divine Law and freedom as understood by moral Probabiliorism.[60] The formation imparted at the Convitto, besides practical pastoral experiences, introduced the young priests to a spirituality founded on love as exemplified in the lives of St. Philip Neri, St. Francis de Sales, St. Vincent de Paul, and proposed solutions to moral problems which promoted the glory of God and the good of the person.[61] As he begins his mission as an educator of the young in Turin, Don Bosco realizes that he must mesh together several different points of view.

---

[58] BRAIDO, *Don Bosco prete dei giovani*, vol. 1, p. 125.
[59] See BRAIDO, *Don Bosco prete dei giovani*, vol. 1, p. 329-361, and L. PAZZAGLIA, *Apprendistato e istruzione degli artigiani a Valdocco (1846-1886)*, in F. TRANIELLO (ed.), *Don Bosco nella storia della cultura popolare*, SEI, Torino 1987, pp. 39-46.
[60] See P. STELLA, *Don Bosco. Life and Work*, Don Bosco Publications, New Rochelle NY 1985, pp. 45-54 and BRAIDO, *Don Bosco prete dei giovani*, vol. 1, p. 152-155.
[61] See BRAIDO, Don Bosco prete dei giovani, vol. 1, p. 160-164; STELLA, *Don Bosco. Life and Work*, pp. 88-91 and F. CASELLA, *L'esperienza educativa preventiva di Don Bosco. Studi sull'educazione Salesiana fra tradizione e modernità*, LAS, Roma 2007, pp. 45-49.

"The seminary and the Convitto [...] had instilled in him a basic structure which, given his uncommon intelligence and innate realism, made it possible for him to make the right choices at the beginning of his ministry to the young. The Convitto had induced an evolution in his ecclesiology, in the practice of certain devotions and moral guidelines, which were further enriched through his personal readings. The encounter with the teachings of Alphonsus Liguori and with the reality of the youth in Turin enabled a substantial approach of his methods to the Salesianity understood in a broad sense, including the blending of the Philippian and Vincentian spiritualities".[62]

4. Some of Don Bosco's ingrained economic management methods belonged, on the one hand, to the rural society, and on the other hand, to the industrialized liberal society.[63] Stella describes Don Bosco's antiplanning mindset in the example of balancing his accounts. His works "were entrusted beyond understanding to 'goodwill', deaf to the most elementary demands of statistics or scientific management [...]. Even in handling the finances his practice reflected the organizational culture of the Oratory, lying between urban and rural life, between scientific and illiterate worldview. In many ways Don Bosco's methods were those of the peasant family-like lifestyle but already showing some changes suggested by his experiences in the city. From his rural background Don Bosco had assimilated certain habits, such as keeping oral accounts or assessment of even complex situations based on essential data situated within a horizon of his daily experience".[64]

Very revealing is the reaction of the physician and writer Serafino Biffi who collected data for his report on youth correctional institutions, in which he summarizes Don Bosco's deep roots in the rural culture: "One might say that that respected priest makes light of all that modern

---

[62] BRAIDO, *Don Bosco prete dei giovani*, vol. 1, p. 185.
[63] See STELLA, *Don Bosco*, p. 61; and P. BRAIDO, *Prevention not repression. Don Bosco's Educational System*, Kristu Jyoti Publications, Bengaluru 2013, pp. 154-159.
[64] STELLA, *Don Bosco nella storia economica*, p. 371.

science has to say in this field. For him it seems that it is enough for a person to do good with pious intention, leaving to Providence the care about the good seed to sprout, grow and bear fruit. When speaking of statistics, of making distinctions, of taking precautions, of regulations, he usually responded with a smile sparkling with surprise, incredulity and compassion".[65] In the conclusion of his volume on the organizing activity of the Founder of the Salesian Society Stella gives his summary: "Don Bosco went along with the capitalistic economy always aware of his civil rights. He became an owner of a growing movable and immovable property [...]. While the Marchioness Barolo financed her institutions with the steady income from her rent, Don Bosco based his own finances on the funds available from private donations, public assistance, school tuition, workshops production and publishing activities".[66]

If on the one hand, Don Bosco rejects the liberal frame of mind and certain progressive ideas, on the other hand, he is to be considered a "modern saint" because of his entrepreneurship, his methodological open mindedness, his distinct ability to motivate others in achieving a significant role in the society, his ability to ensure that the Congregation would stand on its own feet even to the point that others, such as businesses, the social media and health services, would want to partner with it.[67]

The four "worlds" mentioned above moulded Don Bosco's personality, his method of action (*work – Providence*), cultural coordinates (*classical studies – craftsmanship*), his spirituality (*austere salvation – benign love*), and his managerial style (*rural – modern*). In every one of these dimensions there is a polarity enabling the existence of a tension

---

[65] S. BIFFI, *Sui riformatori pei giovani*, in STELLA, *Don Bosco nella storia economica*, p. 369.

[66] STELLA, *Don Bosco nella storia economica*, p. 398.

[67] See P. BAIRATI, *Cultura Salesiana e società industriale*, in TRANIELLO, *Don Bosco nella storia della cultura popolare*, pp. 331-357; F. MOTTO, *Start afresh from Don Bosco*, s.e., Roma 2006, pp. 29-31 and 34-35; G. COSTA, *Don Bosco in terza pagina. La stampa e il Fondatore dei Salesiani*, Istituto Teologico S. Tommaso, Messina 1991.

which becomes the spark of Don Bosco's synergy and creativity in his education and pastoral ministry.

3.3.2 Don Bosco's Childhood and Formation (1815-1841)

From the day of his birth until his residence in the "Convitto Ecclesi-astico" in Turin John Bosco adopted his own cultural and spiritual standards laying the initial foundations for his educative-pastoral style, which then matured in the following years. When he began his studies, immersed in the cultural environment of the Piedmontese countryside, "he had to adjust to the experience of 'two cultures'."[68] He writes in the *Memoirs of the Oratory*: "The walk to and from school afforded me some time to study. When I got home I would take the hoe in one hand and my grammar in the other".[69] Studying as a symbol of the ideal future and the practical struggles of the waiter, the tailor and the bookbinder, became the forces that were part of young Bosco's everyday life.[70] From the perspective of this article one can say that the dynamic principle operating in this period of his life was the binomial *duties – vocation*. John's priestly vocation at such a young age constitutes the essence of leadership he exercised throughout his entire life, broadening the horizon of his vision in which he effectively placed the managerial duties of study, work and prayer.

The harmony and the blending of both components are apparent in his proactivity, his passion and joy which were the elements of a successful although difficult synthesis. "Reading became a passion. John's relish for literary works deprived him of sleep, but it also encouraged reflection

---

[68] BRAIDO, *Don Bosco prete dei giovani*, vol. 1, p. 120.
[69] G. BOSCO, *Memoirs of the Oratory of Saint Francis de Sales from 1815 to 1855. The Autobiography of Saint John Bosco*, trans. Daniel Lyons, Don Bosco Publications, New Rochelle NY 1989, pp. 41.
[70] See STELLA, *Life and Work*, pp. 23-26; S. CASELLE, *Giovanni Bosco a Chieri 1831 – 1841. Dieci anni che valgono una vita*, Edizioni Acclaim, Torino 1988, pp. 24–25; 46; 79; 84-85; and 121. See also M. BAY, *Giovanni Bosco a Chieri 1831-1841. Scuola pubblica e seminario*, LAS, Roma 2010.

and introspection".[71] His proactivity is visible not only in his love for study, but also in his determination to be quickly promoted to advanced classes.[72] The glue that bonded all of the above was the cheerful attitude that characterized all of his activity as a sign of his inner serenity. Linking the fulfillment of one's duties with the cheerfulness of a youth group, which he founded in Chieri and was known as "the Society of Good Cheer", became a paradigm for the future. This duty-cheerfulness link will be part of his educational method[73] as we can see it testified in the biographies of Dominic Savio, Michael Magone and Francis Besucco.[74]

Don Bosco's daily bread is study, work and prayer, guaranteed by the structures of public education and that of the Chieri seminary and the Convitto in Turin. "Cultural, moral and religious formation were mandatory",[75] not only in the Seminary and the Convitto, but also in the secondary school in Chieri as dictated by the School Regulations of 1822, fruit of the Restoration and based on the *Ratio Studiorum* of the Jesuits. John lived each day as prescribed by the regulations[76] spurred on by the lists of resolutions that became his first experience of planning. We may recall the bits of advice given by his mother Margaret on the occasion of his First Communion, the seven resolutions along with the advice of his Mother when he donned the cassock, his decisions during his stay in the seminary, the nine resolutions prior to his ordination and

---

[71] STELLA, *Don Bosco. Life and Work*, p. 26. See also BRAIDO, *Don Bosco prete dei giovani*, vol.1, p. 127.

[72] BRAIDO, *Don Bosco prete dei giovani*, vol.1, p. 126 and F. DESRAMAUT, *Don Bosco en son temps (1815-1888)*, SEI, Torino 1996, pp. 49-50 and 56-57.

[73] See BRAIDO, *Prevention not repression*, pp. 233-251 and 307-319. See also J.M. PRELLEZO, *Sistema educativo ed esperienza oratoriana di Don Bosco*, LDC, Leumann TO 2000, pp. 69-77.

[74] See G. BOSCO, *Vite di giovani. Le biografie di Domenico Savio, Michele Magone e Francesco Besucco*. Saggio introduttivo e note storiche, ed. Aldo Giraudo, LAS, Roma 2012, pp. 61-62; 19-120; and 195-196. See also A. GIRAUDO, *Maestri e discepoli in azione*, in BOSCO, *Vite di giovani*, pp. 27-28.

[75] BRAIDO, *Don Bosco prete dei giovani*, vol. 1, p. 129.

[76] See BOSCO, *Memoirs of the Oratory*, pp. 71-73.

the three resolutions for priestly life in 1842.[77] Braido describes the relationship between his proposals and the existing regulations in these
words: "The seven resolutions reflect to a certain degree the rules prescribed for students as found in the Regulations for schools as of 1822."[78]
So, Don Bosco's first method of planning consists, in brief terms, in the
fulfillment of one's daily duties as required by existing regulations and
in selecting a few chosen ones as resolutions.

A second way to plan the future and his life goes beyond the day-to-
day reality and is connected to his vocational choice. Discernment and
advancement along this second path were not of immediate realization.
In the mindset of the time the vocational choice was given an exaggerated importance even to the point of seeing it as decisive for one's
salvation or damnation. This setting combined with the conviction that
everything was already predisposed by God caused John some moments
of anxiety.[79] There were two steps for a managerial handling of the vocational dilemma: following the path of obedience and/or the path of
logic. As to obedience to his confessor Giuseppe Maria Maloria, es-
teemed as the most learned ecclesiastic in Chieri, John would have
expected more concrete advice that would help him decide on his vocation.[80] Young John was pleased with his guide[81] and would continue to
go to him for confession while in the seminary; however, he was not
satisfied with his advice in regards to vocational discernment: "In this
matter everyone must follow his own inclinations and not the advice of
others."[82] There might be many reasons why Maloria was not more concrete; it is the fact that John simply could not blindly obey the advice of
another person. The remaining alternative was to make a well thought-

---

[77] See BOSCO, *Memoirs of the Oratory*, pp. 32-33; 122-123; 144-146, and 172. See also
F. MOTTO (ed.), *Memorie dal 1841 al 1884-5-6 pel Sac. Gio. Bosco a' suoi figli Salesiani (Testamento spirituale)*, LAS, Roma 1985, pp. 21-22.
[78] BRAIDO, *Don Bosco prete dei giovani*, vol.1, p. 138.
[79] See STELLA, *Don Bosco. Life and Work*, pp. 28-30.
[80] See BOSCO, *Memoirs of the Oratory*, p. 110.
[81] See *Idem*, p. 72.
[82] *Idem*, p. 111.

out choice. Several elements came into play: the appropriate time for making a decision (the last year of high school), the esteem he had for the dignity of the priesthood, his awareness of his own weaknesses and the dangers of the world, and finally the question of finances. The real and rational result of this discernment logic was the application to join the Franciscans.[83]

Although a rational decision was made, he was beset by anxiety and indecision, as is evident in the dream of the Reformed Conventuals.[84] In this context of managerial logic and voluntaristic spirituality of salvation that produces anxiety, Don Bosco develops a further step of "planning" linked to trust in a vision of the future with faith as the key, activating the inner motivational energy, giving inner peace that has no semblance of the rigidity of a cold rational process.

This second method of planning the future is connected to the leadership aspect of human action, giving a fundamental compass to the life, and not only a set of criteria to be applied. This typically Bosconian way of envisioning his future life path requires a context of prayer in order to focus, with a deeper attention to the process of discernment. It can be described phenomenologically as the creation of a vision of the future totally permeated by trust in Divine Providence.

We must understand that John entrusts himself to Providence while engaged in prayer: he is making a novena with this intention in mind and receives the Sacraments with great fervour. With the help of his friend Luigi Comollo, he then seeks advice once more. The counsel given by a priest, the uncle of Luigi Comollo, is very important. He suggests that John enter the seminary where he might better come to know God's plans for him.[85] Rather than being a final decision, this is an act of surrender to a slow lifelong process of discernment.

---

[83] See BRAIDO, *Don Bosco prete dei giovani*, vol. 1, p. 135 and BOSCO, *Memoirs of the Oratory*, pp. 110-111.

[84] See BOSCO, *Memoirs of the Oratory*, pp. 18-19 and 110-111.

[85] See *Idem*, p. 111.

The question of dreams is not indifferent as it is related to the envisioning process lived by Don Bosco, as we have seen with the uneasy dream of the Conventuals. There is a more important dream connected to his vocational discernment process which happened at the age of nine years. Compared with the dream of the Conventuals, this one is not only a signal of an uneasy dilemma but has a pro-positive message, a call. Stella writes about its importance: "This particular dream affected Don Bosco's whole way of thinking and acting".[86]

We agree only to a certain degree with Braido that "the dream at the age of nine or ten [...] was nothing other than his desire to become a priest",[87] because it reduces the richness of the envisioning process only to the result of it. And that result could be then planned and pursued in a rational-voluntaristic way. In important moments of John's life, we see instead a strong vocational dynamic at play. His vocational discernment is a more interior, passive and receptive process lived as both listening and searching for God's will. In that sense the form of a dream is an ideal narrative form of the discernment process: passivity of the subject, visualization and story-evolving are common to both of them. In these events of Don Bosco's life, we can find the roots of his leadership qualities: his identity of a disciple. Only an authentic follower can evolve into an authentic and inspired leader in the future. The leadership type of process

---

[86] STELLA, *Don Bosco. Life and Work*, p. 10.

[87] BRAIDO, *Don Bosco prete dei giovani*, vol. 1, p. 114. It is to be noted that Braido is more concerned about historical critics and the nature of Don Bosco dreams. Our aim is not to answer these questions; our purpose is to insert the dreams in the context of Don Bosco's motivational and decision making processes. For historical-critical approach see P. STELLA, *Don Bosco's Dreams. A historico-documentary analysis of selected samples*, Salesiana Publishers, New Rochelle NY 1996; BRAIDO, *Don Bosco prete dei giovani*, vol. 1, pp. 373-376; M. GUASCO, *Don Bosco nella storia religiosa del suo tempo*, in *Don Bosco e le sfide della modernità*, Centro Studi «Carlo Trabucco», Torino 1988, p. 34 and A. LENTI, *I sogni di Don Bosco. Esame storico-critico, significato e ruolo profetico-missionario per l'America Latina*, in *Don Bosco e Brasilia: profezia, realtà sociale e diritto*, ed. Cosimo Semeraro, CEDAM, Padova 1990, pp. 85-130.

comes first in John's vocation as a priest and educator, whereas the managerial aspect of his action is located, among other factors, in the context of the institutional regulations, pursuing his resolutions, as part of the product of the discernment process.

There is a second use of dreams which is connected to Don Bosco, a leader. It is the educational and formational use of dreams in his later years. This kind of story- and dream-telling is essential because, in addition to offering material that is understandable and in vivid and attractive language, it also stimulates the motivations of the listeners. Don Bosco is a visionary type of leader, and his dreams should not be seen merely as a functional part of the story; they are the very expression of his identity and his mission. Only in that identifying sense they are transmitting the educative-motivational power to the young people formed by Don Bosco through those dreams. The intention of the narrator was not to convince to take a path that was technically within reach, but to follow and have others follow the same path traced by Providence to which he entrusted himself.[88]

The link between the two methods of planning thus becomes most important.[89] Fifty years later, in a letter to John Cagliero, Don Bosco attested the balance between ideals as expressed in visions and regulations that guide the day-to-day reality: "Once again I beg you, do not pay much attention to dreams, etc. If they happen to clarify some moral problem or explain some of our rules, that is fine. Make use of them. Otherwise see no value in them".[90]

Don Bosco's ability to create a harmonic synthesis between the management and leadership approach to action is visible in the importance

---

[88] See STELLA, *Don Bosco's Dreams*, pp. 71-76. It is worth noting how this trust in Providence is stressed especially when he recalls the difficult moments in his life, for example, the time he spent in Capriglio after the death of Don Calosso. See STELLA, *Don Bosco. Life and Work*, pp. 19-20.

[89] See MOTTO, *Start afresh from Don Bosco*, pp. 49-52.

[90] Don Bosco's letter to mons. Giovanni Cagliero of 10th february 1885, in BRAIDO, *Don Bosco prete dei giovani*, vol. 1, p. 3.

he gives to cheerfulness, as already mentioned, in his ability to build relationships and in his commitment to the good of others. His vision that
guided him day by day did not consist only in the fulfillment of his responsibilities in the formative path in being a priest, but also in living
already the mission in situations and with people he found himself with.
In his formative years, for instance, he assumes the role of an acrobat
prior to repeating the homily,[91] he teaches catechism and tells edifying
stories, he nurtures friendships in the Society of Good Cheer with Gug-
lielmo Garigliano, Paolo Braja, the Jewish boy Giona, and Luigi
Comollo.[92] In his relationships his leadership qualities were evident; they
were also based on being a follower of the priests such as Giovanni
Calosso, Pietro Banaudi and Giuseppe Maloria. Already visible were the
signs of his ability to create synergy in organizing events that combine
enjoyable recreation and edifying storytelling or in leading youth groups
such as the Society of Good Cheer within the coordinates of cheerfulness
and duties.

In conclusion, we may say that the element of Don Bosco's daily duties, managed by resolutions, went hand in hand with his vocation to
being a leader eventually as a priest and an educator, as seen in his
dreams, and with his passion for study and his commitment to be an active part in the web of relationships, with followers and friends.

3.3.3 Encounter with the Reality of the Young in Turin (1841-1846)

During the first five years of his priesthood, Don Bosco's desire to
spend his life for the needy young people is achieved by moving forward

---

[91] See STELLA, *Don Bosco. Life and Work*, pp. 11-13; BRAIDO, *Don Bosco prete dei giovani*, vol. 1, p. 119; BOSCO, *Memoirs of the Oratory*, pp. 27-29 and 98-105.
[92] See BRAIDO, *Don Bosco prete dei giovani*, vol. 1, pp. 132-135; STELLA, *Don Bosco.
Life and Work*, pp. 30-32 and 70-74; BOSCO, *Memoirs of the Oratory*, pp. 71-80 and
90-93.

different educative and pastoral activities. In 1846 it found concrete synthesis in his full-time devotion to the Oratory of Saint Francis de Sales in the Valdocco quarter of Turin. Observing Don Bosco's encounter with the reality of the young in Turin in the early 1840s, we can detect three underlying dynamics: the typical style of his presence among the young, the choice of prevention, and the total commitment to the educative mission.

In the first place there is the decision to be with them, to mingle with them, and to take part in their world. This attitude is shown in two different ways. Not only does Don Bosco fulfill his ministerial responsibilities, as for example, catechizing, preaching, visiting the prisons of Turin;[93] but he also feels comfortable in the informal world of the young. While in the Convitto "he also found the moral conferences and lessons in sacred eloquence congenial. Posing practical cases, they did not teach a theological system or a theory of the apostolate but the art of caring for souls. Situations from everyday life were presented, and then put to the test in such priestly activities as preaching, giving catechism lessons, and so forth".[94]

Taking part in these formative courses offered at the Convitto, such as catechesis, preaching and prison ministry in Turin, was in reality a training in pastoral management. But his style of presence among the young went beyond that; it was directed towards the realization of his vision, open to "originality and creativity, hand in hand with his sensitivity towards the preferences of the young and for what was for their benefit".[95]

His style of leadership, reflecting what he saw in his dream, urged him to be totally involved with the young, without formal structures, and

---

[93] See STELLA, *Don Bosco. Life and Work*, pp. 91-99; BRAIDO, *Don Bosco prete dei giovani*, vol. 1, p. 205-208 and BOSCO, *Memoirs of the Oratory*, p. 182.
[94] STELLA, *Don Bosco. Life and Work*, p. 98.
[95] A. GIRAUDO, *L'importanza storica e pedagogico – spirituale delle Memorie dell'Oratorio*, in G. BOSCO, *Memorie dell'Oratorio di S. Francesco di Sales dal 1815 al 1855.* ed. Aldo Giraudo, LAS, Roma 2011, p. 47.

supporting their aspirations. Pietro Stella speaks of "a rowing apostolate to shops, offices and markets"[96] carried on by a new generation of priests. Don Bosco, "starting from the catechetical experiences of the Convitto, felt driven to initiate new models of the oratory, which he wanted to consist of more than the usual methods of religious instruction or a school of Christian doctrine. It was the prelude to his final decision".[97] Before 1844 Don Bosco participated in every activity of the programme at the Convitto, however he also worked with a group of boys on his own initiative.

In 1844 Don Bosco transferred to the Refuge and the little hospital or infirmary (Ospedaletto) of the Marchioness Barolo, serving as an assistant to Father Borel. He was followed there by the group of youths who had gathered around him at the Convitto, and he did not send them away. Then and there he started the Oratory, which he named after St. Francis de Sales. If he did that with all due consideration, then it was one of the most carefully calculated and decisive steps he had ever taken in his life so far.[98] Then followed the months of the wandering Oratory from St. Peter in Chains to St. Martin of the Mills, then to the Moretta house and the Filippi fields.

There is a second dynamic operating here, namely how he responds to the needs of the young. Don Bosco does have an answer, even if it is initially only a part-time solution. It consists in the activities of the festive oratory: offering friendship in an anonymous city undergoing a demographic and early industrial expansion; religious instruction of the young who do not belong to a parish; healthy entertainment for the youngsters who spend most of their time at work; and evening schools for the unlettered.[99] This is a management type of answer to a single dimension need

---

[96] STELLA, *Don Bosco. Life and Work*, p. 105.
[97] BRAIDO, *Don Bosco prete dei giovani*, vol. 1, p. 166.
[98] STELLA, *Don Bosco. Life and Work*, p. 107.
[99] BRAIDO, *Don Bosco prete dei giovani*, vol. 1, pp. 200-202.

of the young that could be reduced to mere assistentialism were it not characterized by a deeper intention: education understood as prevention. Don Bosco, in fact, inserts his activity into a rich tradition of prevention that shaped his times.[100] Leadership in the mind of Don Bosco, who saw the need for prevention, consists in finding the causes of the problems that afflict the young that he meets. Obviously he is interested in psychological or educational individual causality, leaving behind the sociological or political solutions. So he observes the underlying structures behind the behaviour of the street urchins and their gangs in order to develop a programme of prevention.[101] His ultimate mission as a leader is the choice of prevention-education that has managerial implications seen in his decision to abandon the pastoral work in prisons and in re-education institutions as practised by the Marchioness Barolo. He chooses an insecure long-term mission over a clear role in a system that provides a salary. Don Bosco writes his thoughts during his visits to the jails: "On such occasions I found out how quite a few ended up once again in that place; it was because they were abandoned to their own resources. 'Who knows?' I thought to myself, 'if these youngsters had a friend outside who would take care of them, help them, teach them religion on feast days… Who knows but they could be steered away from ruin, or at least the number of those who return to prison could be lessened?' "[102]

Lastly, there is a third dynamic apparent in the life of Don Bosco in the early 1840s, and it is his ability to grasp the relationship existing between the education of the young and his identity. During his stay in the *Convitto Ecclesiastico* Don Bosco, on the one hand, is totally involved

---

[100] See the good analysis by Braido in four chapters of his *Prevention not repression*, pp. 17-114.

[101] See the two paragraphs "Prevenzione in senso socio-assistenziale" e "Prevenzione in senso pedagogico", in Francesco Motto, *Un sistema educativo sempre attuale*, LDC, Leumann TO 2000, pp. 22-30 and the paragraph "Fuggire il male e fare esperienza del bene", in J.M. PRELLEZO, *Sistema educativo ed esperienza oratoriana di Don Bosco*, LDC, Leumann TO 2000, pp. 36-37.

[102] BOSCO, *Memoirs of the Oratory*, p. 182.

in various activities of the formation programme, but at the same time, he continues to question himself regarding the realization of his vocation as a priest and educator. Pietro Braido states that during these years Don Bosco, "priest and shepherd, becomes more and more an educator and his ministry more and more directed towards the young".[103] There is an evident vocational pattern in the recurrence of his childhood dream in 1844 with some new details: the lambs are transformed into shepherds and there is the presence of a magnificent church. Pietro Stella sees behind it the development of the project, the need of collaborators and of a place of worship for himself and his boys.[104] Don Bosco allows the transformation of his own life, he discards other possibilities, committing himself to the work of the Oratory.

It is during these years that his new identity matures: "Don Bosco's activity was [...] a conscious, willed 'consecration'; a 'mission' with a precise objective: 'The full accomplishment of the salvation of the young'."[105] Don Bosco's mission becomes clearer and more defined due to the synergy between the two factors of the binomial *formative activity – vocational choice* which is a reflection of the *management – leadership* dynamic. The study of pastoral theology and the many apostolic ministries available in the Convitto are the context where he develops the certainty of his educative and preventive vocation. There is an impossibility to manage the equilibrium between his choice of the Oratory and other pastoral activities as seen in his health crisis in the 1846. This difficulty and the lead of his recurring dream facilitate the totalizing choice to dedicate himself totally to the preventive education of the youngsters of the Oratory.[106]

---

[103] BRAIDO, *Don Bosco prete dei giovani*, vol. 1, p. 185. See also MOTTO, *Start afresh from Don Bosco*, pp. 69-73.
[104] See STELLA, *Don Bosco. Life and Work*, pp. 93-94; and BOSCO, *Memoirs of the Oratory*, pp. 209-210.
[105] BRAIDO, *Prevention not repression*, pp. 166-167.
[106] See BRAIDO, *Don Bosco prete dei giovani*, vol. 1, pp. 181-183.

The three dispositions mentioned above point to a two-fold sensitivity in Don Bosco which could be described as a synergy between a structured, linear, operative aspect and an informal, systemic, integral and mission-driven aspect of education/ministry. Pietro Stella states that already in these early years Don Bosco appears as a leader, an "active, appealing priest, a kindly man of the people who was ready to participate in sports and games when the occasion arose. But he was already gaining a reputation as an extraordinary priest as well [...]; there was something singular about him, something that came from the Lord. He seemed to know the innermost secrets of conscience, he could switch from light-hearted jests to stunning private revelations, and he somehow made people appreciate the problems of their soul and their eternal salvation".[107]

3.3.4 Development of the Oratory and the Adjoined House (1846-1863)

Pietro Braido describes the years between 1846 and 1852 as the "rapid take-off of a diocesan institution that was virtually universal".[108] The Oratory with its activities was an ingenious answer to a fundamental need that was part of the reality on the fringe districts of Turin. Don Bosco's powerful vision of the integral salvation of the young fueled several new activities of the Oratory marked by a strong creative tension between the ideal and the actual everyday reality. It is during this time that the Oratory gives birth to Sunday and evening classes, the hospice, and the sodalities.

After the difficulties of Don Cocchi, Don Bosco takes over the management of the Oratory of the Guardian Angel. Later, in 1852, the Archbishop confirms Don Bosco as the Director of the three Oratories of St. Francis de Sales, Guardian Angel and St. Aloysius. The expansion continues and it is in the next decade, between 1853 and 1863, that "most

---

[107] STELLA, *Don Bosco. Life and Work*, pp. 108-109.
[108] BRAIDO, *Don Bosco prete dei giovani*, vol. 1, p. 212.

of Don Bosco's initiatives took firm root or reached full maturation".[109]
These are the golden years of his educational activity: the presence of
Savio, Magone and Besucco marked the Oratory ideal and expanded the
possibilities of his educative method. It is also a period in which the Congregation is founded; Don Bosco publishes his most innovative books,
and guides a series of construction projects at Valdocco. Finally it is a
time filled with extraordinary phenomena, which Don Bosco does not
hesitate to publish.[110] Through all of this growth and expansion Don
Bosco developed a more evolved and deeper sense of balance.

Don Bosco's decision to work full time among the youngsters in the
Oratory carried with it an underlying uncertainty about his role as a
priest. Pietro Stella writes: "In the 1840s the composition of boys visiting
the so-called oratories in the Vanchiglia district and in the fields of Valdocco reflected both the influx of young seasonal workers, not yet
anchored in the city, and the sons of the working class who had already
lived in the growing outskirts of the city for years [...]. Don Cocchi and
Don Bosco did not compete with other clerics in the area of the traditional ecclesiastical roles; yet responding to the urgent critical situation
and accepting the risk of an uncertain future, they proved able to successfully solicit subsidies and other resources which the clergy would have
been unable to gather".[111]

Thanks to his practical managerial style and the growing number of
cooperators who believed in his ideal, Don Bosco, unlike Don Cocchi,
knew how to balance the situation of uncertainty which arose from his
educational vision.[112] The balance between the uncertainty in following
his bold dream and his prudent management is the primary fundamental

---

[109] STELLA, *Don Bosco. Life and Work*, p. 119. See also MOTTO, *Start afresh from Don Bosco*, pp. 73-75.

[110] See STELLA, *Don Bosco. Life and Work*, p. 119 and STELLA, *Don Bosco nella storia economica*, pp. 71-100.

[111] STELLA, *Don Bosco nella storia economica*, pp. 394-395.

[112] G. CHIOSSO, *Carità educatrice e istruzione in Piemonte. Aristocratici, filantropi e preti di fronte all'educazione del popolo nel primo '800*, SEI, Torino 2007, pp. 199-200 and 207-212.

dynamic during this period of expansion. Braido states clearly: "Don Bosco had acquired the patience of the farmer. He could harbor grand dreams, but he knew that they would become a reality only a step at a time and as long as the means and the people were available".[113]

A second dynamic results from the teamwork with other priests and lay persons. In the Turin of that period a new class of students and priests was born. They were no longer tagged as nobility or common people, instead, they were instead attracted by a project, a future, an idea.[114] In the case of Don Bosco his colleagues included Giovanni Battista Borel, Sebastiano Pacchiotti, Antonio Bosco, Sebastiano Trivero, Giovanni Battista Vola, Roberto Murialdo, Pietro Ponte and Giovanni Marengo. The existing cooperation implied sharing basic values, a certain comradeship and frankness; there was also room for disagreement regarding methods and management.[115] Historians have detected the *collaboration – personal identity* binomial. Stella writes: "Even before 1848 Don Bosco had fought for the autonomy of his own Oratory. When meetings were held to unify the management of the Turin oratories, he had turned down amalgamation with the other oratories. He supported collaboration between various oratories and the priests connected with them, it seems, and he may even have offered his own services in that cause. But he refused to submit to any sort of formal subordination to others, whose ideas he did not fully share".[116]

He maintained that same balance even after 1848. Don Bosco held to his independence, slowly arriving at a point of advantage compared to other oratories. While his preeminence was reinforced by the decree of 1952, he did not belittle other models as, for example, the oratory of Don Cocchi and Don Ponte. Stella annotates: "Some priests and laymen began

---

[113] BRAIDO, *Don Bosco prete dei giovani*, vol. 1, p. 235.
[114] See STELLA, *Don Bosco. Life and Work*, pp. 104-107.
[115] See BRAIDO, *Don Bosco prete dei giovani*, vol. 1, pp. 197-199 and 240-243.
[116] STELLA, *Don Bosco. Life and Work*, p. 110.

as helpers of Fathers Cocchi and Ponte, went on to help Don Bosco between 1848 and 1856 (perhaps noticing his neediness), and then returned
to Father Cocchi's circle without giving up their friendship and collaboration with Don Bosco".[117]

In the expansion of the Oratory a third dynamic emerged: *expansion
of the works – growth of self-donation.* Stella sums it up describing Don
Bosco's state of mind when founding the Adjoined House (boarding fa-
cility): "If you choose to go out and make personal contact with poverty
and misery, and if you do not succumb to compromises in trying to do
something about it, you will be drawn irresistibly to give your all: your
time, your possessions, your whole life".[118] It was precisely in the situation of material poverty and in the midst of the everyday life of an
educator that his total self-donation became a reality. "At the Valdocco
oratory the boarders, who later came to be called the interns, led a simple
and rather rustic life as one big family. There was no pretentiousness
because all were convinced that they could not ask more of Don Bosco
or others".[119]

Although Don Bosco's transformation was hardly noticeable at an
empirical level, yet there were some indicators of something extraordinary being connected to his profound spirituality of total self-donation.
Pietro Stella quotes a paragraph from the records of 1861 which describe
the atmosphere that reigned in Valdocco because of the image his young
helpers had of him: "Don Bosco's outstanding brilliant gifts, his extraordinary experiences which we admire to this day, his unique guidance of
young people along virtue's arduous paths, and his grand plans for the
future are indications to us of some supernatural intervention; they por-
tend a glorious career for him and for the Oratory".[120]

---

[117] *Idem*, p. 112.
[118] *Idem*, p. 113.
[119] *Idem*, p. 116.
[120] AS 110 Ruffino as quoted in Stella, *Don Bosco. Life and Work*, p. 118.

The fourth and final dynamic is the deepening of one a mentioned before: *managerial boldness – trust in Divine Providence.* The extraordinary phenomena surrounding Don Bosco and his trust in God, which made him undertake plans beyond his possibilities, were not detached from a careful examination of the situation.[121] He was certainly not the first person that joined the spiritual and managerial elements in the youth ministry. Pietro Braido sees different patterns and traditions describing Don Bosco's approach: "In all of his affairs Don Bosco made every effort to follow the steps not only of his liguorian moral tradition mentors, but as well as of persons, such as the theologian Guala and Don Cafasso, prudent and honest in the financial management of resources, originating mostly from donations. From the very beginning his benefactors knew that their contributions were being deposited into honest and skillful hands that would administer them for the benefit of his charitable institutions".[122]

The power of the vision which was becoming a reality has to be seen as the driving force of the expansion of Don Bosco's work. Braido gives us this description of the years that followed 1848: "Don Bosco is a countryman coming from the rural world. He could have been unnoticed and his accomplishments could have been confined to a neighborhood, or at most at the urban level of events. Instead the methods and the style of the oratorian initiative, born at the right moment between the old and the new regime, the resourcefulness of the developer, the favorable conditions, all of these guaranteed him a quick establishment and an astonishing resonance".[123]

---

[121] See STELLA, *Don Bosco nella storia economica*, pp. 71-100.
[122] BRAIDO, *Don Bosco prete dei giovani*, vol. 1, p.218.
[123] *Idem*, vol. 1, p. 233.

3.3.5 Collegialization, Foundations and Missions (1863-1888)

From the 1860s onward, we see another trait in Don Bosco which well explains the indisputable development of his works and of his leadership: generativity and the co-responsibility. The best evidence of these traits is the courage, identification and entrepreneurship shown by the first generation of the Salesians that shared the vision and mission of Don Bosco. The fundamental dynamic in this period springs from the binomial *shared vision – search for stability.*

The first prototype of the expansion out of Turin was the brief experiment with the minor seminary in Giaveno that was discontinued after a short time. The year 1863 marks the Salesian Congregation's move into the boarding school education with the opening of the minor seminary in Mirabello.[124] The structure of the secondary boarding school (collegio), which found itself between Restoration tendencies and the laws of the liberal state, responded to many needs of Don Bosco's institutions at that historical moment.[125]

His boarding high schools ensured a population of students less transient and more organizable than the population of the oratories. His schools took their place among the educational institutions specializing in private high school education just as those institutions were being demanded by the milieu. This ensured greater growth, a larger range of action, and more solid support. There were less creative demands on these schools than on the Festive Oratories; but they served as multiple seedbeds from which to draw new recruits into the family of his educators.[126]

---

[124] See STELLA, *Don Bosco. Life and Work*, pp. 124-131; BRAIDO, *Don Bosco prete dei giovani*, vol. 1, pp. 363-469; and STELLA, *Don Bosco nella storia economica*, pp. 123-153.

[125] See STELLA, *Don Bosco. Life and Work*, pp. 124-127 which describes the Piedmontese context of the early 1800s, when educators with some authority, such as Lorenzo Martini, supported the boarding school education. See L. MARTINI, *Emilio*, 12 vols., Tip. Marietti, Torino 1821-1823.

[126] STELLA, *Don Bosco. Life and Work*, p. 127.

Stella uses the term "collegialization" (collegializzazione), meaning the predominance of secondary boarding schools, to describe the new paradigm created in the 1860s. Because of the rising number of boarding schools, the college type of structured education became the standard for Salesian education, marginalizing the oratory style of catechesis and free-time education. Together with it changed also the nomenclature: "house" turned into to "boarding school". During this period Don Bosco "often thought primarily or even exclusively of collegial communities and the Salesians as educators in 'collegi'."[127]

The predominance of the *managerial pole* of the dynamic we are considering stands out clearly, assuring the stability of the growing institutions. The same can be said of the personnel: "The experience showed that volunteers did not guarantee stability, continuity, or standards of action".[128] Securing stability for both the educational institutions and the personnel is bound historically with the commitment to boarding schools combined with the approval process of the Salesian Society. The other *pole of* Don Bosco's *leadership* is linked to his capacity to share the inspirational vision which is in the process of development. This vision of Christian education of the young, so much at the heart of Don Bosco, starts to grow and to spread through Piedmont and later to other countries. From the '60s onward it is precisely the synergy between Don Bosco's leadership (dynamic of growth and sharing his vision) and prudent management (creating sustainable conditions of growth) that accompanies the rise of his new religious family.[129]

Unfortunately, the shift towards boarding schools as related to the founding of the Salesian Society could be seen as a turn towards a rigorous institutionalized type of stability. Some historical clarifications are

---

[127] *Idem*, p. 128.
[128] BRAIDO, *Don Bosco prete dei giovani*, vol. 1, p. 364.
[129] See the concept of reinforcing and balancing feedback and their role in management as described by P.M. SENGE, *The Fifth Discipline. The Art and Practice of the Learning Organization*, Doubleday, New York 2006, pp. 79-91.

necessary in order to overcome a simplified idea of the process of stabilization. The "college" was an institution which not only guaranteed constancy but also freedom in the educative process as compared to the expectations and stereotypes typical of the parish.[130] The Congregation in an analogous way providing some ministerial autonomy in its activity not enjoyed by the Diocesan clergy. Pietro Stella identifies 1864 as the year in which Don Bosco realized that to be successful and expand the Congregation he would need the guarantee of self-government, free from Diocesan control.[131]

During those years there were several growth limiting factors which demanded a different managerial approach. Motivated by two reasons, there was need for defining the educators, teachers and the administrators' roles. The first are the government inspections in Valdocco at the onset of the 1860s which demanded better organization. The second reason is the need of a certain managerial standardization because not every Salesian house in the years of expansion could be governed directly by Don Bosco. The third reason was the need to define better the procedures for admitting youngsters and personnel because of the growing administrative complexity as the number of persons involved grew.[132]

Later, during the '80s we can detect a thrust in the Salesian schools towards a balance between the multiplying regulations and the original identity of the Valdocco Oratory, which was characterized by openness, spontaneity, and absence of formality.[133] We will deal with this later when commenting on the Preventive System.

Don Bosco wanted the Salesian Congregation to have an institutional form that balances the relationship both to the Church and to the state.

---

[130] See *Deliberazioni del terzo e quarto capitolo generale della Pia Società Salesiana. Tenuti in Valsalice nel settembre 1883-86*, tip. Salesiana, S. Benigno Canavese 1887, p. 5; E. CERIA, *Annali della Società Salesiana*, SEI, Torino 1941, vol. 1, pp. 247-260; See also STELLA, *Don Bosco. Life and Work*, pp. 127-129.

[131] See STELLA, *Don Bosco. Life and Work*, pp. 127-171.

[132] See *Idem*, pp. 159-171.

[133] See STELLA, *Don Bosco*, pp. 66-70.

He creates an association of consecrated citizens who live in a community with public vows recognized by the Church.[134] The Salesians are bound "in conscience" to the superiors, "who together with their subjects are bound to the Head of the Church, and as a consequence, to God Himself".[135] Meanwhile in the eyes of the state the Congregation appears as "an association of free citizens, who gather and live in community for the purpose of charitable works [...]. Any such society of free citizens has a right to exist as long as its purpose and activity are not contrary to the laws and the institutions of the state".[136]

During the drawn-out struggle leading to the approval of the Congregation, Don Bosco is blending the divine with the human, the ideal with the practical.[137] At the end of the chapter dealing with the foundation of the Salesian Society, Stella summarizes: "Notice that it is not easy to pinpoint Don Bosco's outlook between reality on the one hand and the dreams he takes to be prophetic on the other. One gets the impression that his actions are based on the conviction that he has a mandate from heaven, a goal to be reached, something to accomplish, even though his dreams do not make evident what exactly that thing is going to be.

Don Bosco indicates that the course of events gave the congregation a configuration that was not exactly what he had wanted or thought it should be. This does not mean he did not like the way it turned out, or that he was unsatisfied. Don Bosco's attitude seems to be that of a person explaining how things happened, not that of a person indulging in recriminations and clinging fondly to a fanciful ideal in preference to

---

[134] See the study of Don Bosco's mindset as a man of the Church and as a founder in K. BOPP, *Kirchenbild und pastorale praxis bei Don Bosco. Eine pastoralgeschichtliche Studie zum Problem des Theorie-Praxis-Bezugs innerhalb der Praktischen Theologie*, Don Bosco Verlag, München 1992, pp. 199-218.

[135] *Regole o Costituzioni della Società di S. Francesco di Sales secondo il decreto di approvazione del 3 aprile 1874*, in G. BOSCO, *Opere edite*, LAS, Roma 1977, vol. 29, p. 217.

[136] *Storia dell'Oratorio de S. Francesco di Sales*, in «Bollettino Salesiano» 7 (1883) 97.

[137] See *L'evoluzione dei testi delle Costituzioni*, in F. MOTTO (ed.), *Costituzioni della Società di S. Francesco di Sales 1858-1875*, LAS, Roma 1982, pp. 6-20.

reality. [...] Here again his temperament is revealed: practical and aggressive rather than passive; extrovert rather than introvert. His ideas were modified and defined more precisely by the course of actual events. He always paid close attention to the latter, not to accept them in a passive way but to adapt to them in a constructive and creative way. [...] This is not pragmatism because the whole project is governed by a well-established goal and a series of religious and moral principles. It is the ability to seek and find the right moment, a radical optimism based on the conviction that the course of events will always provide suitable ground in which to plant one's own seeds. It is a feeling of confidence that those seeds, however affected by 'sorry weather', will somehow find a way to survive disasters and bear fruit".[138]

His realism stands out in his awareness of a mission given him from on high, in his trust that the good seeds would, in the long run, produce dividends, all of which point to the harmonic *leadership – management* synergy that are part of Don Bosco's personality. The *Constitutions of the Society of St. Francis de Sales*[139] and the *Regulations for the Houses of the Society of St. Francis de Sales*[140] are guidelines, "a firm, secure, and, I [Don Bosco] may add, infallible basis"[141] for Salesian ministry. The way in which he composed and published these documents is significant. In the first place, Don Bosco describes the leadership dimension, his vision, the reasons for the existence, aspirations, and the identity of the Congregation, and its members.[142] Then follows the managerial aspect: the description of roles within the community, the behaviours

---

[138] STELLA, *Don Bosco. Life and Work*, pp. 173-174.
[139] See *Regole o Costituzioni della Società di S. Francesco di Sales 1874*, in BOSCO, *Opere edite*, vol. 29, pp. 199-288.
[140] See *Regolamento per le case della Società di S. Francesco di Sales*, in BOSCO, *Opere edite*, vol. 29, pp. 97-196.
[141] *Costituzioni della Società di S. Francesco di Sales 1874*, in BOSCO, *Opere edite*, vol. 29, p. 201.
[142] See *Il Sistema Preventivo nell'educazione della gioventù* which precedes the *Regolamenti* and *Ai soci Salesiani* precedes the *Costituzioni* in the 1877 edition. See Bosco, *Opere edite*, vol. 29, pp. 97-113 and 201-241.

needed in community, the regulations to be observed. These are understood as norms essential to their identity which must not be changed. In the language of management researchers we might say with Scharmer that after twenty years of prototyping it was time for the implementation phase.[143]

In the founding of the Daughters of Mary Help of Christians (FMA) there are several differences arising from the experience with the Salesian Congregation. These reveal Don Bosco's managerial acumen in adapting his vision to a different situation: roots of the FMA are found in a pre-existing group of "virtually consecrated women in the world";[144] Don Bosco prefers not to be personally involved (he acts through the priests Domenico Pestarino, Giuseppe Cagliero, Giacomo Costamagna and Giovanni Battista Lemoyne);[145] the juridical recognition of the Institute by the local Bishops and a certain "merge" with the Salesian Congregation was to be preferred for practical reasons seeing the probable decennial independent recognition process through the Sacred Congregation of Bishops and of Consecrated Life.[146] In the founding of the FMA (Don Bosco and Mary Mazzarello) and in that of the Salesian Cooperators, besides the classical equation of *vision – context*, we can find also the interdependent dynamic of autonomy and centralization in view of the synergy binding the educative-pastoral action.

According to Stella, although Don Bosco, being in tune with the thinking of Catholic Italy in the 1870s, accepted the autonomy of the Institute and the Association, "the idea of unity dominated his thinking: '*vis unita fortior*'. In it was reflected another solid idea from his own religious heritage: that of a single family in the image and likeness of the human family whose Father is God, and the ecclesial family whose father

---

[143] C.O. SCHARMER, *Theory U. Leading from the Future as it Emerges. The Social Technology of Presencing*, Society for Organizational Learning, Cambridge MA 2007, pp. 191-229.
[144] BRAIDO, *Don Bosco prete dei giovani*, vol. 2, p. 56.
[145] See STELLA, *Don Bosco. Life and Work*, pp. 221-223.
[146] See *Idem*, pp. 223-231.

is the pope. [...] This centralism was certainly one of the reasons for the vitality of the Union of Cooperators, which was solidly bound to the Salesians and dependent on the same center. It was also one of the reasons behind the respectable growth of the Salesian Cooperators".[147]

There is accord between the juridical and administrative elements of unity and the bonding resulting from friendship, trust and the shared vision that had become reality. Braido states: "Don Bosco certainly did not believe that regulations and conferences by themselves could create community and communion. There were prescribed meetings for the Association of the Cooperators. But Salesian brotherhood was created especially through personal relationships, kindness, gratitude, faith-sharing, prayer, working together".[148] Not only were there strong bonds of affection with the benefactors, but they were also offered spiritual direction.[149]

The missionary expeditions to Latin America, beginning with 1875, are a good example to see the interdependency between the missionary effort, as Don Bosco visualized it, and the practical running of the mission entrusted to the first generation of missionaries. His vision of a Salesian missionary approach generated a complex of strategies binding missionary posts, education and Salesian lifestyle: "Schools, boarding schools, shelters, orphanages must be opened on the frontiers. This will attract the young; while you are educating the young, begin catechizing their parents. There are two ways of doing this: by natural instinct the parents will listen to whoever treats their children with kindness or better, once the children have been instructed they will share the Good News with their families, who will accept the word of God proclaimed by their young ones".[150]

---

[147] *Idem*, p. 255.
[148] BRAIDO, *Don Bosco prete dei giovani*, vol. 2, p. 192.
[149] *Idem*, vol. 2, pp. 35-43 and 192-195.
[150] J. BORREGO, *La Patagonia e le terre australi del continente Americano [pel] sac. Giovanni Bosco*, in «Ricerche Storiche Salesiane» 7 (1988) 13, 413-414.

Don Bosco's was an ingenious method: take advantage of the indirect missionary effects of education which is the standard Salesian mission ("children have been instructed and will share the Good News") in a Salesian way ("treat them with kindness") but also with direct evangelization of the adult population ("begin catechizing their parents").[151]

The leadership dynamic characteristics are seen in the various ways Don Bosco operates from a distance guiding the missionary effort. He is not a planner who develops plans for what must be done from far away; rather he fuels the dream by creating a climate in Italy that makes missionary work an "epic saga" in progress.[152] At the same time he knows how to instill the gift of leadership in his followers creating an "environment of orderly, yet not constraining, interdependence."[153] The first generation of the Salesians sent to the Americas, among them Giovanni Cagliero, Francesco Bodrato, Giacomo Costamagna and Luigi Lasagna, were known for their strong leadership in laying the foundations for Salesian work in this new context.[154] In his famous three letters sent to the Salesians in America[155] it is clear that his concern is the family spirit and the method of education, based on the Valdocco experience, and not the exact imitation of his earlier plans.

After reflecting the various phases of the evolution of Don Bosco's educative-pastoral activity we can distinguish three stages which also define Don Bosco's mindset: the first is the *call to be an educator* as

---

[151] See M.G. VANZINI, *El Sistema Preventivo en los internados de Viedma y Rawson (Patagonia Argentina)*, in J.G. GONZÁLES – G. LOPARCO – F. MOTTO – S. ZIMNIAK (eds.), *L'educazione Salesiana dal 1880 al 1922. Istanze e attuazioni in diversi contesti.* Atti del 4° Convegno Internazionale di Storia dell'Opera Salesiana Ciudad de México, 12-18 febbraio 2006, LAS, Roma 2007, vol. 2, pp. 79-80.

[152] See STELLA, *Don Bosco. Life and Work*, pp. 200-203.

[153] BRAIDO, *Don Bosco prete dei giovani*, vol. 2, p. 148. See also MOTTO, *Start afresh from Don Bosco*, pp. 94-95.

[154] See BRAIDO, *Don Bosco prete dei giovani*, vol. 2, pp. 147-161.

[155] G. BOSCO, *Tre lettere a Salesiani in America*, ed. Francesco Motto, in BRAIDO (ed.), *Don Bosco educatore*, pp. 439-450.

expressed in a dream but not yet as a clear project as we would understand it today. There follows the phase of experiments *creating a
prototype*. Finally there is the *regulation of best practices* that attempts
to describe the more efficient procedures and the decennial lived experience.[156] This can be applied to the development of the festive oratory
(1841-52), the Annexed Home and the boarding schools (1853-1877).

All of this planning comes to a definitive point in 1877 with two sets
of regulations. The *Regulations for the Oratory of St. Francis de Sales
for externs* has three sections dealing with the roles within the festive
oratory, the regulations for various activities, and the regulations for the
elementary grades in the oratory.[157] The *Regulations for the Houses of
the Society of St. Francis de Sales* has four sections: "The Preventive
System in the Education of the Young", which is his synthetic essay on
pedagogy; ten "General Notions" describing the young and their attitudes; the "Particular Regulations" which define the roles of the staff;
and lastly, the "Regulations for Houses of the Congregation" which deals
with the various areas and activities in the life of a Salesian house.[158]

3.3.6 The Preventive System, Leadership and Management

In the following paragraphs we will examine in a concise manner the
dynamics at work in Don Bosco's educative experience intrinsic to the
binomial *leadership – management*. Pietro Braido defines Don Bosco's
Preventive System as "an adequate expression of everything he said and
did as an educator,"[159] in which the concept of prevention transcends the
managerial idea of prevention as mere discipline or organization.[160] His

---

[156] See P. BRAIDO, *Pedagogia perseverante tra sfide e scommesse*, in «Orientamenti Pedagogici» 38 (1991) 906-911.
[157] See *Regolamento dell'Oratorio di S. Francesco di Sales per gli esterni*, in BOSCO,
Opere edite, vol. 29, pp. 31-92.
[158] See *Regolamento per le case della Società de S. Francesco di Sales*, in BOSCO, *Opere
edite*, vol. 29, pp. 97-196.
[159] BRAIDO, *Prevention not repression*, p. 1.
[160] See *Idem*, pp. 2-3.

Preventive System "is not exhausted by simply protecting or watching over".[161] Preventive management becomes meaningful when joined with a pro-positive style of education which encourages the student to become an upright citizen and a good Christian.

Joined to this pro-positive leadership is the concept of assistance which differs significantly from an oppressive surveillance,[162] instead, as we read in the 1884 letter from Rome, it has a dual synergic operational way. It is bound to the "soul of recreation" creating a familiarity and life-sharing that leads to trust, and it is linked to the "exact observance of the rules of the house" which integrates the supervision dimension.[163] In this way discipline and management are not only held in a balance, but they are also facilitated with a proximity and assistance of a leadership style that empowers the student. The Salesian style of assistance and supervision is not far away from the concept of servant leadership as theorized by Robert Greenleaf.[164]

There is another important kind of balance to keep in mind. It is the dynamic which exists among the three pillars of Salesian education: reason – religion – loving kindness. Braido writes: "Reason, Religion and Loving kindness are not simply juxtaposed; they are interrelated; rather, they co-penetrate one another. This occurs not only at the level of objectives and content but also [at the level of] means and methods".[165] This attraction existing among them appears in kindness as the preferred method, and in reason and religion as the preferred content.[166] Reason and religion go hand in hand with the goals of Salesian education, namely

---

[161] H. HENZ, *Lehrbuch der systematischen Pädagogik*, in BRAIDO, *Prevention not repression*, p. 3.

[162] See the Jansenistic conception of the *petit écoles de Port-Royal* intended as a small "monitored universe" in BRAIDO, *Prevention not repression*, pp. 54-59.

[163] See G. BOSCO, *Lettera ai giovani dell'Oratorio di Torino – Valdocco del 10 Maggio 1884*, in BRAIDO *Don Bosco educatore*, pp. 382-386.

[164] See R.K. GREENLEAF, *Servant Leadership. A Journey into the Nature of Legitimate Power and Greatness*. 25th Anniversary Edition, Paulist press, New York 2002.

[165] BRAIDO, Prevention not repression, p. 276.

[166] See *Idem*, pp. 276-277.

forming "the upright citizen" through the humanities, while forming "the good Christian" through the religious education programme. Both of these components include a content to be assimilated and competences to be acquired which are beyond the scope of loving kindness. The Salesian education theorist Reinhold Weinschenk describes this dynamic very well in his book *Grundlagen der Pädagogik Don Boscos* (Fundamentals of Don Bosco's Pedagogy). He understands reason and religion as the fundamental ideas behind Don Bosco's educative project, while kindness is the basis of his educative style.[167]

The second dynamic at work among these three elements of the Preventive System indicates that the managerial aspect of education, which includes the contents and strategies of the various programmes and activities that help achieve the goals of the educational project, is acquired in a specific form of leadership that includes loving kindness, trust and friendship. This type of leadership, seen as trust and kindness, gives greater depth to the educative process. According to Stella, loving kindness is the art of "winning the heart" and expresses "the most profound understanding and symbiosis between educator and student (or former student). Winning or stealing the 'heart', or to say it another way, creating the most profound interpersonal relationship between educator and student, is the premise for a successful educational program; that is to say, the sharing of both, the goals and the chosen means".[168]

There is a third dynamic at work among the three elements of reason – religion – loving kindness: the primacy of religion. "The search for salvation is presented to the young as the lesson needed to learn the highest profession of being a Christian, for it is the one which gives meaning and fulfilment to all other professions".[169] For Don Bosco the phrase "good Christian" does not denote a mediocre Christian (efficacy); for

---

[167] See R. WEINSCHENK, *Grundlagen der Pädagogik Don Boscos*, Don Bosco Verlag, München 1987, pp. 40-44 and 116-129.
[168] STELLA, *Don Bosco*, p. 60.
[169] BRAIDO, *Prevention not repression*, p. 223.

him it directs his entire ministry as an educator towards holiness (excellence). Dominic Savio is his most significant example. With Braido we can say that the ideal of holiness becomes the most important objective of the entire educative project.[170] Don Bosco's sermon on holiness, found in the biography of Dominic Savio, is directed to everyone as the goal of educative – pastoral ministry: "The will of God is that we all become saints; it is God's will that we become saints; it is quite easy to do so; there is a great reward in heaven for one who becomes a saint."[171] The biography of Dominic Savio, intended as a model for the boys of the Oratory, is in part idealized; but it is also "an autobiography of Don Bosco himself, the mirror image of the spirituality he lived and taught. The spiritual journey of the pupil is at the same time the story of Don Bosco, the priest and educator, in his role as a guide in the 'story of a soul' […]. The two paths are intertwined."[172]

The educative-pastoral ministry transcends the mere fulfillment of one's duties, or in the management language, the realization of the activities and strategies in pursuit of the goals of the project.[173] The dynamics of the theological virtues, or in the language of leadership, the habits which incorporate the creative tension pointing towards a dream, a vision, are introduced. The Exercise of a Happy Death, which reflects the view of life as seen through the lens of eternity and is typical of the spirituality of the times, does not end in a spirituality that agonizes over one's salvation; instead it finds balance in a spirituality of love which fills the soul with inner joy.[174] Braido says: "From his first writings, with wisdom and normality, in a moral system consisting of obligations he introduced

---

[170] See *Idem*, p. 225.
[171] G. BOSCO, *Vita del giovanetto Savio Domenico allievo dell'oratorio di San Francesco di Sales*, Tipografia e Libreria Salesiana, Torino 1880, pp. 140-141.
[172] BRAIDO, *Don Bosco prete dei giovani*, vol. 1, p. 324.
[173] See *Idem*, vol. 1, pp. 185-195.
[174] See BOSCO, *Vite di giovani*, ed. Aldo Giraudo, pp. 27-28.

the bright sunshine of the theological virtues."[175] Stella describes "religion" as the unitive power which has not to be referred "solely to obligatory religious practices or the educational value of frequenting the sacraments. He goes beyond a fragmentary view of sacramental piety and the task of education, not stopping at merely methodological issues. For him religion does not have merely external and instrumental functions. He sees the sacraments as instruments of grace enabling us to attain holiness and eternal salvation".[176]

There is a fourth dynamic: put into practice the vision of *Give me souls, take away the rest* among both educators and pupils, even though their roles are different. The difference between the roles is of minor importance because "educators and students would work together, each party in its own proper way to carry out God's saving plan. [...] In short, the sole nucleus of Don Bosco's pedagogy and spirituality was a soteriology that had become personal conviction. It balanced a wide variety of elements that had their proper place: e.g., outings, music, theater, and the full liberty for the boys to 'run, jump, and shout as much as they pleased'."[177]

This is the dynamic behind the one and only project leading to salvation which transforms the lives of educators and students in fulfilling their call to holiness.[178]

Upon these four dynamics lie other equilibriums that are part of the Preventive System. Below follows a list of some of them, by no means exhaustive:

---

[175] BRAIDO, *Don Bosco prete dei giovani*, vol. 1, p. 187. See also G. GATTI, *Dall'osservanza della legge alla crescita delle virtù. Lettura etica della "Vita"*, in A. GIRAUDO (ed.), *Domenico Savio raccontato da Don Bosco. Riflessioni sulla Vita*. Atti del Simposio, Università Pontificia Salesiana, Roma 8 maggio 2004, LAS, Roma 2005, pp. 177-183.

[176] STELLA, *Don Bosco. Life and Work*, p. 483.

[177] *Idem*, p. 484.

[178] See Pietro BRAIDO, *"Memorie" del futuro*, in «Ricerche Storiche Salesiane» 11 (1992) 20, 97-127.

- a balance between the pedagogy of duties (discipline) and the pedagogy of cheerfulness (spontaneity);[179]
- a complementarity of the goals of the education of a good Christian and an honest citizen;[180]
- a continuity, development and integration among the several "versions" of the Preventive System as applied in the various institutions (oratory, boarding school, day school, vocational training, university, parish, social works, etc.);[181]
- a feasibility of Don Bosco's educative-pastoral project which finds a balance between regulations and formulation of projects on the one hand, and assimilation of the vision in the form of a narrative pedagogy on the other;[182]
- a managerial and leadership balance;
- among the roles of Director, Prefect, Catechist, counselors and Assistants;[183]
- between the strong educative-pastoral Salesian identity and the openness in the creation of a network of cooperators;[184]
- between spontaneity and discipline in the running of the house[185] which finds its expression in the exercise of formal and informal direction;[186]

---

[179] See BRAIDO, *Prevention not repression*, pp. 307-319 and P. BRAIDO, *Il Sistema Preventivo di Don Bosco alle origini (1841-1862). Il cammino del "preventivo" nella realtà e nei documenti*, in «Ricerche Storiche Salesiane» 14 (1995) 27, pp. 283-287.

[180] See BRAIDO, *Prevention not repression*, pp. 213-232.

[181] See *Idem*, pp. 335-359 and BRAIDO, *Il Sistema Preventivo di Don Bosco alle origini*, 255-320.

[182] See the three biographies of Savio, Besucco and Magone written by Don Bosco. See also the Preface in Bosco, *Memoirs of the Oratory*, 3.

[183] See BRAIDO, *Prevention not repression*, pp. 295-301. See also BRAIDO, *Don Bosco prete dei giovani*, vol. 1, pp. 306-308.

[184] BRAIDO, *Don Bosco prete dei giovani*, vol. 1, pp. 208-212 and 222-225; STELLA, *Don Bosco nella storia economica*, pp. 397-398 and CASELLA, *L'esperienza educativa preventiva di Don Bosco*, pp. 123-137.

[185] See BRAIDO, *Prevention not repression*, pp. 292-295.

[186] See F. MOTTO, *I "Ricordi confidenziali ai direttori" di Don Bosco*, in «Ricerche Storiche Salesiane» 3 (1984) 4, 150-160; BRAIDO, *Prevention not repression*, pp. 295-299

- between an intervention affecting the entire student body and the personal accompaniment which finds in youth groups an intermediate level of realization;[187]

In the pursuit of his desire to save the whole person Don Bosco does not choose a theoretical systematic path; instead he offers practical steps with simple words, not all of them original, which demonstrate the brilliant managerial-educative vision of an inspiring leader. "Don Bosco, unlike Therese of Lisieux, does not write of 'the little way' to holiness. But he does suggest easy ways for boys that some might consider too trivial. These trivial means were undoubtedly not a royal road, but they were a path that led 'to a marvelous level of perfection'."[188]

3.4 Conclusion: Leadership – Management Synergy in Don Bosco

After having analyzed the person and the accomplishments of Don Bosco, although not in great depth, we can verify the presence and the synergetic connectedness between leadership and management in his life and mindset. The following dual concepts are a synthesis of the relationship existing between leadership and management as he exercised them:

1. *Manual work – trust in Providence* that so deeply enriched his early years immersed in the rural setting constitute his point of departure as well as main mindset. His leadership is God-centred and he is simultaneously called to entrust himself to Providence and to work effectively as his gifts and knowledge allow;

2. *Prudent management – powerful dream* binomial becomes the operative translation of the previous one. His vocation as a priest and

---

and C. COLLI, *La direzione spirituale nella prassi e nel pensiero di Don Bosco: "memoria" e "profezia"*, in M. COGLIANDRO (ed.), *La direzione spirituale nella famiglia Salesiana*, SDB, Roma 1983, pp. 53-77.
[187] See BRAIDO, *Don Bosco prete dei giovani*, vol. 1, pp. 214-214 and 318-320. See also BRAIDO, *Prevention not repression*, pp. 302-306.
[188] See STELLA, *Don Bosco. Life and Work*, p. 206.

educator gives direction to all later choices and creates a horizon of meaning where his skills as entrepreneur and prudent manager find their realization;

3. *Expansion of the work – developing of self-giving* explains the inner harmony existing between the man and his activity. His total dedication to his vocation is not limited to the spiritual dimension; it penetrates all of his activity, also in the educative-pastoral and managerial-organizational sense;

4. *Personal identity – team collaboration* represents the bonding which Don Bosco created and which led to a huge movement of persons involved is his mission. His ability to be a leader with a mighty dream, capable to appreciate and combine the gifts and differences of everyone is a typically Salesian trait;

5. *Answer to a need – preventive action* which describes the synergy between education that both responds to the actual needs of the young and at the same time offers a way to escape the conditions that cause their neediness or poverty. They are empowered, given education, knowledge and the tools that prepare them for a better life;

6. *Structured education – narrative education.* Here reference is made to a style of leadership that excites and spurs involvement and knows how to share the dream. It is complemented by the necessary regulations, different roles and tasks. As for spiritual growth, management is equated with forming resolutions, while leadership is exercised through the biographies of exemplary students;

7. *Reason and religion – loving kindness in a family environment* expresses the managerial aspect of education, which includes contents, strategies, programmes and activities, all directed towards the attainment of the goals (good Christian and honest citizen); all of this done with love and a style of leadership that is characterized by trust, friendship and familiarity;

8. *Stability management – expansion of a vision.* Here we refer to how Don Bosco now mature, balances the expansion in Piedmont, in Italy and

in the missions with the opening of boarding schools which were financially sound and would nurture new vocations. In this way there is a balance between productivity and care of resources;

9. *Enacted regulations – informal osmotic education* shows the complementarity within Don Bosco's educative method. Study, work and prayer are "tasks" in a programme but realized in an environment that is forward-looking and informal, expressed in recreation, trust and friendship.

4. Innovation of Salesian Leadership and Project Management

In order to bring some answers to the organizational issues of the Salesian Youth Ministry, we have studied its post-Vatican II evolution (1st Chapter) and its theoretical background (2nd Chapter). In this Chapter we will be guided by the permanent criterion of renewal called "Don Bosco in the Oratory" (3rd Chapter) with the purpose of: putting in place a dialogue with organizational sciences; tracing a set of necessary operative virtues of a Salesian leader and, finally, proposing an updated methodology of Educative and Pastoral Project management.[1]

4.1 Dialogue with Organizational Theories

The SEPP methodology was influenced substantially by the Management by Objectives logic, diffused in the '60 and '70s. In a successive period, from the late '80s, there has been a paradigm shift in the organizational field. Until now, we can find too many different theories and practices that go beyond a reductive MBO anthropology and methodology. We have to choose a set of criteria for the choice of theories to be dialogued with, in order not to be paralyzed by their differences and also to remain faithful to the Salesian charism and its fundamental anthropology.

4.1.1 Criteria for the Selection of Organizational Models

Before doing that, let us specify the differences between different types of criteria. The Oratorian criterion (Don Bosco in the Oratory) will be a constant criterion, so we will dialogue between the Salesian tradition

---

[1] See a more extended argumentation in M. VOJTÁŠ, *Progettare e discernere. Progettazione educativo-pastorale Salesiana tra storia, teorie e proposte innovative*, LAS, Roma 2015.

and organizational theories. A second type of criteria is needed for the selection of significant organizational theories. These are:
1. overcoming the pure Management by Objectives logic;
2. compatibility with the four dimensions of the SEPP anthropology;
3. balance between the scientific nature of the theory and its consolidated application in different cultural contexts.

The first criterion relates to the overcoming of Management by Objectives that has influenced the Salesian projects methodology. It adopts an analytical approach to reality, dividing it in parallel dimensions often losing the wholeness of the man or the community. The linearity of its method analyzes the situation with its needs, formulates objectives that respond to the needs, chooses activities or other means and finally ends a project cycle with the evaluation of the results. In the MBO mindset, a leader is fundamentally a project manager. For an update of the Salesian Youth Ministry organizational model it is necessary that the theories in the dialogue elaborate substantial steps beyond MBO reaching a balance between management and leadership. This synergic and complementary balance is seen in various keys described earlier: systemic logic, transformative change, organizational ethics, spiritual leadership, empowerment and community integration, organizational learning, resource-based approach.

In a second place we choose a simple anthropologic criterion. Adopting MBO in the Salesian project methodology there has been a lack of processes that put focus on discernment; evangelical interpretation of the situation; search for meaning and deeper motivations. Practically, the SEPP method often remained in the position of a purely rational educational planning.[2] The biggest challenge, addressed in the study presented,

---

[2] Since GC25 (2002), the method of discernment has created two types of methodological paths: the discernment of the Provincial Structural Plan, the Community Project and the Project of Life on one side and the educational and pastoral planning on the other. The third edition of the YM Frame of Reference tries to introduce the discernment in the SEPP design, but more like an external focus, not touching the steps of a project cycle.

is to consider man integrally or holistically not only at the level of theoretical content but also at the level of methodological processes. Theories we dialogue with should have an integral vision of man as expressed in the unity of the four SEPP dimensions: the dynamic of the educational transformation within the educational-cultural dimension; the dynamic of spiritual growth as the core dimension of evangelization and catechesis; the dynamic of the call as the cornerstone of the vocational dimension; the dynamic of community-building within the group experience dimension.

The last criterion puts in place a balance between scientific and practical nature of organizational models. The union of theory and practice is of primary importance for the SEPP[3] as we often noticed the failure "to pass from paper to life".[4] The practical use of a theory in project management also follows two principles of knowledge validity proposed by Chris Argyris and Edgar H. Schein, two scholars of organizational behaviour: "I know that I know when my knowledge is actionable – that is, when I can produce it [...] I know that I know when my knowledge is helpful to the various clients and practitioners in the field".[5] An organizational model's proliferation on a global scale becomes an important indicator of the explanatory and practical power beyond limits of a specific culture. The possibility of using a method in different cultures is an obligatory requirement, because the SEPP was established primarily to

---

[3] Juan Vecchi proposes an interesting harmonic concept: "Intelligence of love is the constant fusion of experience, wisdom and scientific knowledge with which we approach the youth, and responds to the 'synthetic' attitude of Don Bosco's 'unity', who did not miss any means or way to understand better the world of young people and to get to them effectively", in J.E. VECCHI, *Per riattualizzare il Sistema Preventivo*, in ISPETTORIA SALESIANA LOMBARDO-EMILIANA, *Convegno sul Sistema Preventivo*, Milano-Bologna 3-4 novembre 1978, [s.e.], [s.l.] [s.d.], p. 14.
[4] See E. VIGANÒ, *Opening address of the Rector Major*, in GC22 (1984), n. 19.
[5] C.O. SCHARMER, *Theory U. Leading from the Future as it Emerges. The Social Technology of Presencing*, SoL, Cambridge MA 2007, p. 98.

favor the inculturation of the Preventive System in local cultures and in different situations.[6]

Following the criteria, we will be considering the following three models: Peter M. Senge's Organizational Learning diffused by the Society for Organizational Learning; Stephen R. Covey's Principle-centered Leadership applied by FranklinCovey; C. Otto Scharmer's Theory U and linked proposals of the Presencing Institute. The choice of the three theories has also been motivated by the following factors. First, the recognition of the educational and the spiritual dimension within the organizational processes could make the models suitable for a dialogue with the SEPP. Covey's Principle-centered Leadership proposes a set of organizational habits based on ethical principles. His character ethics has had a great impact throughout the world and is a neglected, or taken for granted, aspect in the SEPP model. The implementation of Senge's systemic and holistic vision in leadership theory centered on learning could balance the linearity of the MBO's logic. Scharmer's emphasis on the study of the project cycle processes could balance the SEPP's emphasis on objectives. It could provide instruments to go beyond the product paradigm inherited from curricular theories. Each model, of course, has its weaknesses and so we have chosen to dialogue with multiple authors in order to balance one model with another.

In the following brief presentation of the theories and connected educative practices we want to offer a concise understanding of the authors' paradigms and proposals. After the presentation, a synthesis will follow with the goal to sum up the three models' overcoming of the MBO and the compatibility with SEPP dimensions of the Youth Ministry.

---

[6] See GC21 (1978), nn. 82-83 that quotes PAUL VI, *Evangelii Nuntiandi* (1975), nn. 20; 38-39 and GC21 (1978), nn. 91 that integrates *Nostra Aetate*, n. 2.

4.1.2 Peter M. Senge's Organizational Learning

Peter Michal Senge is a senior lecturer in leadership and sustainability at the Massachusetts Institute of Technology School of Management. His consulting and lecturing activity dates back to the middle 1970s. His 1990 publication of *The Fifth Discipline: The art and practice of the learning organization* has influenced organizational thinkers on a global scale through the activities of the Society for Organizational Learning.[7] After a decade, the focus of his studies shifted to issues concerning education and deep social transformation.[8]

His model approaches leadership and management from a systemic perspective focusing on the evolving dynamics of living systems. The core of his leadership theory views the organization as an interconnected whole that is greater than the sum of the parts. Therefore, the long-term sustainable and responsible growth of the organization is linked to life-long learning of its members and teams. The view on the wholeness of reality implies such concepts as circular causality, deep transformation, organizational culture or process consultation.

The central term "discipline" is linked to its original Latin meaning "to learn" (*discere*). The practice of the five disciplines is to be a lifelong learning process of a single person and an organization. Living a discipline is not putting in place a planning technology; it is not an emulation

---

[7] See P.M. SENGE, *The Fifth Discipline. The art and practice of the learning organization*, Doubleday, New York 1990; ID et al., *The Fifth Discipline Fieldbook. Strategies and Tools for Building a Learning Organization*, Doubleday, New York 1994 and ID et al., *The Dance of Change. The Challenges of Sustaining Momentum in Learning Organizations*, Doubleday, New York 1999.

[8] See P.M. SENGE et al., *Schools That Learn. A Fifth Discipline Fieldbook for Educators, Parents, and Everyone Who Cares About Education*, Doubleday, New York 2000; C.O. SCHARMER – P.M. SENGE – J. JAWORSKI – B.S. FLOWERS, *Presence. Exploring Profound Change in People, Organizations, and Society*, Currency Doubleday, New York 2004 and P.M. SENGE et al., *The Necessary Revolution. How Individuals and Organizations Are Working Together to Create a Sustainable World*, Doubleday, New York 2008.

of a model or copying a best practice. It is rather a flow of experimentation and advancement.[9] For Senge "metanoia", in the sense of a change in mentality, is the more appropriate term to describe a learning organization. He argues that the "real learning goes to the heart of what it means to be human".[10] The disciplines are not implemented in an organization at a formal or managerial level. They have to be lived by the practitioners and teams. Only then an organization can "learn" in a genuine way. The disciplines are the following:

1. *Personal Mastery* is the discipline of continually clarifying and deepening our personal vision, of focusing energies, of developing patience, and of seeing reality objectively. As such, it is an essential cornerstone of the learning organization – the learning organization's spiritual foundation. An organization's commitment to and capacity for learning can be no greater than that of its members. This discipline starts with clarifying the things that really matter to us, living our lives in the service of our highest spiritual aspirations.[11]

2. Working with *Mental Models*. The models are deeply ingrained assumptions, generalizations, or even pictures or images that influence how we understand the world and how we take action. Working with mental models is a discipline that helps to get our representations of the world, bring them to the surface and keep them under rigorous examination. Part of the discipline deals with the ability to conduct meaningful dialogues that balance inquiry advocacy.[12]

3. *Building Shared Vision*. When there is a genuine vision (as opposed to the all too familiar vision statements), people excel and learn, not

---

[9] For quotations we will refer to the second updated and revised edition: P.M. Senge, *The Fifth Discipline. The art and practice of the learning organization*, Doubleday, New York ²2006. Note the similarities with Stenhouse's curriculum research model adopted partially by Vecchi.

[10] *Idem*, p. 13.

[11] See *Idem*, pp. 7-8.

[12] See *Idem*, pp. 8 and 163-190.

because they are told to do so, but because they want to. Too often different objectives and visions of the organization are focused on the personal charisma of a leader or a crisis that galvanizes temporarily. The practice of the shared vision discipline implies unearthing shared images of the future that foster shared, genuine, heartfelt and voluntary commitment, rather than compliance.[13]

4. *Team Learning.* We know that teams can learn and the intelligence of the group can exceed the intelligence of the individuals with an extraordinary ability of coordinated thinking and action. This discipline starts with dialogue that, unlike the discussion, suspends assumptions and moves to a genuine "thinking together". It is also the ability to recognize patterns of interaction within the group that can promote or compromise learning. Often some patterns of defensiveness are deeply ingrained in how a team operates.[14]

5. *Systems Thinking.* Senge considers the organization as a set of many components arranged in an interconnected system. The application of systems thinking does not conclude at the level of the whole organization, it is also a methodology applied to the five disciplines of organizational learning. "It is vital that the five disciplines develop as an ensemble [...] This is why systems thinking is the fifth discipline. It is the discipline that integrates the disciplines, fusing them into a coherent body of theory and practice. It keeps them from becoming separated gimmicks, or the latest organization change fads. Without a systemic orientation, there is no motivation to look at how the disciplines interrelate. By enhancing each of the other disciplines, it continually reminds us that the whole can exceed the sum of its parts".[15]

---

[13] See *Idem*, p. 9.
[14] See *Idem*, pp. 9-10.
[15] *Idem*, pp. 11-12.

The interconnectedness goes both ways: not only does systems thinking keep together the other disciplines, but it also needs them to realize its potential. "Building shared vision fosters a commitment to the long term. Mental models focus on the openness needed to unearth shortcomings in our present ways of seeing the world. Team learning develops the skills of groups of people to look for the larger picture beyond individual perspectives. And personal mastery fosters the personal motivation to continually learn how our actions affect our world".[16]

The learning organization does no longer see itself as detached from the world, but connected to it. Consequently, all issues and challenges are not caused by external influences, the "enemy", the "condition" or "situation" that are out there and independent. The issues of an organization are mostly related to how we think and operate, it is our actions that create the problems which we experience. In this way systems thinking is the discipline to see the whole. It is a framework for seeing interrelation rather than things, to see the patterns of change rather than static snapshots. Our language shapes the perception of reality that in many cases is not linear and cannot be described by a linear causal logic following the basic structure of subject-verb-object.

To understand the complexity, Senge uses the "circle of causality" and "feedback process". The two terms describe processes where many variables are organized in circles of cause-effect relations. The classical examples are cases of a self-fulfilling prophecy or virtuous and vicious circles. Often the effects of actions occur with a considerable delay or with a short-term effect linked to a different long-term effect. Virtually all feedback processes contain some delay, but often the delays are not recognized and accepted. Consequently, delays are not taken into account in the operational planning and evaluation. The work with the delays constitutes therefore another brick of systems thinking.[17] Alongside the basics of circular causality, feedback process and delays, Senge

---

[16] *Idem*, p. 12.
[17] See *Idem*, pp. 68-91.

introduces ten systemic archetypes, which make explicit many typical situations in an organization. Here, we present two fundamental archetypes because they illuminate real issues linked to the Salesian Project Management model.

"Shifting the burden" archetype is characteristic for problem solving processes. Usually a problem shows symptoms that require attention. People often have a difficulty dealing with the underlying problem, because it is complex and its solution requires a lot of energy. So they transfer their attention to a symptomatic solution that is easier and less expensive. After some time, the underlying problem gets worse and because the symptoms have for a moment, the system loses ability to solve it with a fundamental solution.[18]

"Erosion of the objectives" archetype is typical for Management by Objectives. There is always a gap between reality and the ideal expressed in a set of objectives. Since actions to improve the actual conditions produce effects with some delay, there is a tendency to adopt a short-term solution to erode or to reformulate the objectives the easy or generic way. While this produces a brief breather from the operational pressure, it leads to a long-term operational mediocrity. In the presence of dynamic erosion of the objectives we must be adhered to the vision and invest in actions that will produce real effects of improvement.[19]

Senge's systems thinking also tries to deal with deeper levels of human action going beyond the reactive mindset that puts its attention on the events. If an organization wants to learn in a sustainable way, it has to focus on "patterns of behaviour" and more profoundly on "systemic structures". Systemic structures are connected with our deep mental models and artifacts of the organization that may be of real, symbolic or legislative nature. The more we go in depth into the circles of causality, the greater is the possibility of influence on the process, but with the risk

---

[18] See *Idem*, pp. 103-112.
[19] See *Idem*, pp. 394-395.

of a longer delay. The following Scheme D correlates the depth of analysis with the type of actions:[20]

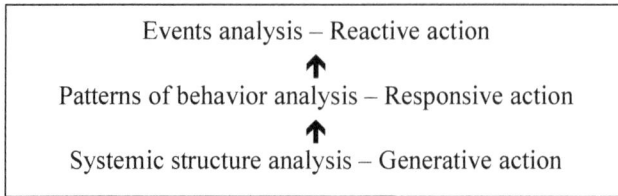

```
Events analysis – Reactive action
            ↑
Patterns of behavior analysis – Responsive action
            ↑
Systemic structure analysis – Generative action
```

Scheme D: Senge's Levels of Analysis and Action

Senge's publication of *Schools That Learn* applies systems thinking to education after two decades of experiments and experiences in the field.[21] The theoretical background is built upon the critics of the current model of public education that is based on industrial-age management of Taylorian mindset: "Primary and Secondary education is a more purely industrial-age institution than is business".[22] This model breaks the system into pieces, creates specialists, lets everybody do his or her piece, and assumes that someone else makes sure that the whole system works.[23] The authors propose a systemic integration of classes, schools and communities referring to real-life experiences and to education theorists such as John Dewey, Jean Piaget, Paolo Freire, Howard Gardner and Parker Palmer. The school should provide, as part of its core purpose, the promotion, development and care of its teachers. The teacher is seen as a life-long learner and a steward for all students. Students should be

---

[20] See *Idem*, pp. 51-54. The risk of being a victim of activism is connected with management paradoxes and "learning disabilities" of an organization. We mention only four: illusion of taking charge; paradox of the cure that is worse than the disease; paradox of acting fast in short run that becomes slow for long distances; paradox of small changes that produce big results. See *Idem*, pp. 20-21 and 61-65.

[21] The publication refers to experiences at the level of schools, communities, school districts and also at national level in the context of the United States, Latin America, Middle East, Asia and Europe.

[22] SENGE et al., *Schools That Learn*, p. 33.

[23] See *Idem*, p. 43.

empowered to be co-creators of knowledge and participants in the evolution of the school.

4.1.3 Stephen R. Covey's Principle-Centered Ethical Leadership

Stephen Richards Covey provides a summary of organizational and
ethical thoughts in his best-selling book *The 7 Habits of Highly Effective
People. Restoring the Character Ethic.*[24] If we compare the two authors
according to Schön's rigor-relevance criterion, we can state that Senge's
theory is more scientifically rigorous (while having good practical applications) and Covey's principles are primarily relevant for practical use
(with a sufficient scientific basis).[25] In the first decade of the third millennium, Covey was considered as the pre-eminent management guru of
North America with a global impact of his consulting firm Franklin-
Covey in more than 140 nations around the world.[26]

The basis of the seven habits theory was born during the eight years
of research that concluded with the interdisciplinary doctorate in educational and managerial sciences in 1976. Covey conducted a critical study
on the "success literature" published in the United States over the past
200 years. He noted a fundamental shift in the concept of success in the
1920s from "character ethics" to a "personality ethics".

---

[24] See S.R. COVEY, *The 7 Habits of Highly Effective People. Restoring the Character
Ethic*, Simon & Schuster, New York ¹1989 and ²2004. In this study we will quote the
second edition.

[25] The *7 Habits* has had a strong impact on the practice of leadership selling over 25
million copies in 38 languages. His theory was further applied to leadership for families, young people and kids. See S.R. COVEY, *The 7 Habits of Highly Effective Families*,
Simon & Schuster, New York 1999; S. COVEY, *The 7 Habits of Highly Effective Teens*,
Simon & Schuster, New York 1998 e ID., *The 7 Habits of Happy Kids*, Simon & Schuster Books for Young Readers, New York 2008.

[26] See B. JACKSON, *Management Gurus and Management Fashions. A Dramatistic In-
quiry*, Routledge, London 2001, p. 94-99; S. GANDEL, *The 7 Habits of Highly Effective
People (1989) by Stephen R. Covey*, in *The 25 Most Influential Business Management
Books*, in «Time» (9 August 2011). For a list of received awards see COVEY, *The 7
Habits*, p. 373.

The character ethics is grounded on the notion that there are basic principles of effective living, and that people can only experience true success and enduring happiness as they learn and integrate these principles into their character. The personality ethics is based on ideas of public image, behaviours, skills and techniques that solve problems and facilitate interpersonal relations. This "quick-fix" ethic incorporates techniques of public relations techniques, positive mental attitude combined with manipulative techniques and different strategies of power gaining.[27] For Covey "it becomes obvious that if we want to make relatively minor changes in our lives, we can perhaps appropriately focus on our attitudes and behaviours, But if we want to make significant, quantum change, we need to work on our basic paradigms".[28] These paradigms should be aligned to a few key principles, natural laws, real, immutable and unquestionably present. The basic principles are present in all the great religions and ethical systems: fairness, integrity, honesty, justice, consistency, human dignity, service and growth understood as development of one's potential. "Although people may argue about how these principles are defined or manifested or achieved, there seems to be an innate consciousness and awareness that they exist".[29]

The growth in effectiveness is a continuous passage from dependence through independence to interdependence. Covey offers an insightful reading of the independence social paradigm as a reaction to dependence, to control and manipulation. In this way, independence is taken by the majority as the absolute value, while communication, teamwork, cooperation and synergy are marginalized as if they were second degree

---

[27] COVEY, *The 7 Habits*, pp. 18-21.
[28] *Idem*, p. 31.
[29] *Idem*, p. 35. See also an interesting remark: T.K. SMITH, *What's so effective about Stephen Covey? The author of The Seven Habits of Highly Effective People sells a message of moral renewal, and corporate America is buying it. Is this a good thing?*, in «Fortune Magazine» 12 December 1994, in money.cnn.com/magazines/fortune/fortune_ archive/1994/12/12/80049/index.htm (accessed 1.1. 2017).

values. For this theory, independence is only a passage to a more integrated or systemic concept of interdependence of teams, families or
communities. Also the structure of the seven habits follows this path of
maturity. The first three habits bring the person from dependence to independence and self-realization, while the fourth, fifth and sixth habit
helps the construction of social relations with the transition from independence to interdependence. The seventh habit is linked to the
integration of the whole and to the continuous renewal. The growth path
is defined "inside-out" because the interior change has to come before
the attempts of an external or social change. Personal change and coher-
ence build trust, a key element for building interdependence.[30]

The concept of trust and trustworthiness is the common denominator
in the so-called "continuum of growth" from dependence through independence to interdependence as shown in Scheme E:

1. *Be proactive.* Pro-active is used as opposed to re-active. Reactive
   strategies are only adaptations to the environment that do not allow
   acting in freedom, given their dependence on external stimuli. Proactivity is the ability to control the space between stimulus and
   response, using self-awareness, imagination, conscience and independent will.

2. *Begin with the End in Mind.* Persons wishing to act with the utmost
   freedom and efficiency must develop the habit of having a vision of
   life. This vision can integrate roles they have and orient individual
   actions to the overall goals.

3. *Put First Things First* is the ability to put the vision or the project in
   everyday reality. The second habit develops a "mental creation" while
   this habit creates the vision in reality.

---

[30] See *Idem*, pp. 42-44 and the publication of S.R. Covey's son: S.M.R. COVEY – R.
MERRILL, *The Speed of Trust. The One Thing That Changes Everything*, Free Press,
New York 2006.

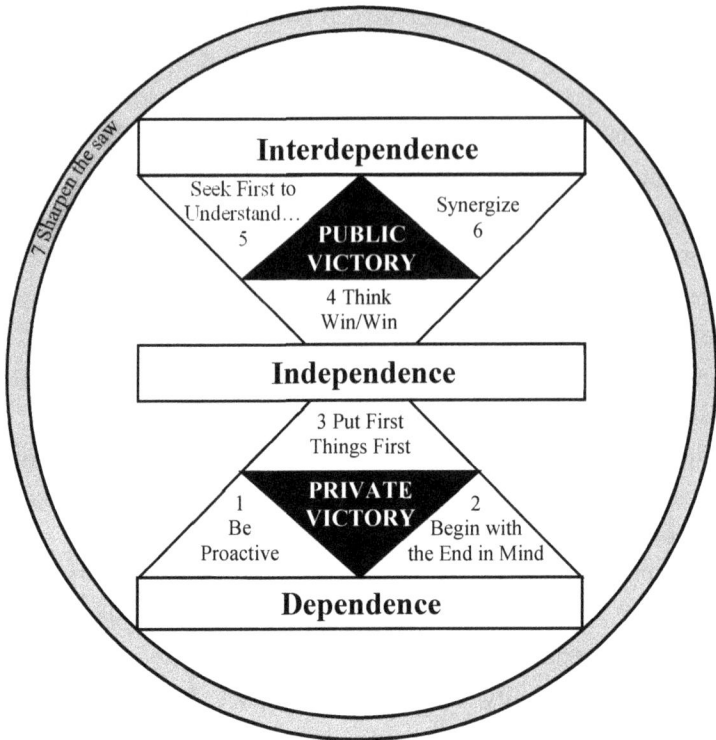

Scheme E: Covey's Continuum of Growth

4. *Think win-win.* A big part of the quality of human life is based on joint efforts. Consequently, the purpose of decision-making must be to find win-win solutions for all, overcoming the competitive attitude that is based on the resource scarcity mindset.

5. *Seek First to Understand ... then to be Understood.* Trustworthy people start from the needs of those who they meet. The person has to be understood first if we want to develop and maintain a positive relationship that is necessary for any type of collaboration.

6. *Synergize* is the habit of creative cooperation that allows to accomplish more than could be achieved by individuals working

independently, according to the conception of the whole that is greater than the sum of its parts.

7. *Sharpen the saw*. Self-care and continuous self-improvement is one of the most important habits in order to perform any activity in a sustainable way, maintaining the balance between "production" and "production capacity".

These seven habits and the underlying principles seem to be rather simple and obvious. We think that the strength of Covey's theory is grounded on two aspects. First, the whole picture of the intertwined habits with the underlying principles is presented in an understandable way and lights up the purpose of single instruments. The second strength is the application of every habit with concrete instruments or practices so they can be experimented immediately right. Of course it also implies a weak theoretical grounding and arbitrary interpretations.[31]

Covey's Seven Habits theory was further enriched and found instant applications in the education sector. Hundreds of school district teams and half a million teachers participated in the formation seminars. The 2008 publication named *Leader in Me* describes experiences of different schools and lays an implementation methodology in the everyday school life.[32] Covey's book begins with the analysis of the expectations of students, teachers, parents and business leaders of the local community. He claims that decision-making, interpersonal, collaborative, ethical, creative and problem-solving skills are more important for the stakeholders

---

[31] See some critical viewpoints in T. CLARK – G. SALAMAN, *The Management Guru as Organizational Witchdoctor*, in «Organization» 3 (1996) 85-107; B. JACKSON, *Management Gurus and Management Fashions. A Dramatistic Inquiry*, Routledge, London 2001 e D. CARLONE, *The Ambiguous Nature of a Management Guru Lecture. Providing Answers While Deepening Uncertainty*, in «Journal of Business Communication» 43 (2006) 2, 89-112.

[32] See S.R. COVEY, *The Leader in Me. How Schools and Parents Around the World Are Inspiring Greatness, One Child at a Time*, Free Press, New York 2008 and SMITH, *What's so effective about Stephen Covey*.

than the performance in a single academic subject suggesting a distinction between primary and secondary greatness. The first has to do with the integrity of the person, work ethic, interaction with others, motivation and initiative. The secondary greatness is the quality of the specific skills achieved by comparing a person with the standards in connection with votes, positions, awards, fame etc. Education for leadership, proposed in the *Leader in Me*, focuses on primary greatness in schools integrating the aspects of secondary greatness.

The applicative approach of integrating the primary and secondary greatness is called "Ubiquitous Strategy". Principles and habits permeate every subject and almost everything students and teachers do. In other words, leadership is not "one more thing" teachers have to teach. It is part of everything they teach. A new culture of the school is created through the selection of discussion topics, examples in teaching, change of language, artifacts in the environment, traditions and folklore of the school. The strategy is accomplished in four phases: inspire trust; clarify purpose; align systems; unleash the talent. The whole proposal integrates educational research with different didactical instrumentation.[33]

Comparing Covey's and Senge's perspective on school education change, we can see fundamental points of contact: both authors interpret a series of experiments that were inspired by their theories. Senge's view is wider because it proposes a change of the school organizational culture integrating the systems theory. At the same time, one can observe Covey's strength in proposing a unified strategy – a point where the complexity of systems theory often fails.

---

[33] See COVEY, *The Leader in Me*, pp. 165-190. Integrated are education studies of Robert J. Marzano from the Association for Supervision and Curriculum Development, Larry W. Lezotte's school effectiveness studies, studies on school change sustainability by Richard DuFour and Robert Eaker, Daniel Goleman's multiple intelligence theory and both Balridge and Deming's quality tools.

4.1.4 Otto C. Scharmer's "Vocational" Theory Linked to Second Senge and Covey

The year 2004 can be considered a turning point for both Senge and Covey. The latter published *The 8th Habit: From Effectiveness to Greatness* in which he integrates the concept of "voice". For Covey, voice is not an 8th habit to be simply added to the previous seven – it is rather a new dimension that shifts the attention from effectiveness to everyone's greatness and uniqueness. There is a deep and almost inexpressible yearning within each one of us to find our voice in life. It is often revealed as we face our greatest challenges in life. The voice or calling or soul's code lies "at the nexus of talent (your natural gifts and strengths), passion (those things that naturally energize, excite, motivate and inspire you), need (including what the world needs enough to pay you for), and conscience (that still, small voice within that assures you of what is right and that prompts you to actually do it)".[34]

In the same year, Peter Senge together with Claus Otto Scharmer and two other co-authors published *Presence: Exploring Profound Change in People, Organizations, and Society.* Senge shifts his focus from systems theory to cognitive studies of profound change, which is Scharmer's field of interest. The vocation is a "call to service that most of us deny throughout our whole life [...] this call to give ourselves to something larger than ourselves and to become what were meant to become".[35] The moment of vocation is identified with the time of "Presence" conceptualized by Scharmer in which the person and the community find their new identity and their future emerges. The authors also refer to the Bible, but choose to use more universal not explicitly religious terms.[36] Their

---

[34] S.R. COVEY, *The 8th Habit. From Effectiveness to Greatness*, Free Press, New York 2004, p. 5.

[35] SENGE – SCHARMER et al., *Presence*, p. 223.

[36] The authors are aware that universal non-religious formulations can be sterile and abstract. So they choose the analysis of the "call experience" as the central point of their endeavor. See *Idem*, pp. 226-230.

concept is inspired by the philosophy of Martin Buber that writes about "freedom and destiny [...] solemnly promised to one another and connected together in meaning".[37] Senge applies the concepts of "Presence" in his next book *The Necessary Revolution* (2008),putting together themes of cooperation, new ways of thinking and perceiving the change, the emerging "vocation" of the future and a world that needs sustainability.

Claus Otto Scharmer is a German organization researcher and P.M. Senge's colleague at the MIT School of Management. He is the founder of the Presencing Institute and works on different development and sustainability projects.[38] His research is in continuity with the organizational learning theory and focuses on the cognitive processes of deep transformation of persons and communities. His theory and practice has a developed philosophical grounding, taking inspiration from Husserl's phenomenology, Buber's philosophy of dialogue, different existentialist philosophies with a fundamental reference to Kurt Lewin's action research.[39] The central point, both theoretical and methodological, is the notion of "presencing" that is the moment of spiritual insight into the identity and mission of a person or community.

Scharmer's so-called "Theory U" is born of the integration of various influences: previous research in the area of strategic leadership, change theories of Friedrich Glasl from the Netherlands Pedagogical Institute; action research projects in global business companies at MIT and the qualitative research with the participation of 150 prominent thinkers in the field of strategy, innovation, leadership and learning. One of the reasons that led Scharmer to the development of the Theory U was the fact

---

[37] M. BUBER, *I and Thou*, as quoted in SENGE – SCHARMER et al., *Presence*, p. 222.

[38] C.O. Scharmer is also the founder and co-director of "Emerging Leaders for Innovations Across Systems", a development joint initiative of the leadership of the United Nations Global Compact, the SOL, the World Bank and various NGOs. Scharmer takes part in projects of Transforming Capitalism Initiative, MIT's Green Hub Project, the African Public Health Leadership Initiative and the Global Dialogue Project.

[39] See C.O. SCHARMER, *Theory U. Leading from the Future as it Emerges. The Social Technology of Presencing*, SoL, Cambridge MA 2007, pp. 105-109.

of not being "able to create schools and institutions of higher education that develop people's innate capacity to sense and shape their future", perceived as "most important core capability for this century's knowledge and co-creation".[40]

Scharmer uses the artistic creation analogy to understand the distinction between three different perspectives on human action: focus on the product (work of art), process (painting), or the person before he takes action (artist as he stands in front of a blank canvas). Scharmer argues that the third perspective has been the most neglected in the recent organization theory, forming a hardly noticeable blind spot. In the argumentation, the most important leaders in various fields of human endeavor are different not for "what" they do or the "how" they run the process, but for the answer to the question: "Where is the source of your actions?" The notion of "presencing" is the combination of "presence" and "sensing" trying to express the state of a person that slows down, becomes connected to the real self and connects to something larger than the self-identity. Scharmer tries to express in a non-religious way the human experience we are used to describing theologically with terms of "grace", "communion" and "call".[41] The core capacity of presencing is the contemporary connection to the inner self and the future that is emerging from which we act and operate with most energy, profundity

---

[40] *Idem*, p. 3. See also Scharmer's previous publications about education: ID, *Neues Wohl-standsmodell als Bildungsaufgabe*, in F-T. GOTTWALD et al. (Eds.), *Bildung und Wohlstand, Auf dem Weg zu einer verträglichen Lebensweise*, Wiesbaden 1994, pp. 14-25; ID, *Kopf, Herz und Hand. Die Anforderungen eines zukunftsfähigen Wohlstands-modells an die Universitäten*, in «Politische Ökologie» 39 (1994) 51-54; K. KÄUFER – C.O. SCHARMER, *Universität als Schauplatz für den unternehmenden Menschen, Hoch-schulen als "Landestationen" für das In-die-Welt-Kommen des Neuen*, in S. LASKE – T. SCHEYTT – C. MEISTER-SCHEYTT – C.O. SCHARMER (Eds.), *Universität im 21. Jahr-hundert. Zur Interdependenz von Begriff und Organisation der Wissenschaft*, Rainer Hampp Verlag, Mering 2000, 109-134.

[41] See *Idem*, pp. 6-13.

and impact. The "U process" is a description of key moments of this deep transformation (see Scheme F):[42]

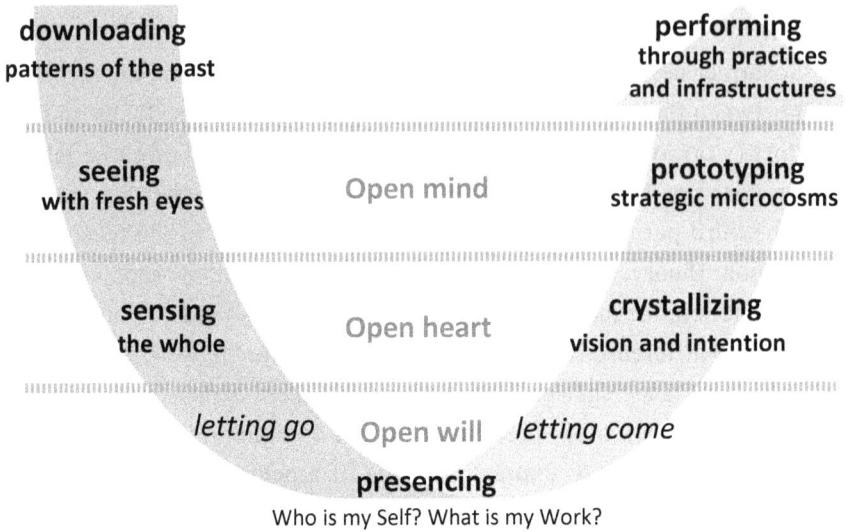

downloading
patterns of the past

performing
through practices
and infrastructures

seeing
with fresh eyes   Open mind   **prototyping**
strategic microcosms

sensing
the whole   Open heart   **crystallizing**
vision and intention

letting go   Open will   *letting come*
presencing
Who is my Self? What is my Work?

Scheme F: Scharmer's Transformational Process

1. *Stopping to download the patterns of the past.* The first step of the shift in focus begins in the recognition of habitual patterns of action and thought derived from the experiences of the past. People often use the models that have worked in the past without inquiring about them. Stop to download is the precondition for entering the U process of deep change. There are four organizational barriers that hinder the awareness about old habits: not recognizing what you see; not saying what you think; not doing what you say; not seeing what you do.

2. *Looking with fresh eyes.* To move from repetition to a new way of seeing, there are three different principles to be practised: clarify the

---

[42] See *Idem*, pp. 119-226.

question and the intent; move in a context that matters and can offer new inputs; suspend the judgement and connect to wonder. These principles practically form Husserl's *epoché* in a procedural context with the goal to push the observer outside the margins of his usual perception. A genuine dialogue is proposed as a positive attitude to be practised. Dialogue is a genuine "thinking together" process which is beyond simple discussion or debate.

3. *Sensing the whole.* In Scharmer's theory, when a person moves from seeing to sensing, perception begins to refer to the whole rather than to isolated objects. In this sense the person closes the feedback loop between the subjective experience of reality (what the system does to us) and the participation in the process (what we are doing to ourselves). There are four principles to feel a whole: creation of a collective physical and relational space; deep diving in the living presence of the phenomenon which suspends judgment; redirecting attention to the connections that form the whole; opening the heart, where heart is seen as the central point of a deeper emotional perception.[43]

4. *Presencing – connecting to the source.* Presencing is similar to sensing, but it goes deeper in the perception and connects "to the source of an emerging future whole – to a future possibility that is seeking to emerge".[44] In this step there are two constitutive moments, in which the subject is contemplatively passive: "letting go" of the past and "letting come" of an emerging future. In a more concrete way presencing answers two questions: "who is my Self?" and "what is my

---

[43] Scharmer links the notions of "deeper knowledge" and "heart" to Eleanor Rosch and Henri Bortoft's cognitive research. See F.J. VARELA – E. THOMPSON – E. ROSCH, *The embodied mind. Cognitive science and human experience*, MIT Press, Cambridge MA 1991; E. ROSCH – B.B. LLOYD (Eds.), *Cognition and categorization*, Erlbaum, Hillsdale NJ 1978 and H. BORTOFT, *Wholeness of Nature. Goethe's Way of Science*, Floris, Edinburgh 1996.

[44] SCHARMER, *Theory U*, p. 163.

Work?". The "Self" is the highest self that transcends pettiness and signifies one's best future possibility and "Work" is the purpose of human existence, what you are here on earth to do. Scharmer agrees with Eleanor Rosch, a researcher in the field of cognitive psychology, distinguishing between two kinds of knowledge: analytical knowledge and primary knowledge. Presencing is a moment of primary knowledge of an interconnected whole, without time limits, direct, open and bearing a non-instrumental value in itself. Scharmer links presencing to the Heideggerian concept of the "self from an emerging future" (German *zukünftiges Dasein*).[45]

5. *Crystallizing vision and intentions.* Presentiment "is connecting to source. Crystallizing means sustaining that connection and beginning to operate from it".[46] It is the clarification of the vision and intent of the emerging future that is brought into reality. It is a narrative process located in a given linguistic context. More precisely, Scharmer offers four principles: create a clear and shared intention; tune in the new intention logic and practise the letting go and letting come cognitive processes; reinforce the call understood as Martin Buber's "Grand Will" sacrificing the arbitrary self-will;[47] create environments that favor crystallization process.[48]

6. *Prototyping strategic microcosms.* Having established a connection to the source and having clarified the sense in a vision, the next stage in the U process is explore the future by doing and experimenting. Prototyping means "modeling or simulating your best current understandings precisely so you can have a shared set of understandings

[45] See M. HEIDEGGER, *Sein und Zeit*, as quoted in SCHARMER, *Theory U*, p. 477.
[46] SCHARMER, *Theory U*, p. 195.
[47] See M. BUBER, *I and Thou.* First Scribner Classics Edition, Scribner, New York 2000, pp. 64-65.
[48] See *Idem*, pp. 197-202.

that enable communication, especially between people with very different discipline bases".[49] The concrete attitudes associated with prototyping are: connect daily to the source; seize opportunities when they arise; fail often to succeed sooner; protect the organizational prototypes that are strategic but vulnerable microcosms.

7. *Performing through practices and infrastructure.* This stage is the shift from small experiments to larger institutional organizational systems. It is about creating a systemic infrastructure of persons that incorporates: vision, roles within teams, shared principles, practices, tools, processes, learning facilities and work environments. The whole process should go beyond the modern analytical Management by Objectives logic of an Ego-system to an interconnected organizational Eco-system.[50]

4.1.5 Evaluation of Selected Models

As we have stated earlier, we will use three criteria to evaluate the selection of Senge, Covey and Scharmer's leadership-management models: 1. overcoming the pure Management by Objectives logic; 2. compatibility with the four dimensions of the Salesian Youth Ministry anthropology; 3. balance between the scientific nature of the theory and its consolidated application in different cultural contexts.

The first aspect to be verified is if the theory and practice go beyond the linear objectives logic. The following Scheme G makes a synthesis of the authors' key concepts linked to the different aspects that characterize the paradigm shift from MBO to more integrated models:[51]

---

[49] SENGE – SCHARMER, *Presence*, p. 147.
[50] See SCHARMER, *Theory U*, pp. 220-226.
[51] For a deeper analysis see VOJTÁŠ, *Progettare e discernere*, pp. 201-213.

Overcoming MBO	Senge	Covey	Scharmer
Systemic approach	5th discipline	interdependence	wholeness
Transformational change	metanoia	paradigm change	U process
Participative complementarity	organizational learning	public victory	organizational ecosystems
From effectiveness to greatness	organizational learning	8th habit	learning from emerging future
Resource-based management	resource archetypes	balance between production and production capacity	resources imply creative responses to challenges

Scheme G: Overcoming of the MBO

The second criterion of evaluation requires the theories to have an integral anthropology. As a reference we consider the four-dimensional model of the Salesian Youth Ministry. It consists in four fundamental aspects which are mutually linked and complementary to one another: education to the faith; education-culture; social experience; vocation. In the following Scheme H we link the anthropological dimensions with the key aspects of the organizational theories.

The third point of view considers the equilibrium between the theoretical scientific grounding and a significant application in different cultures and contexts. All three models have a good diffusion all over the world through the activities of consulting organizations (Society for Organizational learning, FranklinCovey, Presencing Institute). We can state that the models are scientifically grounded as a result of doctoral research and further developments and applications in the context of scientific communities in different universities. Covey was a professor at Brigham

Young and Utah State universities. His model is based on an interdisciplinary research in the field of success manuals. Senge and Scharmer are professors at the Massachusetts Institute of Technology. Senge's model is based on a research in organizational aspects of systems engineering. Scharmer developed his model combining a philosophical basis with cognitive psychology and organizational applications.

SEPP dimensions	Senge	Covey	Scharmer
education to the faith	deeper systemic archetypes, presencing	spiritual dimension, spiritual intelligence	presencing, source, spiritual intelligence
education and culture	5 disciplines of learning	character education through 8 habits	deep transformation process
social experience	shared leadership	public victory	collective field
vocation	presencing	voice	Presencing

Scheme H: Integral Leadership Anthropology

Although the authors make a good contribution to the dialogue with the Salesian leadership and project management model, it is necessary to note some limitations of their theories. The first limit of Covey and Senge regards the rigor-relevance balance.[52] According to Senge's critics, it seems that his organizational learning model, having a good theoretical grounding, was admired rather than practised.[53] Differently Covey, wanting to be relevant to the practice, slipped especially in public lectures into

---

[52] See S. KÜHL, *Sisyphos im Management. Die vergebliche Suche nach der optimalen Organisationsstruktur*, Wiley, Weinheim 2002, pp. 32-36.
[53] See WITZEL, *A History of Management Thought*, p. 224.

simplifications and generalizations that did not take account of different contexts and complexity of the change processes.[54] Scharmer, trying to bring a secular spiritual perspective, invented a "Grammar of the Social Field" with many neologisms that made his theory cryptic and in some way gnostic.[55]

4.2 Integral Methodological Framework

The Salesian Youth Ministry and the SEPP are expressed in four dimension of human growth. These "can be understood as inter-communicating vessels that not only refer to one another ideally but nurture one another. Although in any description they seem to follow one after the other it is worth noting that they form a whole, a unity: each lends its own specific nature to the whole but also receives direction and certain original features from the others. They are inseparable and present themselves in reciprocal manner such that one cannot develop without explicit reference to the others. The logic behind them is that of system, where the dynamics of one element provokes adaptation in all the others".[56]

This statement describes the wholeness of the four dimensions at the level of thought. In this study, our concern is to propose a method that puts the wholeness "on the practical plane of existence".[57] It is obvious that the concrete educative and pastoral actions are always specific and reflect concrete circumstances. Therefore, they cannot be planned *in se*. The question is: how can we insert these single actions in an integral ubiquitous framework that would have a concrete educative and pastoral impact on the single action? We think that only an intellectual integration is not enough, it is too abstract and distant. We need some more concrete

---

[54] See CARLONE, *The Ambiguous Nature of a Management Guru Lecture*, pp. 89-112.
[55] See J. REAMS, *Illuminating the Blind Spot: An Overview and Response to Theory U*, in «Integral Review» 3 (2007) 5, 255.
[56] YM DEPARTMENT, *Frame of Reference*, ³2014, pp. 148-149.
[57] GC21 (1978), n. 14.

operational and methodological paradigms that mediate between the "wholeness mindset" and concrete actions (see Scheme I). Previously, we have seen that the Management by Objectives methodological paradigms are very analytical and favor a sectorial approach – every dimension is parallel to the other. In the following sections we would like to present an integral methodological framework that implies concrete virtues of a minister and an updated series of methodological steps for an integral SEPP planning. We will consider the contributions of Senge, Covey and Scharmer who have taken seriously the wholeness paradigm at a methodological level.

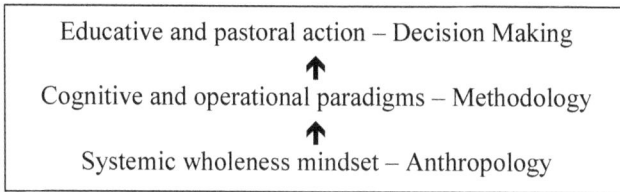

> Educative and pastoral action – Decision Making
> ↑
> Cognitive and operational paradigms – Methodology
> ↑
> Systemic wholeness mindset – Anthropology

Scheme I: Levels of the "Wholeness Mindset"

4.2.1 Knowing the Whole

Peter Senge starts his famous publication with an analysis: "From a very early age, we are taught to break apart problems, to fragment the world. This apparently makes complex tasks and subjects more manageable, but we pay a hidden, enormous price. We can no longer see the consequences of our actions; we lose our intrinsic sense of connection to a larger whole. When we try to 'see the big picture', we try to reassemble the fragments in our minds, to list and organize all the pieces. But, as physicist David Bohm says, the task is futile – similar to trying to reassemble the fragments of a broken mirror to see a true reflection. Thus, after a while we give up trying to see the whole altogether".[58] Senge then

---

[58] SENGE, *Fifth Discipline*, p. 3.

proposes the fifth discipline as an art and science of knowing the whole through feedback processes, circular causality, delays in causality and different organizational archetypes.

Knowing the systems is not the only way of seeing the whole. Howard Gardner and Daniel Goleman's multiple intelligences framework is also shared by all three above mentioned authors. In this context, Scharmer makes interesting references to Aristotle, seeing him as the greatest pioneer and innovator of Western inquiry and thought. Scharmer quotes and puts into practice the notion of different ways, faculties or capacities in the human soul to grasp the truth: "Science (episteme), according to Aristotle, is limited to the things that cannot be otherwise than they are (in other words, things that are determined by necessity). By contrast, the other four ways and capacities of grasping the truth apply to all the other contexts of reality and life. They are: art or producing (*techne*), practical wisdom (*phronesis*), theoretical wisdom (*sophia*), and intuition or the capacity to grasp first principles or sources (*nous*)".[59] Covey, especially in the *8th Habit*, makes references to a general synthesis of the Greek gnoseology speaking about *logos* (rational intelligence, analysis, abstract thinking, language understanding); *pathos* (emotional intelligence that determines effective communication, relationships and leadership); *ethos* (ethical nature, personal credibility and trust that others are placing in one's consistency and competence). Ethos at its highest is linked with the concept of spiritual intelligence, which is the ability of consciousness to perceive and process meanings and find a vocation (voice).[60] In this sense, the authors go beyond the modern progress logic, they make references to classical authors affirming "older is often better".[61]

Senge's systems theory and the notion of multiple intelligences are integrated with contemporary research coming from the area of action research, Gestalt psychology, Francisco Varela and Eleanor Rosch's

[59] SCHARMER, *Theory U*, p. 16.
[60] SEE COVEY, *8th Habit*, pp. 50-58 and 129-131.
[61] Cfr. SENGE – SCHARMER et al., *Presence*, pp. 177-179 and COVEY, *7 Habits*, pp. 18-21.

cognitive psychology, but find also references with philosophical cognitive concepts of Gottfried Wilhelm von Leibniz and Johann Wolfgang von Göthe.[62] These points of view could be useful to enlarge the type of analysis proposed in the Salesian Educative and Pastoral Project. There is not only a scientific (often only sociological) analysis of the situation. The situation has to be interpreted in order to live a real dynamic of discernment and vocation discovery. An enlarged view on cognitive processes can also help us understand better Don Bosco's creative ways of thinking and operating, overcoming a strict modern gnoseology. In fact, a historical and critical view of Don Bosco, focusing mainly on facts and rational reconstruction, very often misses the point of his leadership genius (vocation, vision, narrations, charisma, etc.) and levels his action mainly to managerial abilities. We propose these forms of knowledge:

- *Knowledge of the whole* that comes from the study of the phenomenon from within. The knowledge of the whole is inspired by a growing ecological awareness and by cognitive models that refer to phenomenology, hermeneutics and the Gestalt theory. Scharmer uses Kurt Lewin's holistic term "field" in the sense of "the totality of coexisting facts, which are conceived of as mutually interdependent".[63]

- *Reflection in action* developed by Chris Argyris and Donald A. Schön. "Phrases like 'think on your feet', 'keeping your wits about you', and 'learning by doing' suggest not only that we can think about doing but that we can think about doing something while doing it".[64] A reflective practitioner goes beyond the axiom of the detachment from the object

---

[62] See references of the authors to F.J. VARELA – E. THOMPSON – E. ROSCH, *The Embodied Mind: Cognitive Science and Human Experience*, MIT Press, Cambridge MA 1991; F.J. VARELA, *Ethical Know-How: Action, Wisdom and Cognition*. Edited by Timothy Lenoir and Hans Ulrich Gumbrecht, Stanford University Press, Stanford CA 1999 and H. BORTOFT, *Wholeness of Nature: Goethe's Way of Science*, Floris, Edinburgh 1996.

[63] K. LEWIN, *Resolving Social Conflicts & Field Theory in Social Science*, as quoted in SCHARMER, *Theory U*, p. 232.

[64] D.A. SCHÖN, *The Reflective Practitioner: How Professional Think in Action*, as quoted in SENGE, *Fifth Discipline*, p. 176.

212 REVIVING DON BOSCO'S ORATORY

and moves towards a phenomenological *epoché* (blocking biases and assumptions in order to let the phenomenon presents itself to the world of the participant in terms of its own inherent system of meaning).

- *Intuitive knowing* integrates the *analytical-rational knowledge*. Grounded on leadership studies and on examples of great thinkers who were characterized by a synergy of reason and intuition, Senge aims to foster brilliant insights which are converted into rationally verifiable propositions.[65] As people become familiar with systems thinking, long-term effects, circles of causality, as an alternative language, they discover that many of their intuitions become explicable.[66]

- *Narrative and imaginative knowledge*. The narrative is very useful in both interpretation of the situation and in the description of a vocation. In the project design process, the narrative is useful for downloading the mindsets. The linguistic analysis discovers the paradigms that guide the action. In a second area, narratives and imaginative language are fit to express the ideal of a vocation. An immediate translation of a vocation into a series of objectives is a reductive operation and diminishes the motivational impact.[67] In this sense Don Bosco's *Memoirs of the Oratory* are an excellent example of vision formulation.

- *Tacit knowledge* regarded as an embodied knowledge that is simply known and carried out in everyday actions.[68] Scharmer and Senge use the iceberg image to describe the levels of knowledge: explicit knowledge is known and measurable over the surface; tacit knowledge is already below the surface as embodied in behavioural and cognitive

---

[65] See studies of Weston Agor and Henry Mintzberg in SENGE, *Fifth Discipline*, p. 412 and also the notion of intuition as a key connection between Covey's and Scharmer's model in A.R. SZAMEITAT – H. NESTLER, *Intuition as a Key Factor for Implementing Theory U*, in «The Systems Thinker» 21 (2011) 8, pp. 8-10.
[66] See SENGE, *Fifth Discipline*, pp. 157-158.
[67] See SCHARMER, *Theory U*, pp. 120-122; 195-202; COVEY, *7 Habits*, pp. 130-135; SENGE, *Fifth Discipline*, pp. 136-156.
[68] See SCHARMER, *Theory U*, p. 69.

paradigms of persons; systemic structure knowledge is a deeper level that is not yet embodied and transcends the individual. Ikujiro Nonaka and Hirotaka Takeuchi state in their groundbreaking publication that the real knowledge is a "situational living process that evolves in a spiraling movement between explicit and tacit dimensions of knowledge held by individuals, teams, and the organization".[69]

- *Metaphysically based ethics.* Although different scholars contest metaphysical references in organizational studies, our three authors connect their methodological and ethical reasoning with "reality as it is". Covey's ethical leadership presumes principles which are real, immutable and unquestionably present laws of nature, e.g. the principle of impartiality, justice and human dignity.[70] These principles are the measure of the adequacy for our paradigms. Senge similarly speaks of "deep systemic structures" and Scharmer postulates a "source of social field" but they use more caution and a "critical realism approach" than Covey. The reality is the last instance for the commitment to the truth seen as a whole.[71]

4.2.2 Enacting the Whole

Fragmentation of thought into analytical dimensions and objectives in the MBO also produces projects divided into sectors which then translate into operational lines and finally into isolated actions. Of course, we cannot let go analytical thinking (it is very useful in specific situations), we have to integrate the panorama of cognitive and operational methods backing wisdom, intuitions, contemplation, concrete practical approach, etc.

---

[69] I. NONAKA – H. TAKEUCHI, *The Knowledge-Creating Company*, as quoted in SCHARMER, *Theory U*, p. 70.
[70] See COVEY, *7 Habits*, pp. 31-40 and ID., *8th Habit*, pp. 46-49.
[71] See SENGE, *Fifth Discipline*, pp. 52-54; 92-94; 148-162 and SCHARMER, *Theory U*, pp. 243-245; 436-442.

In recent organizational studies, we can observe a controversy with the reflective learning model used by Dewey which became part of the SEPP methodology through curricular theories.[72] While the connection between learning and experience is the strength of the theory, Scharmer and Senge point out two shortcomings of observation-planning-execution cycles. The first is the fixation on superficial events, ignoring the deeper levels of change processes. The second problem is the implicit reactiveness of the action guided only by the challenges of the situation. See Scheme J for the schematic illustration of the two models.[73]

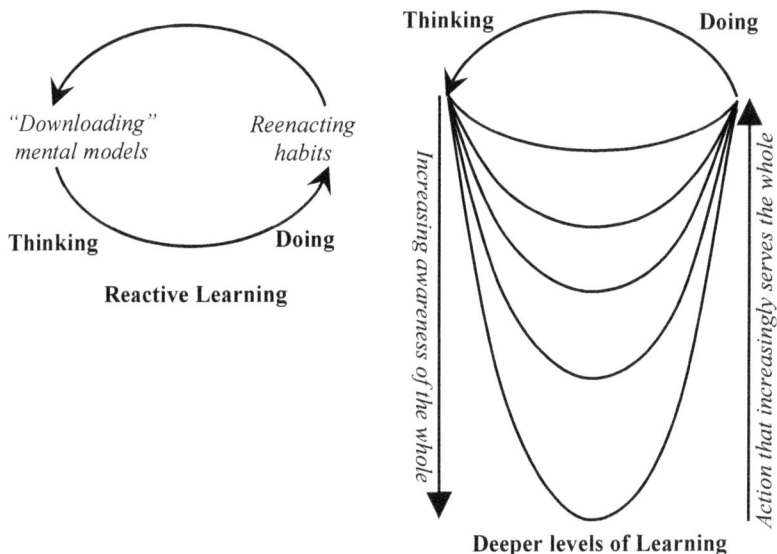

Scheme J: Deeper Reflective Learning

---

[72] See SENGE – SCHARMER et al., *Presence*, pp. 10-12; 86-92 and P.M. SENGE et al., *The Fifth Discipline Fieldbook*, Doubleday, New York 1994, pp. 59-65. For Dewey's theory see J. DEWEY, *How We Think: A Restatement of the Relation of Reflective Thinking to the Educative Process*, D.C. Heath&Co., Boston 1933; ID., *Experience and Education*, Macmillan, New York 1938.
[73] SENGE – SCHARMER et al., *Presence*, pp. 10-11.

Having dealt with integral knowledge in previous paragraphs, now we focus on the reactiveness of Dewey's model. Overcoming reactive behaviour by proactive action is the strong point of Covey's model that focuses more on vision than on events.[74] Senge enumerates 11 paradoxes of behaviour that does not take into account systemic-integral parameters. He fundamentally describes how today's problems come from yesterday's solutions.[75] Adam Kahane, an integral leadership scholar, sums up Senge and Scharmer's position: "Planning, deciding, and monitoring and controlling the ensuing process may be all that are needed in situations where change is essentially about reacting to the new circumstances. [...] When you're facing very difficult issues or dilemmas, when very different people need to align very complex settings, and when the future might really be very different from the past, a different process is required".[76] Overcoming reactiveness begins with stopping the downloading or creating a space between stimulus and response. Then proactive responses come into place acting "for" a big picture ideal, not only "against" a concrete threat. These are the steps in the dynamic discernment process of vocation (voice), which appears when we respect, develop, integrate and balance all the dimensions and intelligences.[77]

It this sense, we agree with the *Frame of Reference* that speaks about the vocational dimension: "The three earlier dimensions converge on this one, the ultimate horizon, reference point for our ministry".[78] Rector Major Pascual Chávez states: "All ministry, and especially youth ministry, is radically vocational in nature: the vocational dimension is what naturally inspires it and is its natural outcome".[79] We therefore consider "Salesian anthropology" dimensions not only as intertwined aspects of

---

[74] See Covey's first two habits: "be proactive" and "begin with the end in mind".
[75] See SENGE, *Fifth Discipline*, pp. 57-67.
[76] SENGE – SCHARMER et al., *Presence*, p. 87.
[77] See COVEY, *8th Habit*, pp. 83-86.
[78] YM DEPARTMENT, *Frame of Reference*, ³2014, p. 160.
[79] P. CHÁVEZ VILLANUEVA, *"Come and see" (Jn 1,39). The need for vocation ministry*, as quoted in YM DEPARTMENT, *Frame of Reference*, ³2014, p. 161.

the educative project towards the development of the young people, but also as organizational attention on different levels of depth. If lived together, they can reinforce one another and lead to creative solutions held together by a vocational logic.

We can find some interesting remarks in this sense made by Egidio Viganò, quoting Alberto Caviglia, in his letter on the SEPP: "In the Preventive System Don Bosco manifests a strong creative ability. His creativity is not a creativity of elements. Creating from nothing is the work of God alone. Don Bosco's creativity is a creative synthesis which is a sign of genius. I call it creative synthesis because its originality, its beauty, its greatness does not reside so much in its novelty of particulars but in the discovery of that idea which bands them into a new and results into a whole".[80] Some pages further, Viganò develops the idea of the creativity linked to the "whole" with proactive, cognitive and spiritual aspects: "Perhaps his early disciples spoke so enthusiastically in a language which pre-dated the development of the science of education and the inevitable changes have created a certain remissness, a certain slackening for serious study which could have negative results on our identity. Don Bosco instead incarnated in this 'system' his own sanctity. He conceived pedagogy 'beyond theory and beyond the narrow confines of methodology' to the realm of a wisdom which is based on the charism and special gift of the Holy Spirit. In this manner 'the originality' of his system has acquired a future dimension".[81]

An integral or holistic way of action or organization is not only proactive, creative, deep, vocational and interdimensional. One can recognize it from the fruits it bears: synergy and trust. Important is the vocation and the correlated vision that is beyond the measurable and,

---

[80] A. CAVIGLIA, *Pedagogy of Don Bosco*, as quoted in VIGANÒ, *The letter on the Preventive System*, pp. 13-14.
[81] VIGANÒ, *The letter on the Preventive System*, pp. 14-15.

once received, permeates all with the "ubiquitous strategy".[82] The vocation does not add one more element, but resets the interrelationships, creates alignment and synergy of particular elements. The concept of synergy translates operationally in the search for "third" solutions, which are not a compromise but a solution that creatively puts together the best energies of two or more (apparently) conflicting solutions.[83] Speaking in the language of Senge and Scharmer, who criticize visions that come from a place of powerlessness, an authentic vocation works on the main levers of the system, because of the deeper awareness of the people and of the mobilizing of motivational energies.

Trust, as a second indicator of an integrated action, begins with the ethical trustworthiness of the educator and only then evolves in the mutual trust throughout the community. Trustworthiness is a key element for creating synergy as well. Without trusting relationships, we hardly manage to exchange rational opinions, not mentioning deeper levels of dialogue, interpretation and discernment.[84] This is the reason in the next section we propose six ethical virtues that facilitate a deepening transformational process.[85] The operational planning is preceded by the creation of an Educative and Pastoral Community with trusting relationships. The virtues and reciprocal trust are key elements for the passage of a project "from paper to life".

---

[82] See COVEY, *The Leader in Me*, pp. 52-61.

[83] See Covey's 6th habit named "synergize" and the publication by COVEY, *The 3rd Alternative. Solving Life's Most Difficult Problems*, Free Press, New York 2011.

[84] Relationship qualities in the key of loving kindness (*amorevolezza*) are the key to see the whole Salesian Youth Ministry for Viganò. He agrees with Caviglia stating: "This system of Don Bosco is the system of kindness or, for better words, kindness built into a system". See CAVIGLIA, *Pedagogy of Don Bosco*, as quoted in E. VIGANÒ, *The letter on the Preventive System*, p. 15.

[85] We will refer also to Jerome Vallabaraj's transformational and holistic education to the faith, which is partially inspired by Senge's organizational learning. See J. VALLABARAJ, *Animazione e pastorale giovanile. Un'introduzione al paradigma olistico*, LDC, Leumann (TO) 2008, pp. 115-128 and ID., *Educazione catechetica degli adulti. Un approccio multidimensionale*, LAS, Roma 2009.

4.3 Virtues of Salesian Leader-Manager

The theme of virtues is an application of a general idea of authentic leadership: "We must be the change we seek to create".[86] The educational transformation promoted by Educative and Pastoral Community occurs first, and above all, in the interaction of people and not mainly in organizational systems update. Who one is as a person is inseparable from who he or she is as a leader, manager, educator or minister within an educational and pastoral project.

There are different terms that express the notion of more or less stable characteristics of human behaviour: attitude, capacity, competence, discipline, habit, trait or virtue. We have chosen the last term "virtue" with the following motivations: It is a term that expresses best the link between a certain behaviour and an ethical value. It is not only about an effective or functional behaviour in order to get results, as the terms attitude, capacity or competence may suggest. Other terms may have other connotations that could imply misunderstandings: habit could be linked to "routine", discipline to "drill" and trait to "innateness" of the capacities.

The term "virtue" also implies an everyday lived excellence that reflects the shift in organizational studies from effectiveness to excellence (greatness). Virtue-based approaches, or character education, seem to turn back not only in organizational but also in educational sciences.[87]

---

[86] It is a quote of Mohandas Karamchand Gandhi taken as a paradigm in SENGE – SCHARMER et al., *Presence*, p. 147.

[87] See e.g. A. MACINTYRE, *After Virtue*, University of Notre Dame Press, Notre Dame 1981; T. LICKONA, *The return of Character Education*, in «Educational Leadership» 51 (1993) 6-11; C. PETERSON – M.E.P. SELIGMAN, *Character strengths and virtues. A handbook and classification*, American Psychological Association Press – Oxford University Press, Washington DC – New York 2004; H. GARDNER, *Truth, Beauty, and Goodness Reframed: Educating for the Virtues in the Age of Truthiness and Twitter*, Basic Books, New York 2011.

We also do not have problems with a traditional Catholic term, although some specifications have to be made.[88]

	Personal virtues	Prosocial virtues
Mentality	1. Dynamic Fidelity	4. Abundance Mentality
Leadership	2. Call Discernment	5. Generative Accompaniment
Management	3. Operational Consistency	6. Synergic Integration

Scheme K: Virtues of a Salesian Leader-Manager

In the following section we will develop six virtues that are necessary, a *sine qua non* condition for a functional Salesian leader or SEPP manager. These virtues are important in terms of processes in organizational setting, which does not mean they have to be prioritized to theological or classical moral virtues in character education. Of course to build trustworthiness of a leader, a complete character ethics is to be put in place. In this sense, these organizational virtues are cognitive, emotional and operational character qualities that refer to a set of values and express themselves in everyday organizational behaviour.

The set of organizational virtues is organized in Scheme K. The first three personal virtues precede the prosocial virtues in order to respect the inside-out logic: first comes the personal change that builds trustworthiness of a person and only afterwards comes the leading of a community or the management of greater social systems. There is also a certain symmetry between the personal and the prosocial virtues. The first virtues, both personal and prosocial, favor the creation of a cognitive mindset;

---

[88] We agree with Alexandre Havard's argumentation for a leadership based on classical aretology and anthropology, but we find his practical proposals less penetrating . See A. HAVARD, *Virtuous Leadership. An Agenda for Personal Excellence*, Scepter Publishers, New York 2007.

the second virtues develop the aspect of leadership accentuating the emotional dimension in the search for a vision to pursue and, finally, the third virtues of both sets stress out the managerial operational and practical qualities. The next paragraphs about the organizational will follow this structure: definition of the virtue; references to Don Bosco's legacy; the internal dynamic and organizational implications; tools for training and practice.

4.3.1 Dynamic Fidelity

The virtue of dynamic fidelity is the mentality and the connected attitudes of a person who is striving to know the surrounding reality integrally in its complexity, who is inserted in the flow of tradition and who searches spaces for creative intervention. Dynamic fidelity was introduced by the Special General Chapter as a key concept in the Vatican II renewal.[89] In that context it was applied more on the restructuration of the works and not on the underlying balanced mentality. The focus of the '70s was the necessary change that put aside the fidelity aspect. Dynamic fidelity as we understand it here is the cognitive rooting in tradition and open-minded attitude towards the future possibilities without rushing to practical applications.

In the organizational field we can find references to Covey's first habit of proactivity, Senge's discipline of mental models and Scharmer's attitude of looking at the reality with fresh eyes, capable of stopping the downloading of the past solutions and stereotypes. Fidelity and dynamic creativity produce the semantic space that describes the virtue. Fidelity is to be understood both as a true relationship with the world (fidelity to reality) and as continuity with the good cognitions, beliefs and practices of the past (fidelity to tradition). The dynamic creativity is also meant in

---

[89] See SGC (1972), nn. 192-273.

two ways: the knowledge of the situation that uses all forms of the integral knowledge (cognitive creativity) and the search of possible educational and pastoral interventions (operational creativity).

Don Bosco's Legacy

In the beginning of his ministry in Turin, Don Bosco positioned himself as a creative innovator of various traditions. He operated a creative synthesis from the interweaving of educational, spiritual and organizational mindsets. As a practitioner, he did not tend to design an educational institution from scratch, but rather reorganized creatively other currents of thought and experience. Don Cocchi's educational model of the Oratory was integrated with the influences of Filip Neri's and Lombard oratorian traditions. The same dynamic fidelity approach was used by Don Bosco with the educational model of the Jesuit college revived in the mid-nineteenth century, or with the Combonian missionary method adapted to the reality of Latin America of the last decades of the nineteenth century. At the level of spiritual traditions, he incorporated more practically than theoretically St. Francis de Sales' teachings with St. Alphonsus de Liguori's moral doctrine and with Philippine or Vincentian spirituality. His managerial style combines a fundamental rural family base upgraded with the aspects of modern managerial thought, such as a strong entrepreneurship, economic autonomy, expansive capacity, motivational ability and the striving for the conquest of a significant social role.[90]

Pietro Braido summarizes the operative mentality of Don Bosco: "The project of Don Bosco, beyond certain accidental stiffness, has to be taken not as a 'closed system', but as an 'open system', pro-active and not re-active. It is able to maintain the internal formal and organizational

---

[90] For further details, see the analysis of Don Bosco's leadership and management qualities in Chapter 3.

equilibrium and at the same time to grow in complexity and differentiation to more advanced equilibria, which allow an intense and enriching
transactional relationship with the environment".[91] Dynamic fidelity is
also one of the most important virtues of the first generation of Salesians
who were called to be faithful to the educational heritage of Don Bosco
in many contexts that differed significantly from Valdocco. Historical
studies show that the second Rector Major Michael Rua was strongly
characterized by dynamic fidelity to the Salesian educational method. He
left ample margins for creative action in the Oratories developments, in
the missions in Amazonia, Patagonia, Middle East, Africa and India.[92]

Internal Dynamic

The Salesians of Don Bosco, taking inspiration from the Founder, define in the Special GC the ideal criterion for every renewal as "Don
Bosco in the Oratory" where he is seen as "faithful and dynamic, docile
and creative, firm but at the same time flexible". The formation of a combined mentality of fidelity and creativity will be developed in dialogue
with the three theories of leadership that offer some insight and important
balance.

The Dynamic fidelity is close to Covey's concept of proactivity which is
the first habit and the starting point of the whole growth model. It is
linked to the interdependence paradigm that recognizes the freedom of a
mature person with strong ties that is inserted to a concrete context. This
way, the dynamic fidelity goes beyond a pure mentality of dependence,

---

[91] P. BRAIDO, *Il progetto operativo di Don Bosco e l'utopia della società cristiana*, LAS, Roma 1982, p. 29.

[92] A scientific conference on the person of Michael Rua concludes its deep analysis, stating that Rua's leadership developed original traits of creative fidelity that interpreted
the style of the Don Bosco. See G. LOPARCO – S. ZIMNIAK (Eds.), *Don Michele Rua
primo successore di Don Bosco. Tratti di personalità, governo e opere (1888-1910)*,
Atti del 5° Convegno Internazionale di Storia dell'Opera Salesiana Torino 28 ottobre
– 1° novembre 2009, LAS, Roma 2010, pp. 1039-1040.

which repeats the patterns of the past in an absolute loyalty. The independence mentality is also insufficient, because of the subject's isolation in a fiction of pure creative freedom.[93]

Senge and Scharmer's theoretical framework about creativity refers to the work with mental models. In this setting, dynamic fidelity could be linked with a constant disposition to consider reality as complex and interconnected. In the search for truth that has operative implications dynamic fidelity searches in the complexity of the world for strategic leverages with the contributions of the analytical, rational, intuitive, narrative, tacit knowledge and of reflection in action.

In the Salesian Youth Ministry publications we can find some close positions on the matter. Juan E. Vecchi and Elisabetta Maioli, writing about the educative and pastoral projects for young animators, call the dynamic fidelity a "mentality of change " and suggest the animators fuel the tension between security and crisis in order to bring a group to change.[94] The closest position to the virtue of dynamic fidelity is found in Giuseppe Groppo's module about the "integral promotion" within the publication about educative and pastoral project. Groppo proposes proactivity as opposed to reactivity and describes it as a trait of emotional stability, cognitive realism, inner security, humor that relativizes rigidity and security in carrying out choices in reality. Proactivity is also connected to a wise creativity that comes from experience, intuition, docility, sagacity, discursive rationality, foresight, carefulness and a realistic sense of risk. Groppo then connects proactivity with the theological virtue of hope that "becomes a way of life according to the fundamental

---

[93] There are some limits of Covey's notion of proactivity: risk of activism and an absence of concrete value systems that lead freedom in choosing concrete actions. See also Senge's critics in SENGE, *Fifth discipline*, pp. 20-21.

[94] See E. MAIOLI – J.E. VECCHI, *L'animatore nel gruppo giovanile. Una proposta "Salesiana"*, LDC, Leumann (TO) 1988, pp. 133-147.

trust in God's faithfulness to his promises".[95] This theological hope becomes mature, when the Christian has already moved from reactivity to proactivity. Then, and only then, hope can be a component of Christian maturity.

Tools and Practices

Dynamic fidelity is seen as a cognitive mentality that is part of a deep and sustainable process of change. A practical approach implies not only the description of the internal dynamic, but also some concrete tools to practise that virtue. However, it should be stressed out that a virtue is not "created" by using tools and activities because, saying it with Senge, it is located at the level of systemic structures, not at the level of observable events. In this sense we propose some basic tools in a very concise form:

1. *Listen to your language* in order to become more self-conscious about actual mental models. We can distinguish two types of language: reactive and pro-active. In the reactive mindset, the emphasis is on the description of the external influences of human action that implements a deterministic paradigm ("I cannot", "if only", "I must", "They won't allow", etc.) In proactive language, the emphasis is placed on decisions that are rooted in motivating visions ("I want", "I choose", "I can", "Let's look on our alternatives", etc.).[96]

2. *Cultivate all types of knowledge* regarding the situation, tradition, community and oneself: analytical-rational knowledge of empirical studies about the current situation or historical studies that analyze the tradition; listening to the intuitive knowledge of others that involves imagination and narrative knowledge; reflection in action with analysis of one's mindsets, motivations and stereotypes that influenced the concrete action; search for tacit knowledge patterns.

---

[95] G. GROPPO, *Promozione integrale*, in J.E. VECCHI – J.M. PRELLEZO (Eds.), *Progetto Educativo Pastorale. Elementi modulari*, LAS, Roma 1984, p. 129.

[96] See COVEY, *7 Habits*, pp. 76-90.

3. *Study different educational and pastoral models* in their cultural and historical context. Historical and hermeneutical study of practical models foster critical thinking giving instruments that help understand decisions, mental models, historical development of thought and the history of the effects of ideas.[97]

	enforces the project	hinders the project
internal	**strength**	**weakness**
external	**opportunity**	**threat**

Scheme L: SWOT Matrix

4. *Use alternative representations of the analysis of the situation*, such as the SWOT matrix (see Scheme L), developed by Albert S. Humphrey, which divides the elements into the fields of strengths, weaknesses, opportunities or threats.[98] Other useful tools are dialogue visualization techniques, story walls, mind mapping, visual artifacts design, systemic flow mapping etc.

4.3.2 Call Discernment

The first virtue of dynamic fidelity creates an open cognitive mentality that facilitates many types of knowledge. Discernment, as a second step, accentuates the leadership and orienting part of the process. It is

---

[97] See e.g. Lenti, Stella or Braido's historical critical studies about Don Bosco and the Salesian tradition evolution.
[98] See e.g. L.G. FINE, *The SWOT Analysis: Using your Strength to overcome Weaknesses, Using Opportunities to overcome Threats*, Kick it LLC, Charleston WV 2010.

sensitive to the links between single pieces of information, interprets them spiritually with a deep and unifying view and finally tries to make a vocation emerge. Discernment of the calls is a virtue of personal leadership; it moves from the cognitive domain to the search for direction. It consists in open, deep and unifying listening to different calls of the reality seen as connected to oneself, in a way that welcomes a concrete vocation letting aside various disturbing voices.

The profound harmony of the whole is also understood as beauty, in terms of aesthetics. In the sense of Gardner, it is good to remember that the whole is designed with all the intelligences. It comes from different types of knowledge and tends operatively to a vocation that expresses itself in a vision of the future and afterwards orientates the concrete choices. Discernment accentuates the passive component, discipleship, as the man listens to the Spirit and the reality that precedes and exceeds him.

Call discernment is in connection with the theories of leadership, especially with Covey's second habit (begin with the End in Mind), with the personal vision creation within the discipline of personal mastery of Senge, which in turn, correlates with Scharmer's design phases of sensing the whole, presencing and crystallizing of a vision.[99]

Don Bosco's Legacy

As we have seen in the third Chapter, Don Bosco created a harmony between leadership and management in his life and in his educational model. The personality of Don Bosco was built around a strong leadership centre. If one is not careful, the image of Don Bosco could be falsified by a charismatic and visible aspect of leadership that consisted

---

[99] Darmanin, by referring to the categories of Covey, sees the Ignatian discernment as an exercise of leadership that empowers the emotional intelligence in the analysis of the spiritual experiences of consolation and desolation. See A. DARMANIN, *Ignatian Spirituality and Leadership in Organizations Today*, in «Review of Ignatian Spirituality» 36 (2005) 2, 8.

in a powerful vision involving and energizing many people. The virtue of discernment is the internal aspect of the same authentic leadership. Don Bosco, only by being disciple and steward to a worldwide vision beyond his person, could become a great leader in the accompaniment of others.

Personal discernment is present in many moments of Don Bosco's life. It begins with the dream of nine years that brings the question of vocation. The vision of him being a priest and educator crystallizes slowly in the adolescence, during the seminary years and also in the first years in Turin. Since the tasks and the concreteness of his vocation were changing in different stages of his life, he learned to link the process of discernment with two fundamental attitudes: trust in Providence and dynamic fidelity. At first, he discerned his personal vocation. Being ordained a priest, he sought to understand the concrete way of the commitment to the abandoned young people. Later in the years of the wandering oratory, he discerned step by step the concrete way to put his educational model into practice. Afterwards the building process of the Oratory of Valdocco was to be determined. Subsequently, as the director in the three oratories in Turin, he searched for the right formula other lay and priest cooperators' involvement in the education of the young. The virtue of discernment is lived even later in the expansion of the Salesian work in Piedmont with the boarding school structure. Then came the search for the shaping of the Congregation and, ultimately, for the formula of global expansion.

Among the typical features of Don Bosco's discernment, along with the trust in Providence and the dynamic fidelity, one can notice dreams, dialogues and narrations as typical forms of the vision formulation. This form of knowledge developed a high grade of motivational transfer, conveying the beauty of an integrated life through the vocation to holiness lived with and for young people. The wholeness of Don Bosco's vocation and vision was also expressed in the integration of the *novissimi* (lat. "the last things") and the question of eternal salvation in the concreteness of everyday life. Time and eternity harmonized in his vision and the narrative formulae enforced the wholeness of his "project".

Internal Dynamic

The personal discernment is preceded by a mentality of dynamic fidelity that makes the person stand in the midst of different types of knowledge about the situation, traditions, structures and themselves. Inspired by the theories of leadership, we describe the discernment dynamic in four related steps. First the person has to "feel the whole", which not only means thinking about the connections among traditions, knowledge and oneself, but also feeling existentially involved with the situation that produces a cognitive empathy. Secondly, entering into silence is required. The person focuses on the source of the situations and actions remaining existentially involved. The silent focus is the contemplative attitude of an open heart, seen as the centerpoint, not only as a symbol of emotions.[100] In the third step the spiritual "letting come" attitude is essential. The accepted vocation is a gift of the Spirit that brings together elements of truth, beauty and goodness. In the final fourth step the person describes the vocation in a symbolic, narrative, engaging, cross-disciplinary and short form. This vision thus becomes a point of reference for personal identity.[101]

---

[100] See references to the "knowledge of the whole" by Bortoft, Scharmer, Eleanor Rosch's cognitive psychology and Gestalt psychology in SCHARMER, *Theory U*, pp. 148-159 and H. BORTOFT, *Wholeness of Nature. Goethe's Way of Science*, Floris, Edinburgh 1996. See also the importance of different types of knowledge during discernment process in A. CENCINI, *Discernimento* in J.M. PRELLEZO – G. MALIZIA – C. NANNI (Eds.), *Dizionario di Scienze dell'Educazione. Seconda edizione riveduta e aggiornata*, LAS, Roma 2008, pp. 333-334.

[101] COVEY, *7 Habits*, pp. 107-139; G.P. QUAGLINO, *La vita organizzativa. Difese, collusioni e ostilità nelle relazioni di lavoro*, Fabbri, Milano 2007, pp. 370-385; L. HIRSCHHORN, *The Psychology of Vision*, in E.B. KLEIN – F. GABELNICK – P. HERR (Eds.), *The Psychodynamics of Leadership*, Psychosocial Press, Madison CT 1998, pp. 109-126.

In transactional project management, the challenges of the situation are described first. Afterwards objectives are set to overcome the difficulties of the current state of things. Finally, interventions and activities are planned in a linear logic for every objective. In transformative change, however, the vision is used in a constant correction of the operation course, as shown in Scheme M. [102] A transition plan may also exist, but it does not eliminate the discernment awareness to the feedbacks coming from reality. These are "calling" to be recognized and a personal and organizational learning has to take place. Ultimately discernment recognizes the reality as a whole, puts it in relation with the vision and corrects the course of action or its accents. Discernment is therefore necessary not only in the beginning of the planning but as constant attention during the execution of a project.

In the SEPP management model, we can find some elements that converge with the transformational change and the discernment model. The *Handout No. 1*, speaking about the SEPP methodology, proposes the interpretation of the situation: "We must therefore assess the facts according to their ability to make it easier or more difficult for young people to grow their humanity in faith".[103] Unfortunately, more concrete indications for interpretation are lacking and the entire category is overflown with a list of General Chapter 21 conclusions. The 2nd edition of the Frame of Reference repeated the need of interpretation, but offered

---

[102] Inspired by D. ANDERSON – L.A. ANDERSON, *Beyond Change Management. How to Achieve Breakthrough Results Through Conscious Change Leadership*, Pfeiffer, San Francisco ²2010, p. 66.

[103] DICASTERO PER LA PASTORALE GIOVANILE, *Progetto Educativo Pastorale. Metodologia*, Sussidio 1, [s.e.], Roma 1978, p. 14.

the concept of a vision of the future that must be open, inspiring, detailed and positive.[104]

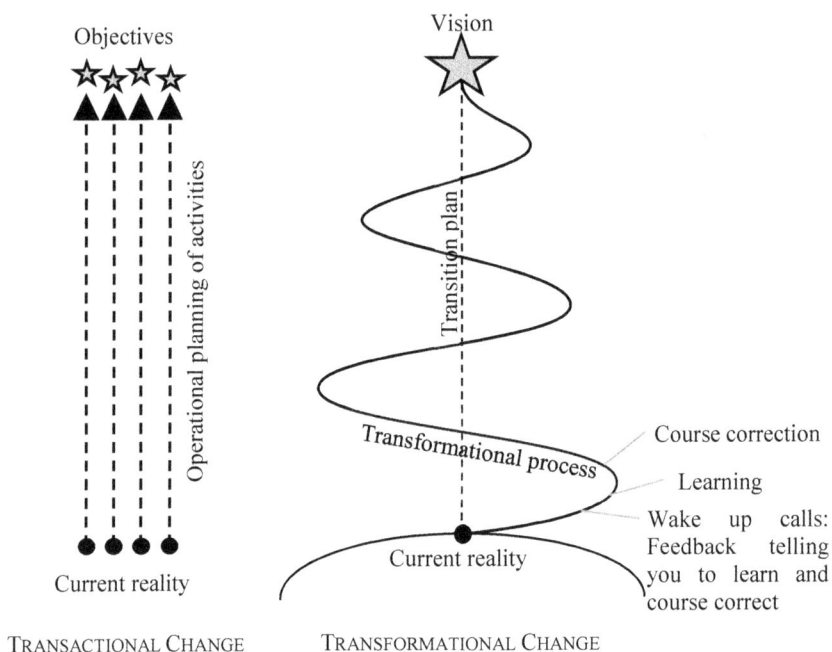

Scheme M: Transformational and Transactional Change

A significant emphasis is offered by Alberich and Vallabaraj in their holistic model of catechetics. Speaking of interpretation, they emphasize the impossibility of operational decisions deduction directly from the analysis of the situation. The authors propose discernment in order to analyze the meanings, look for the causes and connections to get to a new awareness about the situation.[105]

---

[104] YM DEPARTMENT, *Frame of Reference*, [2]2000, pp. 171 and 173.
[105] E. ALBERICH – J. VALLABARAJ, *Communicating a Faith That Transforms. A Handbook of Fundamental Catechetics*, Kristu Jyoti Publications, Bangalore 2004, p. 271.

The method of discernment suggested by Domènech and Cereda declares, of course, the term discernment, but it is perceived as a whole design method. Cereda proposes the creation of a personal vision in an integral way: "It is important that this vision for the future is not described as something intellectual or cold, but as something you are enthusiastic about that is attractive and encouraging, that corresponds with your desires and expectations, that shows the possibilities that can result from the efforts you make. The more the goal attracts you and fills you with enthusiasm the more determined you will be to take the necessary steps to reach it".[106]

Tools and Practices

Creating daily space and time for silence and listening is required for the growth in the virtue of discernment. In the language of Scharmer, it comes to creating fourfold physical space, time space, relational space and intentional space. This still environment allows persons and communities to plunge into the depth of experience, to shift attention from events to the source of the dynamic, and finally, to open the heart. There are different tools inspired by the Jesuit spirituality,[107] but we focus here on a small set of simple and concrete tools:
1. *Writing down a personal vision* by analyzing one's objectives. The question to ask is if the objective is a real purpose in itself or just a means to get to another goal. The chain of these purifying questions and answers should get one to the last inherent desire that can be the basis of vision and is an "end" in itself. The vision conceived in this way has the attributes of definitiveness (end in itself) and concreteness (tied to a concrete personal desire or passion).[108]

---

[106] See CEREDA, *The Personal Plan of Life. Ongoing Formation.*
[107] See e.g. M.E. THIBODEAUX, *Reimagining the Ignatian Examen. Fresh Ways to Pray from Your Day*, Loyola Press, Chicago 2015.
[108] See SENGE, *Fifth Discipline*, pp. 136-139.

2. *Create the personal vision* with the visualization of the future, imagining one's funeral, retirement or other anniversaries of life, in a sort of "exercise of the good death". Within this imagination, one can recall dear or loved people that sum up one's life and legacy in order to distinguish the important objectives or activities from the instrumental ones.[109]

3. *Writing meditation* is proposed by Cereda with the following motivation: "taking notes, writing down what in the Spirit you have seen as the plan of your life. It is a methodology of the spiritual life that our Salesian tradition has always had recourse to and that is effective in the unfolding of the journey. You can refer to what you have written at any time in order to check progress. Writing is a means to prevent you being superficial, to help you with your reflection and prayer, to reach the depth of your life".[110]

4.3.3 Operational Consistency

After the proposal of dynamic fidelity, which creates a necessary precondition for change process, and the virtue of discernment, which concretizes a vocation in a formulated vision, we focus on the operational and managerial aspect. The third and final step of personal change is synthesized in the virtue of operational consistency that is defined as the implementation of the vision in everyday reality. The consistency as a virtue accentuates, therefore, the skills, attitudes and deeper practices of personal management. The triad of personal virtues describes a sustainable change process in three phases: 1. the creation of an open and realistic mentality; 2. the reception of a vocation which is formulated in

---

[109] The praxis of the "exercise of good death" was abandoned by the Salesians as an anachronism and is instead proposed in a secular management setting in COVEY, *7 Habits*, pp. 96-97.

[110] CEREDA, *The Personal Plan of Life. Ongoing Formation.*

a vision; 3. the harmonization of everyday life around and according to the vision.

Operational consistency is connected with the SEPP's third step of "operational planning" that plans and carries out policies, interventions, strategies and activities. The fact of describing a virtue will guide us to provide not only some techniques, but also a connected ethical reasoning. In this sense, operational consistency will have references to Covey's third habit "Put first things first" and to Senge's discipline of personal mastery, which address both the implementation of the vision in the reality of every day. Covey emphasizes more the aspect of time-management and Senge focuses instead on the creative tension between the vision and the current reality.[111]

Don Bosco's Legacy

Referring to the lived harmony between leadership and management in Don Bosco, we can remember some of the binomials that express the connection between his visionary leadership and the organizational rationality, order and operational harmony. "Manual work – Trust in Providence", "Prudent management – Powerful dream" and "Stability management – Expansion of a vision" create the coordinates for the many educative, pastoral and organizational activities inserted and fuelled from the creative tension between his vision and the reality. Also when Don Bosco narrates his dreams or visions, an operational translation follows immediately. After the dream of nine years, he tries out an experimental apostolate with his fellow countryside boys, forming a "kind of oratory". At the end of his life, when he remembered the beginnings of the Oratory, he wrote a letter from Rome and after his return a

---

[111] Cfr. COVEY, *7 Habits*, pp. 146-182; SENGE, *Fifth Discipline*, pp. 129-162 and Covey's publication on operative consistency S.R. COVEY – A.R. MERRILL – R.R. MERRILL, *First Things First*, Simon & Schuster, New York 1994.

series of interventions in Valdocco were carried out according to the vision.[112]

In the Salesian educational model, we can correlate the operational consistency with the so-called "pedagogy of duties". Don Bosco's narratives, especially the *Memoirs of the Oratory*, describe his mindset, where the vocational discernment is often linked with a list of concrete proposals to be carried out. After describing the important place of duties in the biographies of the Oratory boys Dominic Savio, Michael Magone and Francis Besucco, Peter Braido sums up the argumentation: "The pedagogy of duty and work is substantially part of the entire life of an educational institution, with its continuous succession of various occupations and moments of recreation, tight rhythm of activities in the classroom, workshops and study halls, with eagerness to achieve one's best, emulating others, all the while accompanied by the example and energy of the educators".[113]

Internal Dynamic

Operational consistency is the virtue that implements the vision in the daily life. It is important to emphasize that it is not a simple linear translation of the vision into smaller separated operating units (lines of action, interventions, activities, etc.). Following the integral paradigm, operational consistency finds itself in the tension between the vision and the current reality. In the Salesian setting, a proposal by Vecchi and Maioli to the young animators states the need to feed the tension between utopia and the search for practical mediations.[114]

It is important to live all three personal virtues, in order to be and act in this "uncomfortable" position of "tension". If one forgets the dynamic fidelity mentality and does not make the vision concrete and present, he

---

[112] See J.M. PRELLEZO, *Valdocco nell'Ottocento tra reale ed ideale (1866-1889). Documenti e testimonianze*, LAS, Roma 1992, pp. 273-276; 287-307.
[113] BRAIDO, *Prevention not repression*, p. 237.
[114] See MAIOLI – VECCHI, *L'animatore nel gruppo*, p. 146.

is likely to fall in the evasion strategies, mentioned by Senge: 1. *vision erosion* lowers the tension by putting away the challenging parts of the vision; 2. with *conflict manipulation* we try to manipulate ourselves into greater effort by focusing on not wanted consequences of failure; 3. the *willpower strategy*, instead, tries to psych ourselves up to overpower all forms of resistance.[115] Commitment to the truth is suggested by Senge as a positive solution that helps to live creatively the tension between the vision and the reality. Senge's view on creative tension is a good start, but we need a more concrete set of instruments to make the vision happen.

The simplest and most straightforward instrument for operative planning is a to-do list. Covey refers to it as the 1st generation of time management because a to-do list translates the whole vision as a series of often randomly sorted tasks of different nature. The 2nd generation of time management already implements the list within the calendar, the 3rd makes a leap forward by grouping tasks according to priorities and dividing them in successions of long, medium and short-term objectives. These are implemented accordingly in the calendar. The 4th generation of time management proposed by Covey not only plans the objectives and results, but also manages all needed resources. This is the application of his conception of effectiveness: the harmony between "production" and "production capacity".[116]

Time management is a strong point of Covey's model and so he offers other useful categories and distinctions. A second upgrade is the division of tasks between urgent and important. The urgent ones are within the logic of reactivity and demand an immediate response. Urgent tasks "push the buttons" of social pressure, stereotypes, previous commitments

---

[115] See SENGE, *Fifth Discipline*, pp. 146-147.
[116] See COVEY, *7 Habits*, pp. 149-172. It seems that the SEPP and other Salesian projects lack prioritization of objectives. Considered according to Covey's categories, Salesian projects are the second generation of management at best. See e.g. the operative guidelines of the previous General Chapters: CG25 (2002), nn. 14-16; 31-36; 46-48; 56-62; 64; 72-84 or CG26 (2008), nn. 7-22; 31-51; 60-78; 85-97; 104-113.

or manipulation. Important tasks are instead in the logic of creative fidelity as they have a direct relationship with the vision and need to be brought in the current situation. Important tasks' fulfilment can be procrastinated but at elevated long-run costs. For the interrelationship between the two types of tasks see Scheme N describing some typical activities.[117]

	Urgent	Not urgent
Important	*I* crises pressing problems deadline-driven projects	*II* prevention, capacity building, relationship building, recognizing new opportunities, prayer planning, recreation
Not important	*III* interruptions, some calls, some mail, some reports, some meetings proximate pressing matters popular activities	*IV* trivia, busy work some mail, some calls time wasters, compensations pleasant activities

Scheme N: Important and Urgent Activities Matrix

Covey, in its proposal for fourth-generation management, being consistent with what was stated before, emphasizes the role of Quadrant II (important and not urgent activities). The activities in Quadrant I are important and urgent, and thus attract and mobilize many personal

---

[117] See COVEY, *7 Habits*, p. 151. See also M. KROGERUS – R. TSCHÄPPELER, *The Decision Book. Fifty models for strategic thinking*, Profile Books, London 2011, p. 10. See also analogous tools such as PERT (Project Evaluation and Review Technique) and CPM (Critical Path Method) in Y.Y. HAIMES, *Risk Analysis, Systems Analysis, and Covey's Seven Habits*, in «Risk Analysis» 21 (2001) 222 and H. KERZNER, *Project Management. A Systems Approach to Planning, Scheduling, and Controlling*, Wiley, New Jersey [10]2009, pp. 494-500.

resources almost automatically. Quadrants III and IV refer to not important activities, so discipline and determination have to be applied constantly in order to spend less resources and recover time, energy and motivations for the activities related to important issues. Quadrant II is called the effectiveness quadrant because there are activities that nurture the mentality of dynamic fidelity, discernment, creation of the vision, capacity and relationship building, etc. Covey's time management strategy suggests to move the resources allocated to Quadrants III and IV to the important activities of Quadrant II in a logic of prevention of Quadrant I crises and capacity building for unforeseen issues.

Operational consistency, as a personal operational virtue, is not far from the description of the attitude of responsibility described in the "Personal Project of Life": "It is easy to see that it is possible to pass a whole life-time caught up in a whole variety of activities and not be aware of the obstacles that are blocking personal development. You can be living your vocation, following the rules, accepting roles, allowing yourself to be carried along by events, following the current fashions, the accepted ideas, other people's values. It is as though you had all the necessary material available to build your house, but not having any plan you haphazardly pile one thing on top of another. On the other hand, with a personal plan, guided by the Spirit of God and by His grace you take charge of your own growth, using your freedom to assume your identity as a consecrated salesian apostle, priest or brother, and so becoming what God is calling you to be".[118]

Tools and Practices

Operational consistency can be put into practice with many tools. Management handbooks and self-help publications are full of advices and tools. We prefer to stick with Covey's model because of the linearity of the argumentation and the interconnectedness of the virtues within his

---

[118] CEREDA, *The Personal Plan of Life. Ongoing Formation.*

model. There are some practices in the logic of the 4th generation of time (and resource) management:

1. *Move out from Quadrant III*, investing the focus, motivation and time resources from urgent issues to important ones. It is basically an exercise of assertiveness, meaning to say "no" to different pressures of the environment, organizational stereotypes, reactive mental models and manipulative behaviour. Saying a decisive and constant "no" can only occur if there is a previous concrete "yes" to the personal vision that encompasses the important elements of one's life and vocation.

2. *Invest preventively in the Quadrant II*, turning your attention to the discernment, vision fulfillment, relationships care, talent development, study of new opportunities and to the renewal of production capacity. Typical Quadrant II activities are the base for sustainable project management according to the deep transformation paradigm that goes beyond crisis management. Preventive investments help to avoid activism and "fixes that fail" paradox.

3. *Plan weekly involving all your roles* and priorities for each role. Management experts suggest the day is too small a unit to achieve a balanced and holistic investments in all one's roles. A weekly planning, therefore, could be carried out incorporating the vision, identifying the roles, setting priorities for each role, including the investments into the renewal of personal resources.

4.3.4 Abundance Mentality

The virtue of dynamic fidelity creates a mentality needed for sustainable personal leadership and management. The abundance mentality, in a similar way, is the grounding for sustainable caring relationships that build a mutual responsibility in a community. We define it as the mentality and linked attitudes related to a person who recognizes the interrelationships between different persons as an opportunity for synergy. Abundance mentality is built when God's personal love and trust in his providence are experienced in a habitual way. It "flows out of a deep inner sense of personal worth and security. It is the paradigm that there is plenty out there and enough to spare for everybody".[119] The abundance mentality is the opposite to the mentality of scarcity, which leads to reactive behaviour and deep competitive zero-sum mindset. A person with a scarcity mentality deduces their sense of worth from being compared to others, and someone else's success, to some degree, means their failure. Mentality of abundance is also near to Senge's systemic thinking understood as the mentality of seeing the whole rather than separate entities, and the dynamic of change rather than static images of reality.[120]

The Salesian documents do not define directly the mentality of abundance, as if it were automatic for a Christian to think and live according to it. The post-Vatican II terms that recur frequently are sharing, service, shared responsibility, communion, community, experience of the Church, etc. The Educative and Pastoral Community is an important concept that expresses the abundance mentality and occupies a significant place in the structure of the GC21 documents preceding the treatise on the Educative and Pastoral Projects.[121] *The Frame of Reference of Salesian Youth Ministry* states: "Evangelization is always an ecclesial activity. The first key element for realizing Salesian Youth Ministry is the community involving young people and adults, parents and educators in an atmosphere of family, so that it becomes an experience of the Church. It implies a communion whereby the different gifts and services are seen as complementary. There is mutual reciprocity in the service of the same mission".[122] It is interesting to see the authors of the *Frame of Reference* understand that such an EPC "demands a new mature sense of

---

[119] COVEY, *7 Habits*, p. 220.
[120] See SENGE, *Fifth Discipline*, pp. 68-73. For a more detailed description of the two mentalities see L. FREEBAIRN-SMITH, *Abundance and Scarcity Mental Models in Leaders*, ProQuest, Ann Arbor MI 2011.
[121] See *Const.*, articles 44-48; CG21 (1978), n. 62 and GC24 (1996), nn. 61-67.
[122] YM DEPARTMENT, *Frame of Reference*, ³2014, p. 116.

belonging and a new mentality, a new way of thinking, judging and acting, a new way of confronting problems and a new style of
relationships".[123] In the following paragraphs we will develop some basic
traits of this mentality.

Don Bosco's Legacy

The cooperative abundance mentality is evident in Don Bosco's way
of building relationships. The search for cooperation is obvious in the
later years when he was launching a vast movement of persons of different proveniences and vocations for the education of the disadvantaged
and abandoned youth. Most of the times he tried to find a common plat-
form of motivations to promote his projects, appealing both to Christian
values and humanistic principles.

Let us go back in time to see his mentality in its shaping during the
first years of his mission in Turin. Don Bosco, as well as Fr. Cocchi, the
founder of the first oratory in Turin, tried not to put his youth ministry
activities as an opposition to classical ecclesiastical roles. They were
seeking support, cooperation and resources not yet mobilized.[124] An
abundance mentality became a prerequisite for the rise of a new type of
priests who did not identify with a given social status, but united themselves through a common pastoral project for the future. Within this
fledgling group, Don Bosco was trying to keep clear the autonomy of his
work and at the same time to help one another.[125]

At the base of the cooperation and a deep abundance mentality there
is a lived spiritual belief in divine providence that accompanies and
guides human efforts. God provides for the salvation of everyone and
everyone contributes with his work to the building of God's Kingdom.
Don Bosco's combination of hard work and trust in Providence, as we

---

[123] *Idem*, p. 118.
[124] See STELLA, *Don Bosco nella storia economica*, pp. 394-395.
[125] See BRAIDO, *Il prete dei giovani*, vol. 1, pp. 197-199.

CHAPTER 4: INNOVATION 241

have seen in the previous chapter, is a concrete synthesis of dynamic fidelity and abundance mentality.

Internal dynamic

The abundance mentality wants to be a virtue of deep awareness of the value of relationships, trust and the community understood systemically as a whole that is larger than the sum of the individuals and where everyone can find their right place. This virtue is a mentality that precedes cooperation and shared responsibility strategies in educative and pastoral projects. Abundance mentality does not identify itself with the love or charity, it is just a paradigmatic assumption that creates a base for cooperation. In this sense, Antonio Domènech talks about the sense of community as an attitude to be developed during the Salesian pastoral formation.[126]

References to the leadership theories can be summarized in two points: the systemic vision of reality proposed by Senge and Covey's win/win strategy which incorporates concepts of transactional analysis. Senge develops 11 laws of systems thinking[127] that give a good theoretical foundation to Covey's fourth habit "Think Win/Win" which, in turn, enriches Thomas Gordon's transactional scheme.[128] According to Covey, human interactions have six basic paradigms: "Win/Lose" (competitive mentality), "Lose/Win" (losing mentality), "Lose/Lose" (revenge mentality), "I Win" (self-centered mentality), "Win/Win" (mutual benefit

---

[126] See A. DOMÈNECH, *La formazione pastorale salesiana. Atteggiamenti e competenze da sviluppare*, in ACG 87 (2006) 393, 62-63.
[127] See SENGE, *Fifth Discipline*, pp. 57-67.
[128] See P. SCILLIGO, *Gruppo*, in J.E. VECCHI – J.M. PRELLEZO (Eds.), *Progetto Educativo Pastorale. Elementi modulari*, LAS, Roma 1984, pp. 386-398 and T. GORDON, *P.E.T. Parent Effectiveness Training*, P.H. Wyden, New York 1970; ID. – N. BURCH, *T.E.T. Teacher Effectiveness Training*, P.H. Wyden, New York 1974; ID., *Leader Effectiveness Training L.E.T.*, Wyden Books, New York 1977; R. TASSAN, *Leadership & Analisi Transazionale. Come migliorare le proprie capacità manageriali*, Franco Angeli, Milano 2004, pp. 31-54.

mentality), and "Win/Win or No Deal" (realistic mutual benefit mentality).[129] The virtue of abundance mentality gives a grounding to the realistic mutual benefit relationships, which seeks the synergy between people, but also counts with the possibility of no agreement as the best solution in some cases.

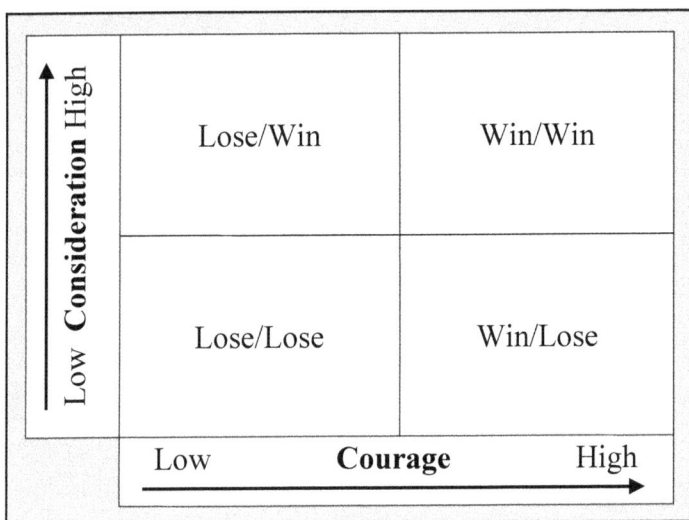

	Lose/Win	Win/Win
High ← Consideration → Low	Lose/Lose	Win/Lose
	Low **Courage** High →	

Scheme O: Cooperative and Competitive Mentality

There is a strong bond between the dynamic fidelity and the mentality of abundance: the integral vision of reality that goes beyond a positivistic, deterministic and mechanistic worldview. The dynamic fidelity surpasses the apparent dilemma between tradition and creativity. The abundance mentality solves instead the seeming negation between "me" and "you". A "win/win or no deal" paradigm is necessary for a SEPP that is designed and carried out with mutual responsibility of the EPC members. A genuine dialogue and praxis cannot exist if the members of the community are rooted in the four scarcity paradigms (win/lose; lose/win; lose/lose; I win). As a maximum result only a debate or discussion can

---

[129] COVEY, *7 Habits*, p. 218.

occur, followed then by individual activities that are coordinated only by force or by appearance. In a scarcity setting, a process of lifelong learning is highly improbable and the intra-communitarian relations are managed as a dynamic of power or as a formal and bureaucratic system. The abundance mentality requires an interior conversion of the EPC members and this way the whole SEPP methodology can be simultaneously a process of personal formation, organizational learning, transformational change, vocational discernment and operative educative and pastoral planning.

Tools and Practices

The abundance mentality can and has to be exercised on many occasions. We offer only a few suggestions:
1. *Explore your beliefs and mentality* using the "Ladder of Inference" by William Isaacs (See Scheme P). This tool helps to analyze the normal process of generalizations, simplifications and hasty inferences that occur naturally in the communication process. First we select data from what we observe; then we add cultural and personal meanings; afterwards we make assumptions linked to the meanings; then we draw conclusions; from them we adopt beliefs about the world; and finally we take actions based on our beliefs.[130]
2. *Grow in multicultural and historical awareness.* Study of other cultures and past times creates an experiential basis for the

---

[130] See P.M. SENGE et al., *The Fifth Discipline Fieldbook. Strategies and Tools for Building a Learning Organization,* Doubleday, New York 1994, pp. 242-246 and P.M. SENGE et al., *Schools That Learn. A Fifth Discipline Fieldbook for Educators, Parents, and Everyone Who Cares About Education,* Doubleday, New York 2000, p. 101-104. See also other tools in T. BENSON – C.S. IMMEDIATO, *Educating the Next Generation of Systems Thinkers: An Interview with Tracy Benson,* in «Reflections. The SoL Journal on Knowledge, Learning and Change» 10 (2011) 4, 13-22.

I take: actions
(based on my beliefs)

I adopt: beliefs
(about the world)

I draw: conclusions

Ladder of Inference

The reflexive loop
(Our beliefs affect
what data we select
next time.)

I make: assumptions
(based on the meanings)

I add: meanings
(cultural and personal)

I select: "data"
(from what I observe)

Observable "data" and ex-
periences (as a video
recording might capture it)

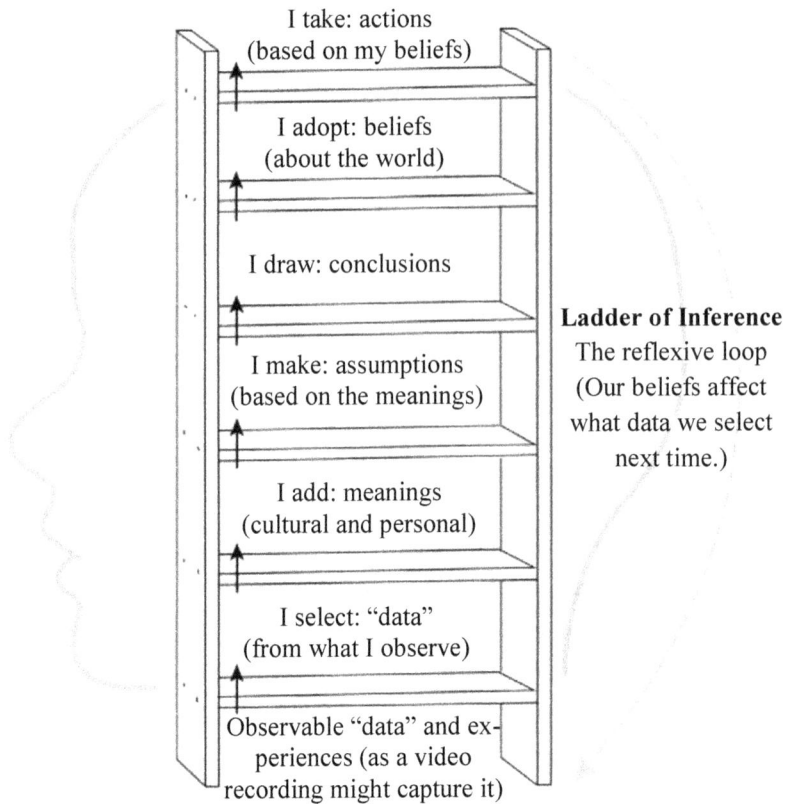

Scheme P: Ladder of Inference

understanding of the other people's paradigms. The historical studies about Don Bosco and the Salesian Youth Ministry applications
in various cultural and historical contexts can be a good start. In
multicultural settings the awareness about different culturally con-
ditioned leadership styles can be useful. Different cultures

understand differently categories like time, loyalty, duty, truth, project, plan, hierarchy, etc.[131]

3. *Build win/win relationships*, growing in mutual trust, which is a concrete expression of abundance mentality and of win/win relationship. Covey advises six main actions that are an investment in trust: understanding the person; attending to little things; keeping commitments; clarifying expectations; showing personal integrity; apologizing sincerely.[132]

4.3.5 Generative Accompaniment

The virtue of the generative accompaniment is built through communication between two or more persons that surpasses the simple exchange of information and generates change in the paradigms and motivations. This type of accompaniment, according to Covey, provides high levels of consideration for other people combined with equally high levels of courage. Consideration for others translates concretely in the ability to listen empathically and courage turns in the ability to clearly express the expectations, requirements and more generally all the aspect of reality involved in the process. Courageous and empathic dialogue has, in the last instance, the goal of creating a shared vision of a community.[133] Scharmer, being inspired by Isaacs, puts an emphasis on the deepening process of dialogue between members of a community. The virtue of

---

[131] See e.g. R.D. LEWIS, *When Cultures Collide. Leading across Cultures*, Nicholas Brealey Publishing, Boston MA ³2005 or A. MOLINSKY, *Global Dexterity. How to Adapt Your Behavior Across Cultures without Losing Yourself in the Process*, Harvard Business School Publishing, Boston MA 2013.

[132] See COVEY, *7 Habits*, pp. 190-199. Stephen M.R. Covey, son of S.R. Covey, offers a more elaborate programme for trusting relationships in S.M.R. COVEY – R. MERRILL, *The Speed of Trust. The One Thing That Changes Everything*, Free Press, New York 2008, pp. 125-232.

[133] See SENGE, *Fifth Discipline*, pp. 191-215.

generative accompaniment highlights the leadership aspect of a community brought together by a shared vision. The management effectiveness will be addressed through the next virtue of synergic integration. The theme of accompaniment is also a central category of the 3rd edition of the *Frame of Reference for Salesian Youth Ministry*. It seems the terms recurring in the previous editions such as communication, dialogue, animation and sharing came together in the accent put on the process of accompaniment. "Every EPC must ensure the promotion and care of the many different ways of animating and accompanying the people. This is why we can speak of an original Salesian style of pastoral accompaniment. We support people at different levels, through the general environment of the EPC, groups, personal relationships and personal guidance".[134] According to Egidio Viganò, the Salesian accompaniment and animation of the community is a synthesis of the capacity for dialogue, the attitude of reciprocity, the ability to listen, discernment of hearts and communication skills.[135]

Don Bosco's Legacy

There are some typical traits of Don Bosco's accompaniment. The main characteristic is the preventive nature of the process. His educative accompaniment is proactive and educational process placed in the area of primary prevention. Therapeutic aspects of an accompaniment intended as cure of bad habits or deviant behaviour come only in a second place. His "Preventive System" is a synergy of protection and promotion of character education through accompaniment of individuals, groups and environment.[136] An excellent example of organizational accompaniment is the building process of the shared vision of the Salesian Congregation. It included personal spiritual accompaniment, dialogue

---

[134] YM DEPARTMENT, *Frame of Reference*, ³2014, p. 122.
[135] See VIGANÒ, *Closing Address*, in GC21 (1978), n. 586.
[136] See M. VOJTÁŠ, *Implicazioni metodologiche del principio religioso nell'educazione salesiana*, in «Orientamenti Pedagogici» 64 (2017) 1, 11-37.

with the traditions of other religious orders, study of legal aspects of a religious order in a liberal state, experimentation with the first committed group, slow process of Constitutions approval, etc.

At a more concrete level, we can focus on Don Bosco's capacity for dialogue and narration. We can find several important dialogues that have affected the progress of his projects. A strong sense of discernment is found in the dialogues with his spiritual directors like Don Maloria in the period of studies in Chieri, and afterwards with Don Giuseppe Cafasso. The dialogue about the future of Don Bosco, as reported in the *Memoirs of the Oratory*, is a turning point in his life. Other examples worth to be mentioned are the paradigmatic educational dialogues with Bartholomew Garelli, Dominic Savio or Michael Magone, or the dialogue with Urbano Rattazzi about the legal form of the Salesian Congregation, to name only a few.[137]

Secondly, we can state that for Don Bosco the dialogue is not only an operational tool, but a paradigm that structures his actions and his thinking. The art of describing meetings, dialogues and dreams reveals a narrative mindset, rather than systematic or abstract. Aldo Giraudo, calling the *Memoirs* "a manual of narrative pedagogy and spirituality", asserts in Don Bosco a strong and structural dialogical frame of mind that prefers a familiar colloquial communication. In fact, the narrated dialogues become generative not only by reproducing an experience, but also by motivating a particular educational style.

Internal Dynamic

The generative type of accompaniment can happen when some basic conditions are met. First of all is the mentality of abundance that "permeates" the community. In such relational environment trusting

---

[137] See G. BOSCO, *Vite di giovani. Le biografie di Domenico Savio, Michele Magone e Francesco Besucco.* Saggio introduttivo e note storiche a cura di Aldo Giraudo, LAS, Roma 2012, pp. 53-55; 115-117 and 120-122.

relationships can be developed. In the second place, a generative dialogue has to be searched as an ideal on the individual and communitarian level.

Abundance mentality would only be a philosophical or theological worldview if it did not permeate the concreteness of the community life. Covey proposes five dimensions of attention in order to build a win/win and trusting environment: win/win character; win/win relationships; win/win agreements; win/win supportive systems and win/win processes (see Scheme Q).[138] Character ethics is the foundation of trusting win/win relationships that can be translated in an organizational setting in win/win agreements where we specify the desired results, guidelines, resources, accountability mode and consequences.[139]

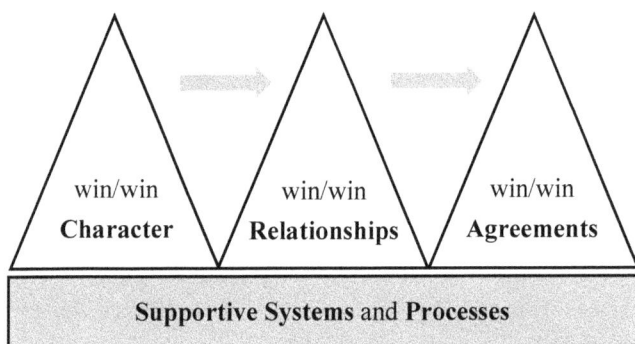

Scheme Q: Supportive Systems and Processes

As a second element, generative dialogue can be searched as one of the highest modes of abundance mentality processes. It happens when the high empathic regard for others is combined with great courage to present one's ideas. The universal principle of "diagnose before prescribing" can be applied as listening that seeks to understand the other

---

[138] See COVEY, *7 Habits*, p. 216.
[139] See COVEY, *7 Habits*, pp. 216-234.

integrally avoiding autobiographical self-centered communication.[140] The *Frame of Reference* reminds us: "The vocation to the service of education requires the ability to question oneself and allow oneself to be questioned on one's deepest convictions, motivations and expectations. Self-knowledge takes away fear and strengthens one's identity".[141] If we do not want to remain only at a level of exhortation, we have to point out some distinctions about different types of conversation and about the fundamental choices connected with the flow of communication.

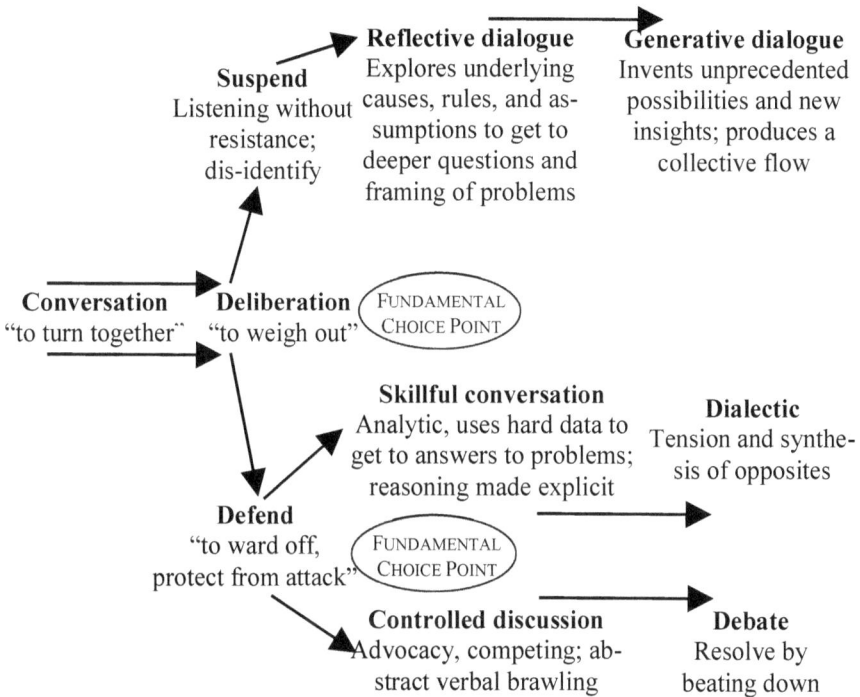

Reflective dialogue
Explores underlying causes, rules, and assumptions to get to deeper questions and framing of problems

Generative dialogue
Invents unprecedented possibilities and new insights; produces a collective flow

Suspend
Listening without resistance; dis-identify

Conversation
"to turn together"

Deliberation
"to weigh out"

FUNDAMENTAL CHOICE POINT

Skillful conversation
Analytic, uses hard data to get to answers to problems; reasoning made explicit

Dialectic
Tension and synthesis of opposites

Defend
"to ward off, protect from attack"

FUNDAMENTAL CHOICE POINT

Controlled discussion
Advocacy, competing; abstract verbal brawling

Debate
Resolve by beating down

Scheme R: Types of Dialogue

---

[140] See Covey's fifth habit "Seek First to Understand ... then to be Understood" in COVEY, *7 Habits*, pp. 235-260. We consider its practical applications too simplistic and fit only to a one-to-one dialogue, not to a community setting.

[141] YM DEPARTMENT, *Frame of Reference*, ³2014, p. 133.

William Isaacs and Peter Senge offer a model of conversational dynamics based on choices participants make (see Scheme R).[142] If people make the first choice to defend themselves, they are assuming to be right and tend to ward off attacks of the others. The chosen defensiveness can be guided in a productive way and will consequently result in a skillful but dialectic conversation with hard data, rigorous argumentation and explicit reasoning in order to solve problems re-actively. If the defensive position escalates in unproductive dynamic, the community finishes in a debate where one wants to defeat the others in a sort of wars. Those do not resolve problems, they generate them by that power dynamic, stereotypes, generalization, shouting, humiliation, etc.

The second scenario opens up if the community, through informal or formal leaders and facilitators, deliberately makes the choice to suspend the judgement not defending contrasting positions. Empathic listening can result in a reflective dialogue where people are willing to think about the rules and assumptions underlying what they think and do. They see more clearly what they have taken for granted, or been doing but not noticing. A genuinely reflective dialogue can give rise to generative dialogue, where we pro-actively begin to create entirely new possibilities and levels of interaction.

A beneficial side-effect of the generative dialogue is the identification with the new shared vision and the new level of relationship ties. Community building is necessary to put the vision into practice and to endure the tension between the current reality and the vision. Probably just a project built with a generative accompaniment dynamic can discern the "vocation" of a community. It brings the benefits listed by Cereda in the motivational part of the Salesian community project: a sense of identity, sense of direction, a sense of communion, sense of responsibility.[143]

---

[142] See W. ISAACS, *Dialogue. The Art of Thinking Together*, Doubleday, New York 1999 and also SENGE et al., *The Fifth Discipline Fieldbook*, p. 361.
[143] See CEREDA, *The Salesian Community Plan* and also Fr. Pascual Chávez Vilanueva's motivations in P. CHÁVEZ VILANUEVA, *Progetto di animazione e governo del Rettor*

Tools and Practices

Any relationship between people, where there is a communication channel, can be a place of growth in generative dialogue. The planning process itself is a good formation opportunity. Animation theory also offers many instruments for the development of communication and accompaniment attitudes.[144] For example, they also suggest other tools, which strengthen one aspect or perspective of the dialogue:

1. *Listen empathically and give feedback*, using both hemispheres of the brain. The effort to comprehend the other person is expressed in the logical and analytical content of the feedback. Understanding is a more integral category that involves emotional, creative, narrative or non-verbal expressions of feedback.

2. *In group, explore different narrations* of the Educative and Pastoral Community members around a concrete issue. The authors of the *Fifth Discipline Fieldbook* propose a narration in the following stages: description of a chronic issue without rushing to conclusions; narration of its historical development; offering explanatory hypotheses; listing the key factors in the narration; drawing an image that represents the underlying dynamic.[145]

3. *Practise the "Two-Column Exercise"*. Think of an accompaniment conversation that captured the moment when you came face-to-face with a significant issue. Take two or three pieces of paper and divide them into two columns. On the right-hand side, write down what you and the other(s) actually said or did in the situation. On the left-hand side of the page write down any thoughts and feelings you might have

---

Maggiore e del suo Consiglio per il sessennio 2002-2008, in ACG 84 (2003) 380, 9-12.

[144] See e.g. M. COMOGLIO, *Abilitare l'animazione. Riflessioni teorico-pratiche sulle competenze dell'animatore*, LDC, Leumann (TO) 1989.

[145] See SENGE et al., *The Fifth Discipline Fieldbook*, pp. 103-108.

had but did not say. Try to understand what happened by linking the content of both columns.[146]

4.3.6 Synergic Integration

As we have seen previously, generative dialogue based on the mentality of abundance is necessary to build an Educative and Pastoral Community around a shared vision. The next step, in a modern rational and voluntarist mindset, would be splitting the vision into dimensions, deduction of objectives, division of roles, planning of activities and interventions. After the operational planning, everyone would execute the assigned tasks and at the end of the project, cycle effectivity would be evaluated. We propose a more integral alternative managerial model.

The virtue of synergic integration is the ability to create sustainably operational wholes (communities, teams, systems) according to a synergic and reinforcing logic. This virtue has a more concrete application in the alignment of managerial systems within the community: system of objectives, communication system, motivational and belief system, system of government and animation roles, financial management and all other formal or informal subsystems. This alignment has two strategies: synergy (cooperation that produces a total effect that is greater than the sum of the individual efforts) and sustainability (investing in people's growth and in resources).

The synergic integration is not based on effectivity motivations, but mainly on a very Salesian ideal of "family spirit" that permeates our living and working together. The *Youth Ministry Frame of Reference* defines the EPC as a community "because it involves young people and adults, parents and educators in a family atmosphere. The thing that unites us is not work or efficiency, but a set of values of life (educational, spiritual, Salesian ...) that form a shared identity willingly accepted by

---

[146] See *Idem*, pp. 235-247.

all".[147] The inspiration and model is the Don Bosco in the Oratory criterion: already "from the early days of the Oratory Don Bosco formed around him a community – a family in which the young people themselves were the key players. He created a youthful environment in which the values of the Preventive System were embodied. There were well-defined spiritual and pastoral characteristics with clear objectives and a convergence of roles designed to suit the needs of the young people".[148]

Don Bosco's Legacy

In the third chapter we have analyzed the synergic integration between leadership and management qualities in the life of Don Bosco. We can go beyond his personal project of life and see briefly how his educative method and the Valdocco Oratory were integrated into one. Pietro Braido agrees with Bartolomeo Fascie, General Councillor and the author of Salesian pedagogy, and asserts that the "one who approaches Don Bosco's education system with the idea of subjecting it to painstaking analysis, dissecting it, dividing it into many parts, rigid patterns, is following the wrong lead. Don Bosco's method of education should be looked at as a living form in its entirety, by studying the principles which gave origin to its life, its bodies, its vitality, and the functions developed from them".[149]

The proximity of integration and generative vitality are confirmed by Stella using the biological term "osmosis" in a broad sense. Don Bosco, his cooperators and the young of the Oratory lived an indelible osmosis which integrated people at Valdocco in a real community. This type of integration was experienced by Don Bosco with an attitude of loving kindness and confidence, lived not only with the people of the Oratory, but also with various categories of people, friends, co-workers, civil or

---

[147] YM DEPARTMENT, *Frame of Reference*, ³2014, p. 118.
[148] *Idem*, p. 117.
[149] B. FASCIE, *Del metodo educativo di Don Bosco. Fonti e commenti*, as quoted in BRAIDO, *Prevention not repression*, p. 122.

religious authorities. Valdocco was an open community that experienced concretely the generativity of open living systems.

Stella speaks about a spiritually based integration at Valdocco and understands the entire educational system of Don Bosco, in his deepest soul, as a spirituality. The education brings educators and students to work together, each in its own way of being, to the saving plan of God.[150]

Management
What do you
do about it?

Mentality
How do you
see reality?

Leadership
Where are
you called
to go to?

	Personal Virtues	*Prosocial Virtues*
Mentality	**1. Dynamic Fidelity**	**4. Abundance Mentality**
Leadership	**2. Call Discernment**	**5. Generative Accompaniment**
Management	**3. Operational Consistency**	**6. Synergic Integration**

Scheme S: Mentality, Leadership and Management Virtues

---

[150] See STELLA, *Don Bosco. Religious Outlook*, pp. 483-487.

Internal Dynamic

The virtue of synergic integration can be lived and practised on three different levels that have different dynamics: personal level, team level and the systems level. Personal integration is a multifaceted issue. At this point, we want to approach it from the point of view of integration around the six operational virtues. In this sense, synergic integration is a special virtue that blends together the others, similarly to Senge's fifth discipline and Covey's eighth habit. It is a final point of a formation cycle that began with the conversion of mentality, proceeded with search for vision within the dimension of leadership, concluding with operational management attitudes. Similarly, it can be said that without the previous virtues the synergistic integration is not possible: without the mentality of dynamic fidelity and abundance (virtues 1 and 4) there is no real vocation and shared vision (virtues 2 and 5) that could guide the operational consistency on the personal and the communitarian level (virtue 3 and 6). The integration of the six virtues also follows a generally accepted principle *inside-out*: the personal change is required before acting to change the community or larger systems.

On the level of team, groups or small communities, it is crucial to practise a generative dialogue in order to find synergic solutions. These consider the good of all (win/win) and through a courageous process that goes beyond compromises and previous alternatives create superior "third solutions". Of course there are real-life situations where a compromise or a no-deal is the best viable solution. The virtue of integration practises synergy when possible, tends to third solutions and develops a sensibility for synergy potential progressively. The synergy in teams is not only a surplus of quality in project management, it is often a necessity in resource shortage situations. In teams, a wise management of talents (natural predispositions) and charisms (gift of the Spirit) is a good beginning of synergic processes.[151]

In organizational settings, everyday systems override rhetorical solutions. If we agree on a shared vision but the systems are designed according to scarcity mentality, nothing significant can happen, only the level of frustration will rise. Covey puts it simply: "alignment is institutionalized trustworthiness. This means that the very principles that people have built into their value system are the basis for designing structures, systems and processes".[152] In scarcity mentality systems not everyone can "win", there is a lack of transparent information and accountability, motivations are personal not shared, differences are a source of conflict not of synergy, etc.

In the Salesian settings, Youth Ministry organizational structures were growing for more than 50 years and the world-wide model has already been set.[153] As we have seen in the first chapter, there are numerous projects, plans and programmes (over 20 to be integrated at the local level), institutions (at the global, regional, provincial and local level), documents (Constitutions, Regulations, directories, manuals, etc.), teams, commissions, councils, chapters, etc. If we add the local Church's hierarchical and collegial structures, plans, NGO projects, governmental legislation, etc., we can gain the impression of a hard-to-manage not synced chaos. With a dose of critical realism, we can state that the official structural level is only an appearance of a system and that many honest and trustworthy persons with a mentality of loyalty are incompetent when it comes to managing. They lose themselves in the bureaucratic complexity and the hidden agendas of informal leaders take over. It seems that synergic solutions in Salesian settings are first of all simplifying and begin with one crucial vision shared by the "animating

---

[151] See e.g. "Called and Gifted" workshops and publications in siena.org.
[152] COVEY, *8th Habit*, p. 235.
[153] See YM DEPARTMENT, *Frame of Reference*, ³2014, pp. 107-111; 119-127; 144-162 and especially 7th Chapter (Activities and Works of Salesian Youth Ministry) and 8th Chapter (Salesian Youth Ministry Animation Structures) in pp. 184-301.

nucleus" patiently implemented in the projects and systems with the "ubiquitous strategy". No new structures are added, only the accompaniment of strategic personnel is reinforced, communication is filled with meaningful content linked to the vision, transparency and correctness criteria are applied. Systems cannot be linked bureaucratically, they have to be loosely coupled with ties based on trust and transparent communication.

Tools and Practices

Preferring Covey's "ubiquitous strategy", which does not create new activities but prefers to implement a new mindset in the existing activities and structures, we offer the following:

1. *Create win/win systems.* First of all, one should know what a real "win" for the other members of the community is. Those objective are often tacit and underlying. Then examine if the systems enable people to execute their top priorities, or they only create roadblocks. Afterwards you can scan if people's real objectives are consistent with the organization's vision and values. Finally, implement small experimental changes and after a successful prototype change the system together as a community.

2. *Search for the third alternative.* For the integration of various points of view, use a three-step process. In the first step check the availability of persons to open up and get in the interaction (abundance mentality), the second step consists in the effort to understand all points of view (generative dialogue) and finally third superior solutions can be proposed (synergic integration). If no solutions are found, return to dialogue or to check the mentality.

3. *Practise mutual accountability.* In collaborative groups there are often monthly or weekly coordination meetings. By applying the three prosocial virtues, the meetings can be managed in a logic of mutual accountability. They consist of these moments: follow-up on everyone's previous commitments; celebration of successes; quick reporting of few

vital issues (important, not urgent); search for third alternatives and new solutions; everyone's proposal of his/her commitment in the direction of the emerged solutions in a logic of mutual accountability.[154]

4.4 Process of an Integral and Transformational Project Management

The Salesian Educative and Pastoral Project methodology started with the *Handout No. 1* produced by Juan Edmundo Vecchi and his team in the Youth Ministry Department in 1978.[155] The planning process proposal did not change substantially in the following years maintaining the structure of three stages: analysis of the situation, operational planning and assessment. The last edition of the *Youth Ministry Frame of Reference* sums up the process:

1. *Analysis of the situation* that consists in careful observation and knowledge of the situation in the locality and of the young people; educative and pastoral interpretation of the situation in the light of the fundamental elements of the Salesian mission; identification of precise options for the future.

2. *Operational planning*: Translation of the precise options into general objectives that are considered the most important, urgent and possible; proposal of procedures through which the general objectives can be put into practice and become operative; setting out practical courses of action, that is activities that are precise, gradual and verifiable.

3. *Assessment* measures the impact of the project on the real situation objectively. It evaluates the results in the light of the proposed objectives, uncovers new possibilities or the needs that emerge and

---

[154] See COVEY, *8th Habit*, pp. 286-288.
[155] See DICASTERO PER LA PASTORALE GIOVANILE, *Progetto Educativo Pastorale. Metodologia*, Sussidio 1, [s.e.], Roma 1978.

determines new steps to be taken. Some important attentions not to be overlooked: involvement of the various interested parties, creation of a real educative and pastoral process, use of precise and measurable indicators, an analysis of the causes that have helped or hindered the process.[156]

As we have seen in the second chapter, this basic method of the SEPP has been influenced by Management by Objectives through the mediation of curriculum planning theories. The analysis-planning-assessment stages are an expression of a rational-analytic mindset that presumes it is possible to describe, plan and assess with precision the whole process of change. We think that the founding experience of Don Bosco in the Oratory and the recent development of organizational models have shown some weaknesses of this planning methodology. For this reason, we offer some updates to the present model that go in the direction of an integral and transformational project methodology.

Our suggestions do not invent a totally new method; we think more in a logic of developing potentially promising ideas from different fields. There are different valuable elements that come either from Don Bosco's organizational experience or from organizational sciences and, last but not least, from the Salesian methodological integrations proposed in the last years. Domènech and his team introduced the concept of "vision" in the second edition of the *Frame of Reference* and enlarged the stage of assessment with an accompaniment processual logic. Through the method of discernment Cereda some new planning stages, such as "God's call" in the GC25 and GC26, or the "interpretation" in the GC27. In the following pages we will start with the fundamental criterion of Don Bosco's experience in order to develop, update and find both a logical and methodological order of the potentially interesting elements that have emerged in the Salesian project management methodology of the past years.

---

[156] See YM DEPARTMENT, *Frame of Reference*, ³2014, pp. 296-298.

4.4.1 Don Bosco's "Project Methodology"

As we have seen before, on the one hand Don Bosco's organizational methods belong to the rural society, and on the other to some dynamic of the industrialized liberal society.[157] We think that Stella's descriptions of the organizational culture of the Oratory, lying between urban and rural life, between the scientific and illiterate worldview, are more a description of Don Bosco's organizational realistic excellence than a limit. His managerial, educational and pastoral "good sense" and the entrusting of important roles more to the young of "good will" than to external "experts", are a sign of his knowledge of the whole. His "project management methodology" was built on the realism of a man close to nature, to young people and to situations which combined rational, emotional, spiritual, social, intuitive, tacit knowledge into a harmonious whole. The generative and synergic fruits of his organizational style and the expansion of his works are a proof of the "knowledge of the whole" and of the dynamic fidelity to his vocation.

If we pass from Don Bosco's general organizational style to his management of single works or projects, some typical traits emerge. A strong visionary leadership, connected to his youth ministry vocation, is clearly foregoing the organizational management aspect. First there is the wandering form of the oratorian activities, then comes the stabilization at Valdocco, experimentation with the boarding facilities of the "Annexed Home", the expansion and only then come the definitive regulations of the 1870s. The Special General Chapter confirms the twofold combination of Don Bosco's dreams (visionary leadership) and Rules of the Oratory (organizational management).[158] The strong grounding in his vocation and in a fundamentally traditional post-Napoleonic Reformation mindset was balanced in a synergic way with his dynamic entrepreneurship, methodological open-mindedness and his distinct ability to

---

[157] See STELLA, *Don Bosco,* p. 61 and BRAIDO, *Prevention not repression*, pp. 154-159.
[158] See SGC (1972), nn. 203-204

motivate others for his vision. More than a contradiction between the tradition and creativity, his organizational synthesis is a dynamic fidelity in action.

Don Bosco's Dream of Nine Years (1825)	Project stage
"A crowd of children were playing there. Some were laughing, some were playing games, and quite a few were swearing. When I heard these evil words, I jumped immediately amongst them and tried to stop them by using my words and my fists".[159]	1. situation analysis - description of facts - symptomatic, quick fix or old solutions emerge
"You will have to win these friends of yours not by blows but by gentleness and love. Start right away to teach them the ugliness of sin and the value of virtue".[160]	2. communitarian interpretation - interpretative dialogue - emotional connection
"This is the field of your work. Make yourself humble, strong, and energetic. And what you will see happening to these animals in a moment is what you must do for my children".[161]	3. embraced vocation - new identity - new mission
"I wasted no time in telling all about my dream [...] Each one gave his own interpretation".[162] "I did what was possible at my age and formed a kind of festive oratory".[163]	4. experimented vision - narration and meaning of the vocation - experiments
Rules of the "Society of a Good Cheer", interiorized rules of the Chieri secondary school and different lists of resolutions.[164]	5. operational guidelines - consolidation of the practice - regulations and guidelines

---

[159] BOSCO, *Memoirs of the Oratory*, p. 18.
[160] *Ibidem.*
[161] *Idem*, p. 19.
[162] *Ibidem.*
[163] *Idem*, p. .
[164] See *Idem*, pp. 32-33; 71-73; 122-123; 144-146; and 172.

Don Bosco's Letter from Rome (1884)	Project stage
Description of the differences between the lively recreation before 1870 and the apathetic one in 1884. "But don't my boys get enough love? ... I have done everything I possibly could for them".[165]	1. situation analysis - description of facts - old solutions emerge
"You see, closeness leads to love and love brings confidence. It is this that opens hearts and the young people express everything without fear to the teachers, to the assistants and to the superiors. They ... will do everything they are asked by one whom they know loves them".[166]	2. communitarian inter-pretation - interpretative dia-logue - emotional connection
"That the youngsters should not only be loved, but that they themselves should know that they are loved ... By being loved in the things they like, ... they are led to see love in those things which they find less attractive".[167]	3. embraced vocation - new identity - new mission
Don Bosco resolves to write his vision in a letter; when he comes home he speaks with the young-sters; discussion of the issue in two council meetings; survey on the state of the Oratory en-trusted to Fr. Bonetti; establishment of a commission; proposals on the assistance of youth or on the 5th grade restructuration.[168]	4. experimented vision - narration, dialogue about the meaning of the vocation - experiments
Change of the Valdocco student section in a small seminar and the reorganization of the lead-ership structure of the Oratory (two directors for the two sections of the house, instead of one).[169] *Scheme T: Don Bosco's Project Methodology*	5. operational guide-lines - managerial decisions - regulations and guidelines

[165] See G. BOSCO, *Due lettere datate da Roma 10 Maggio 1884* in P. BRAIDO (Ed.), *Don Bosco educatore. Scritti e testimonianze*, LAS, Roma ³1997, pp. 373 and 378-380. Translation by P. Laws, with modifications by G. Williams.
[166] *Idem*, pp. 378-379.
[167] *Idem*, pp. 381-382.
[168] See J.M. PRELLEZO, *Valdocco nell'Ottocento tra reale ed ideale (1866-1889). Documenti e testimonianze*, LAS, Roma 1992, pp. 273-276 and 287-307.
[169] See PRELLEZO, *Valdocco nell'Ottocento*, p. 276.

4.4.2 Integral SEPP Methodology

In the current method of the SEPP there are three stages of planning: situation analysis, operational planning and assessment. It seems these have to be updated, taking in account the criterion of Don Bosco in the Oratory, development of the Salesian project management and the paradigm shift of the management-leadership sciences. Some instances can be briefly described in the following way:
- To strengthen the cyclical nature of the project we propose to join the stages of assessment of the previous projects with the stage of **situation analysis** for the new SEPP. If the assessment is an independent stage at the end of a project cycle, it tends to be omitted with the impact of low continuity with the next projects.
- Within the stage of situation analysis, we can see the presence of a singular element - the **interpretation** phase. The importance of the interpretation is emphasized in organizational models and it is seen as an analysis of mental models or paradigms that influence the development and carrying out of the project.[170]
- The stage of the **vocation** or "God's call" was already used in the method of discernment and can be taken into account as a new stage. In this way the project design extends to a spiritually deep discernment. It is not only adopted in various Salesian projects, but also emphasized by Senge – Scharmer in the presencing model and by Vallabaraj – Alberich transformational model speaking not about a call or vocation, but about a "strategic moment" in the planning process.[171]
- There has been an increasing importance of the visionary element, too. The 2nd and 3rd edition of the *Frame of Reference* included the term

---

[170] A special emphasis on the interpretation stage is given also in Alberich and Vallabaraj's transformative catechetics. See E. ALBERICH – J. VALLABARAJ, *Communicating a Faith That Transforms. A Handbook of Fundamental Catechetics*, Kristu Jyoti Publications, Bangalore 2004, pp. 271-273.
[171] See *Idem.*

vision, but the authors had difficulties to collocate it. Cereda states his inspiration from a "vision planning" management for his method of discernment.[172] The vision that involves emotional and motivational elements could be a next stage of the planning cycle.

- The **operational planning** stage has to be maintained in order to bring a concrete and real implications of the vision, although some specific changes have to be made in order to go beyond the Management by Objectives shortcuts and paradoxes.

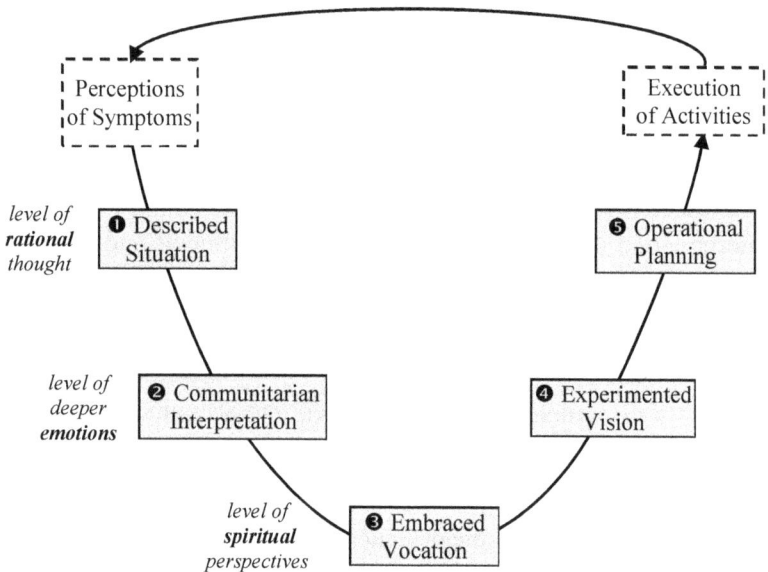

Scheme U: Integral Planning Stages

The five stages of the design will be organized in a "U" form that reflects the different levels of approach to the transformational change

---

[172] See "fcereda@sdb.org to misovojtas@gmail.com" (12. 7. 2012).

planning.[173] In order to propose an integrated model we also connect the five planning stages with the Salesian organizational virtues. The planning process, on the one hand, requires some degree of presence of the virtues and, on the other, we see planning as a process of formation and development of the virtues. (See Scheme V).[174] Planning can be an educational and spiritual transformation journey of the individual members of the CEP and of the CEP as a whole. The management aspect puts attention on the planning outcomes (planning as a product) but we want it to be integrated with the leadership aspect, which emphasizes the personal and communitarian development (planning as a process).

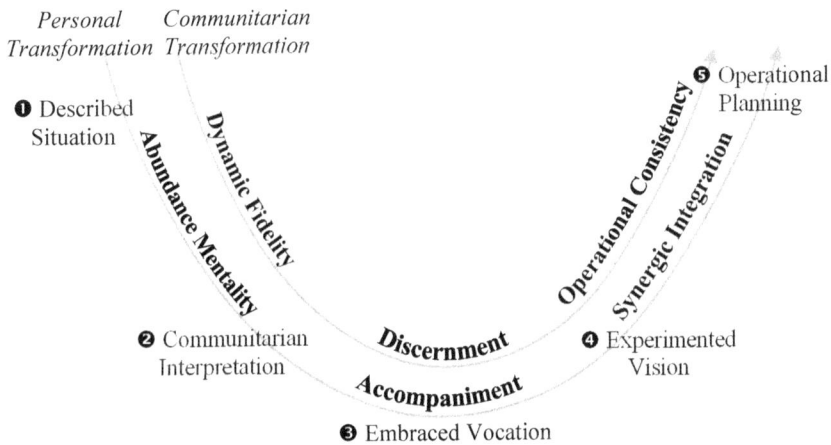

Personal   *Communitarian*
Transformation   *Transformation*

❶ Described Situation

Abundance Mentality

Dynamic Fidelity

❷ Communitarian Interpretation

Discernment

Accompaniment

❸ Embraced Vocation

Operational Consistency

Synergic Integration

❺ Operational Planning

❹ Experimented Vision

Scheme V: Planning Stages and Operational Virtues

---

[173] See Senge and Scharmer's "U process" and Alberich's deep change learning model in SENGE – SCHARMER et. al, *Presence*, pp. 10-12; SCHARMER, *Theory U* and E. ALBERICH, *La catechesi oggi. Manuale di catechetica fondamentale*, LDC, Leumann (TO) 2002, pp. 107-121.

[174] Giuseppe Tacconi, a Salesian scholar of formation in organizational settings sees planning as organizational learning of individuals and of the community. See G. TACCONI, *Alla ricerca di nuove identità. Formazione e organizzazione nelle comunità di vita apostolica attiva nel tempo di crisi*, LDC, Leumann (TO) 2001.

4.4.3 Stage 1: Described Situation

The planning process begins by entering in contact with the current educational and pastoral reality. An increased awareness about the situation is the priority and a desired outcome of this stage of planning. As a second focus, the animator of the planning process should encourage the involvement of all the sub-groups or interest groups within the Educative and Pastoral Community. Every member of the EPC probably has different motivations that can be linked to the curiosity around some issues, the pressure to solve a problem, relational components, the planning seen as a necessary evil of being in the field of the Youth Ministry, etc. The facilitator should not address the different motivations directly, but it is important that he pays attention and makes the involvement grow through his/her choices and interventions. Authentic motivations are vital especially in the next stages of the planning and operating process.

The description of the situation aims to bring out the various types of knowledge present in the EPC. Differently from the *Frame of Reference*, in this stage it is important to keep together the different types of knowledge without rushing to interpretations or objectives. The four-dimension model of the SEPP can be used in order not to forget important issues concerning education, evangelization, the communitarian and vocational dynamic. It is important to assess the impact of past projects at the level of results and processes.

After the assessment, opening the horizons can be useful. Receiving feedback from external learning or youth ministry organizations or experts can break the stereotypes in perception. In Scharmer's language it is stopping the download of old schemes. Learning trips or excursions to different or unfamiliar educational and pastoral realities can have the same impact. We consider as a standard to receive feedback from stakeholders, especially from the young people's parents or from the alumni. The task of "knowing" the situation clearly highlights the rational intelligence rather than the emotional or spiritual intelligences that will be more important in the next stages. The following types of knowledge can be emphasized:

- Historical knowledge of the environment, the Salesian presence and the EPC;
- Assessment of the previous SEPPs;
- Sociological and demographic situation of the young;
- Current cultural trends that influence the education and pastoral care;
- Educational and pastoral policies that affect the youth ministry;
- Management of resources and knowledge of the EPC's limits;
- Intuitive knowledge about causal connections in the educative and pastoral reality;
- Narrative knowledge of the success stories and failures in a learning perspective.

4.4.4 Stage 2: Communitarian Interpretation

After the description of the situation, educational and pastoral interpretation has to follow. The description offers different, and not yet aligned, inputs on the youth situation. The methodology of the description is based on openness, on accumulation of data and on holding of different themes and different types of knowledge with their tensions. An interpretation is not only a rational criticism, comparison, interpretation or hermeneutics of the facts, but it also strengthens the emotional involvement, because the paradigms that are interpreted are connected with the emotional experience of the EPC members. Our paradigms or habitual mental models can be analyzed under two points of view. First come the paradigms that underlie the educational and pastoral action and as second those mental patterns underlying the description of the situation of the young can be scrutinized. There are, therefore, operative and cognitive paradigms. The access and understanding of them is fundamental because without a paradigm shift planning, we do not pursue a transformative change, but only a transitional one.

In order to interpret the situation and analyze the shared paradigms we need a dual cognitive and emotional movement. The first moment of lesser identification with our paradigms can be called with Scharmer "stop downloading". It describes an *epoché* dynamic that shifts people's perceptions of themselves to the border between the observer and the observed.[175] In this detached position we seek to clarify the questions and fundamental intentions regarding the educational and pastoral reality. Besides the virtue of dynamic fidelity, virtue of discernment comes already in play as we operate judgments of value and importance around various elements present in the situation. Some of the paradigms linked to the Gospel and Salesian values have a major importance as criteria of interpretation. It does not mean, however, that our paradigms of faith and the Salesian charism have no need to be purified and updated. In the interpretation stage it is better to leave behind the four-dimension model, because it could leave aside some fundamental challenges concerning the whole. A growing awareness of the whole attitude is to be cultivated by the animator of the process. The establishment of the main challenges, recommended by the second edition of the *Frame of Reference*,[176] does not mean to produce a list of unrelated facts, but to create a shared prioritization of interconnected issues. The systemic issues, like lack of trust or blocked communication that cause other smaller symptomatic problems have a higher priority in our point of view than visible problems of quotas, statistics or public image of single YM leaders.

A second cognitive moment can take place after the community has taken some distance from itself and can see its shared paradigms with a new look. These can be myths about how ministry functions, theological concepts used as magical formulae without a shared understanding, some

---

[175] See influences of Husserl's phenomenology in SCHARMER, *Theory U*, p. 129.
[176] YM DEPARTMENT, *Frame of Reference*, ²2000, pp. 171. Authors of the third edition skip the identification of challenges and go directly to the selection of "precise options". See YM DEPARTMENT, *Frame of Reference*, ³2014, p. 297.

operative mental shortcuts such as: "if we plan it, we will do it" or "define roles and tasks and the YM ministry will produce results", etc. Here begins the deeper journey of an EPC that differs from the classic Management by Objectives logic. Overcoming the rational debate and evidence-based discourse, a genuine dialogue is required in order to make a paradigm shift to a more enlightened understanding of the situation that will bring clarification or a possibility of change of the question.[177] Following Scharmer we could speak of moving in a significant real context where we can find sketches of new responses and begin to wonder.[178] Learning journeys to new youth, educational and pastoral contexts or institutions can be a good stimulus to see the situation with a new and deeper awareness.[179]

In an atmosphere of genuine vulnerability, the community members can act according to the abundance mentality and put into practice the generative dialogue understood as "seeing together" (Scharmer) and as "thinking together" (David Bohm and William Isaacs). The two cognitive moments described before (distance from itself, new look) should favor the passage through the first crisis of dialogue, where the community is called to leave aside discussion and debate, as less productive forms of interaction. In this way, the community moves from a conversation to a reflective dialogue, where deeper issues and underlying paradigms emerge.

The community, especially the animator of the process, has to stand the emotional frustration connected with the loss of secure and certain positions. The ideas and beliefs cease to be absolute. There is no clarity to be taken for granted at the level of vision, theories, management or leadership solutions. Uncertainty is a price to be paid in the logic of trust

---

[177] See ALBERICH – VALLABARAJ, *Communicating a Faith That Transforms*, p. 271.
[178] See SCHARMER, *Theory U*, pp. 133-135 e 245-246.
[179] See *Going on Learning Journeys*, in J. JAWORSKI – A. KAHANE – C.O. SCHARMER, *Presence workbook. A companion guide of capacity-building practices, practical tips, and suggestions for further reading from seasoned practitioners* in allegrosite.be/artikels/Presence Workbook.pdf (accessed 1.1. 2017).

in Providence, so strong in various periods of Don Bosco's life that they brought him to "solutions" at qualitatively new levels of leadership or management. In this sense we understand that "listening to the Scriptures and prayer are the context and the parameters within which the planning process takes place and through which it then becomes a real spiritual experience for the community. Docility to the Spirit creates the conditions necessary to be open to the Gospel and to life, so as not to get lost in the face of uncertainties and mistakes, but to be always ready for renewal and conversion".[180] The communitarian interpretation is the stage of planning that allows the EPC to interpret the situation, seeing the deeper interrelationships with a new awareness. The importance of the "process" at this point is greater than the attention to the "result". Therefore, a genuine dialogue at this point can be pursued only in an environment of mutual trust and confidence in God's plan. The third component of "identity" will be the strong point of the next stage.

4.4.5 Stage 3: Embraced Vocation

The reception of vocation is a planning stage that heightens the importance of the planning process and of the identity (communitarian leadership) compared to the attention to the results (task and structures management). At this moment the EPC discerns the direction and does not walk the path, as illustrated in Scheme W. The stage of embraced vocation is a procedural translation of the primacy of God, the author of the Salesian vocation and mission.[181] The dynamic of a deep community discernment involves a recognition of God's supremacy through two passive steps described by Scharmer. The first step is the "letting go" of unwanted issues, barriers between people and paralyzing paradigms about the reality and the future. This prepares a second step of "letting

---

[180] See CEREDA, *Salesian Community Plan.*
[181] See *Cost.*, articles 1; 2; 3; 20; 26 and GC21 (1978), n. 16; 31. See also references to "god" in a vocational setting in SENGE – SCHARMER et al., *Presence*, pp. 222-225 and SCHARMER, *Theory U*, p. 190.

come" a new future that emerges through the community and that has to be embraced as a new vocation.[182]

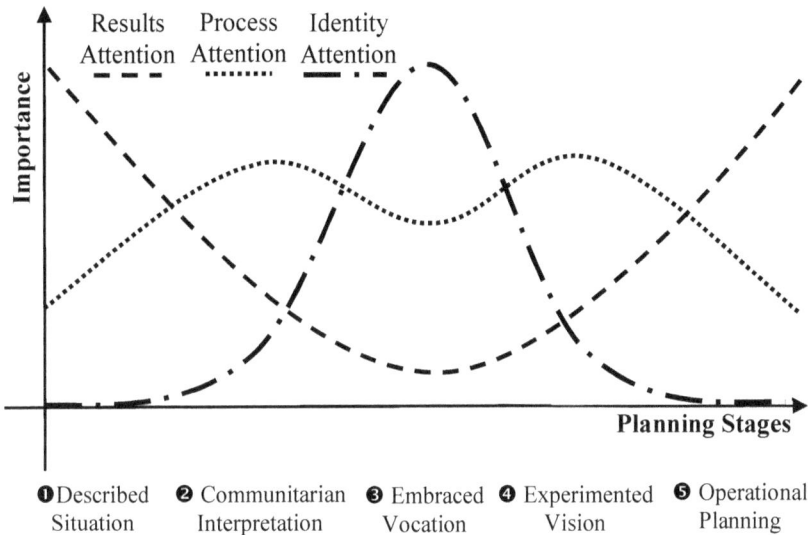

Scheme W: Results – Process – Identity Attention

At the level of dialogue in the community, the moment of receiving the vocation requires a transition to the third level of generative dialogue that involves certain attitudes. The quality to think as a community involves every person that is communicating as a part of the whole. It implies a new empathic sensitivity that finds new "thin threads" which weave together narration themes neglected before. In this way, dialogue generates new prospects and scenarios without trying to find definitive operational solutions. The quality and depth of the dialogue, in a very high level of trust, guides the participants through a "crisis of collective pain"[183] in which the imperfection of each proposal, of each expression

---

[182] See SCHARMER, *Theory U*, pp. 163-190.
[183] David Bohm's description is quoted in SENGE et al., *The Fifth Discipline Fieldbook*, p. 363.

and the poverty of words and signs is felt. "The net of words may not be fine enough to capture the subtle and delicate understandings that begin to emerge; the people may fall silent. Yet the silence is not an empty void, but one replete with richness".[184]

Through this spiritual and transformational stage, a new level of awareness and identity of the community is perceived. It is necessary to remain in the discernment position for a certain time and not to rush towards the operational issues of objectives, strategies, tasks. Building a new identity is crucial not only for planning but especially for the SEPP execution in the everyday ordinary reality. It is vital that the EPC sees itself as participating in a mission that exceeds each of the members and is bigger than the community.[185] Embracing a communitarian educative and pastoral vocation exercises the personal virtue of call discernment and also the generative accompaniment of the whole process at the community level. A critical number of key community members should know how to discern in their own lives, to know themselves, their stereotypes and their own defense mechanisms in order to build a communitarian discernment through generative dialogue.

Embracing a new vocation is close to Scharmer's concept of "running towards an emerging future", to Senge's *metanoia* that means transformative learning, or to Alberich's profound transformation that consists in taking an all-encompassing central attitude linked to a new identity.[186] In this stage, Jaworski and Scharmer invite the community members to share, not ideas, interpretations or analysis, but profound stories of personal transformation. It is not required to formulate the vocation in a definitive way. The linguistic development of a vision that is linked with the vocation comes in the next stage and there is a concrete reason for this delay. Verbalization or narration of the vocation in a form of vision

---

[184] *Ibidem.*
[185] We find interesting Maslow's argumentation about excellence of groups in which identity and mission are identified. See A. MASLOW, *Eupsychian Management*, in SENGE, *Fifth Discipline*, p. 194.
[186] See ALBERICH, *La catechesi oggi*, p. 136.

is always an action of distinguishing, making choices and introducing different stories, metaphors, symbols, references, etc. The community needs to hold the new identity linked to the emerging future in a meta-logic communication. For this to happen the community has to take care of the physical, temporal and relational spaces for deep listening, contemplation and generative dialogue. Obviously there is also the risk of an exaggerated spiritualistic dynamic that can separate the community from the surrounding reality and from a healthy reasonableness of faith and vocation. But we think that in the actual Salesian settings, the problem is an opposite one – superficial, formal, sterile or repetitive planning with a lot of meetings that badly needs leveled-up discernment processes.

4.4.6 Stage 4: Experimented Vision

After the acceptation and identification with the vocation, the next stage is the vision development and making small experimentations in the direction of the emerging vision. The vision in the method of discernment "is only describing how this community should be, not what it needs to do. And it is important that the community's projection of itself into the future, which emerges from what is said by everyone, be not a cold, cerebral thing but something to make all the members of the community enthusiastic. It is something to attract them, to encourage them, and that is realistic; it responds to their wishes and to their expectations; it points to what could be the result of everyone's efforts and sacrifices".[187] There are some characteristic features a vision should have; it:
- refers to the emerging future in between actual problems and a distant utopia;
- talks about being a community more than managing objectives;
- uses a positive and stimulating narration in order to inspire enthusiasm;

---

[187] See CEREDA, *The Salesian Community Plan.*

- responds to the expectations of the people involved because it is a fruit of generative dialogue
- expresses a general strategy or philosophy of action that will align the community and will accompany the operational planning stage.

The chosen leadership models enrich the vision creation with two typical traits of the Salesian charism: narration and experimentation. Once we find ourselves past the paradigm of a technical plan that works in a deductive way, we have to integrate these two focuses. The first is the implementation of various narrative or symbolic languages in order to emphasize the emotional component of the planning process. The vision is a connecting stage between the calling and operation. Therefore, it is important to encourage artistic and narrative expressivity to create a whole interpretive context in which both the vocation and operative planning is located. Following Senge's principle, the focus should not be put in a correct formulation: "It's not what the vision is, it's what the vision does".[188] In their publications, Senge, Scharmer and Covey illustrate the theoretical leadership and management principles through the real-life stories, case studies or success stories. Often these are not only a way to make the content more attractive or readable, but build a framework within which the fairly general principles gain their importance and concreteness.[189] The relationship and the balance between the narrative pedagogy and project-based pedagogy is to be remembered in educational praxis of Don Bosco. The vision narrated through biographies, memoirs, stories or dreams is completed with the concrete regulations, division of roles and tasks.[190] A formulated vision is not only a document,

---

[188] P.M. SENGE et al., *The Necessary Revolution. How Individuals and Organizations Are Working Together to Create a Sustainable World*, Doubleday, New York 2008, p. 324.

[189] See B. JACKSON, *Management Gurus and Management Fashions. A Dramatistic Inquiry*, Routledge, London 2001 and D.A. JAMESON, *Narrative Discourse and Management Action*, in «The Journal of Business Communication» 38 (2001) 4, 476-511.

[190] See P. BRAIDO, *Il progetto operativo di Don Bosco e l'utopia della società cristiana*, LAS, Roma 1982, pp. 6-7.

it is a learning environment built by narratives, stories, symbols and theories that imply a concrete organizational learning culture.[191]

A second connection between the vision creation and experimentation or testing is offered by Scharmer. Integrating the lean management core theory in the Theory U, he proposes the "crystallization" of the vision that clarifies, shares and expands the intentionality born within the vocation. The "prototyping" stage applies the nascent vision instantly in small protected microcosms where the interaction between practice and vision is experimented. Small educational and pastoral experiments offer an early feedback on understanding the vision. Moreover, these prepare the operational planning stage realistically and preventively. It is important that experiments are flexible, not too complex and can be realized in short execution times. In order to enlarge their impact on the whole EPC afterwards, it is important not to bias the prototypes with a link to small elite groups guided by charismatic leaders. Creating the vision is the desired outcome of this stage of educational and pastoral planning. It constitutes the contact point between leadership, accentuated with virtues of discernment and generative accompaniment, and management, consisting in the virtue of operational consistency and synergic integration.

4.4.7 Stage 5: Operational Planning

Speaking about a traditional SEPP, the operational planning is the most typical stage of project creation. The Salesian Youth Ministry *Frame of Reference* proposes the following:
"1. Translation of the precise options into general objectives that are considered the most important, urgent and possible. These objectives lead on to clear proposals taking into account the people in the EPC and the innate effectiveness of the four dimensions of youth ministry.

---

[191] See e.g. E.H. SCHEIN, *Organizational Culture and Leadership*, Jossey-Bass, San Francisco ³2004.

2. Proposal of some procedures through which the general objectives can be put into practice and become operative.

3. Setting out practical courses of action, that is activities that are precise, gradual and verifiable. In these the following are clarified: the group aimed at (for whom?); the responsibilities of the different individuals or teams (by whom?); the employment of the resources available and the time scale (how and when?)".[192]

In the integral perspective we want to go beyond the traps of Management by Objectives and give more importance to the systemic view on the project, objectives and the organization. In our point of view, operational effectiveness of a SEPP is not pursued primarily through organization of activities and events. Therefore, the more or less linear attention to the activities and results related to the virtue of operational consistency is balanced with systemic attention to the virtue of synergic integration.

The modern anthropology that is rationalistic (define objectives) and voluntaristic (carry out activities) is integrated with a more holistic view on the man. The SEPPs of the 1980s had a technical focus on the establishment of precise objectives and interventions. Now the main attention is shifted to the balance between the linear operation and the alignment of the organizational systems according to the vision and vocation. Some tools are offered by Covey's *Leader in Me* and Senge's *Schools That Learn*, who propose an implementation of the vision in various systems: organizational structure, communication systems, didactics, training, tutoring and motivational, economic, IT systems.[193] The systemic perspective is given importance also by Salesian scholars. Pellerey and Grządziel insist on the integration of a linear project with building a relational atmosphere and environment with a narrative perspective. Alberich and Vallabaraj propose the balance between the objectives and

---

[192] YM DEPARTMENT, *Frame of Reference*, ³2014, p. 297.
[193] See the systemic structure of the publication by SENGE et al., *Schools That Learn* and also COVEY, *Leader in Me*, pp. 71-89; 173-179.

activities logic with the alignment of the learning, organizational and financial system.[194]

The alignment of organizational systems in itself is not only a one-time decision of adjustment. Taking seriously the systemic paradigm and synergistic integration virtue, it is rather the constant search for synergy between the various systems and the vision. The vision is not simply implemented, because it is not formulated in a structured and operative way. The vision is more linked to questions, focuses and internal motivators that the community can use for the search of contact points and mutual enrichment situations. We could say that the EPC does not implement the vision, but its logic, values and aspirations.

Operational planning could finish here, but there is the whole question of "execution" that is fairly complicated if we abandon the modern anthropology where everything is clear. Execution is a continuous process of operative attention and evaluation motivated by the creative tension between the vision and the current reality. The processual aspect of execution is also present in the last pages of the *Frame of Reference*: "the creation of a real educative and pastoral process [has not to be overlooked]. It should not be limited to examining the results, but rather to reawakening the individual and community maturing processes, encouraging, improving and providing motivation for better results".[195]

The close link between the results (objectives and activities) and the process (daily running routines) is important for the leadership models. Senge has dedicated the team learning discipline to the link between learning and practice and to overcoming of the defensive routines. Covey introduced the term of the Execution Quotient (XQ) that measures the

---

[194] See M. PELLEREY – D. GRZĄDZIEL, *Educare. Per una pedagogia intesa come scienza pratico-progettuale*, LAS, Roma ²2011, pp. 112-113 and 203-270 and ALBERICH – VALLABARAJ, *Communicating a Faith That Transforms*, p. 273.

[195] YM DEPARTMENT, *Frame of Reference*, ³2014, p. 298. N.B. We think that the collocation of this processual logic in the stage of assessment could be counterproductive, because the EPC has to evaluate only at the end if a process has been put in place. In the planning stage no mention of processes is found.

collective ability to focus and execute and he carried out an empirical study on a sample of 2.5 million people. Scharmer speaks about execution as a spiral movement between learning, commitment and doing.[196] Covey offers the "triage reporting" as a crucial instrument for mutual accountability about the execution of the project. In triage meetings on a weekly or monthly basis each team member reports quickly on the few vital issues of his field of responsibility and previous commitments, preferring the focus on importance not on urgency. Next, the community can focus on the synergy by searching for third alternative solutions emerging from the current reality. Finally, everyone takes a commitment in order to carry out the proposals. Triage meetings are an application of systemic and synergistic execution logic in the daily practice of the project, as people take responsibility in front of the team and later report to it.[197]

4.4.8 Application of the SEPP Integral Methodology

In the preceding pages we have presented the five stages of a full project cycle. We are aware, however, that the full realization of all the stages is neither a simple nor a technical management task. It involves interdependence of many people, it requires an ethical, psychological and spiritual maturity and, last but not least, quite a few resources of the EPC's time, motivation, organizational resources, leadership capacity, etc. The leadership authors offer a good number of examples of integral project management that were developed in a time span of years and implemented in long processes that, in some cases, exceeded a decade.[198]

---

[196] See SENGE, *Fifth Discipline*, pp. 216-252; COVEY, *8th Habit*, pp. 289-290; 369-373 and Scharmer, *Theory U*, pp. 216-218.
[197] See COVEY, *8th Habit*, pp. 286-288.
[198] See e.g. SENGE et al., *The Fifth Discipline Fieldbook*, pp. 366-373; COVEY, *7 Habits*, pp. 16-44; 86-88; 103-106; 309-318; SENGE, *Fifth Discipline*, pp. 253-376; SCHARMER, *Theory U*, pp. 32; 122-126;136-147; 192-195 and 203-205.

We have started our innovative approach with references to the criterion of "Don Bosco in the Oratory". It is right to conclude in the same manner. The development of different projects in Don Bosco's life was also a multi-year process with paradigm shifts, specific calls, experimentation and implementation. As examples we can refer to the project of the Festive Oratory from the late 1841 where he began meeting the first boys to 1852 when Don Bosco stabilized the Oratory model as the Director of the three Turin Oratories. Another project of the Salesian boarding school education took place in the decade between 1853 and 1863. In those years Don Bosco consolidated the Oratory schools and vocational training facilities, and the educational experience with Savio, Magone and Besucco developed a tension towards holiness as the final aim of youth ministry. The founding of the Congregation is a good example of a non-linear project. More than two decades of constant project development challenged Don Bosco's leadership and management virtues and included many paradigm shifts, experimentations and negotiations. Another type of project is the model of the Salesian missions in Latin America. The missionary idea started in 1864 with an inspirational visit of the African missionary Daniele Comboni at the Valdocco Oratory. The project idea grew until 1875 when the first expedition took place and developed further in the 1880s as the model took its dual shape. The first form under the leadership of Giovanni Cagliero developed boarding schools in the missionary territory (focusing especially on Patagonia). The second form, with Giuseppe Fagnano as the protagonist, founded reductions where Salesians took care of an entire population (mostly in Tierra del Fuego).[199]

The SEPP developed in the restructuring after the Vatican II has instead fixed project schedules. The choice was influenced by time

[199] See J. BORREGO (Ed.), *La Patagonia e le terre australi del continente americano [pel]sac. Giovanni Bosco,* in «Ricerche Storiche Salesiane» 13 (1988) 255-442 and D. COMBONI, *Escritos,* Mundo Negro, Madrid 1996, pp. 821-822.

schedules of the school or pastoral year, the three-year period of the leadership of a Salesian Rector, or the six-year period for the General Council. In this sense, the timing of the project is linked to the management structures and not to time periods required by the nature of the different projects. We have seen the projects of the 1980s that suffered too short implementation times or nominalistic projects that focused on the correct vocabulary in the 1990s, etc. Projects linked to the three or six years of the usual governance periods have the implicit risk of no continuity and so every rector or council begins their projects anew. Senge's archetypes of the symptomatic solution and of the erosion of objectives are a good description of a recurrent project management dynamic in Salesian settings.

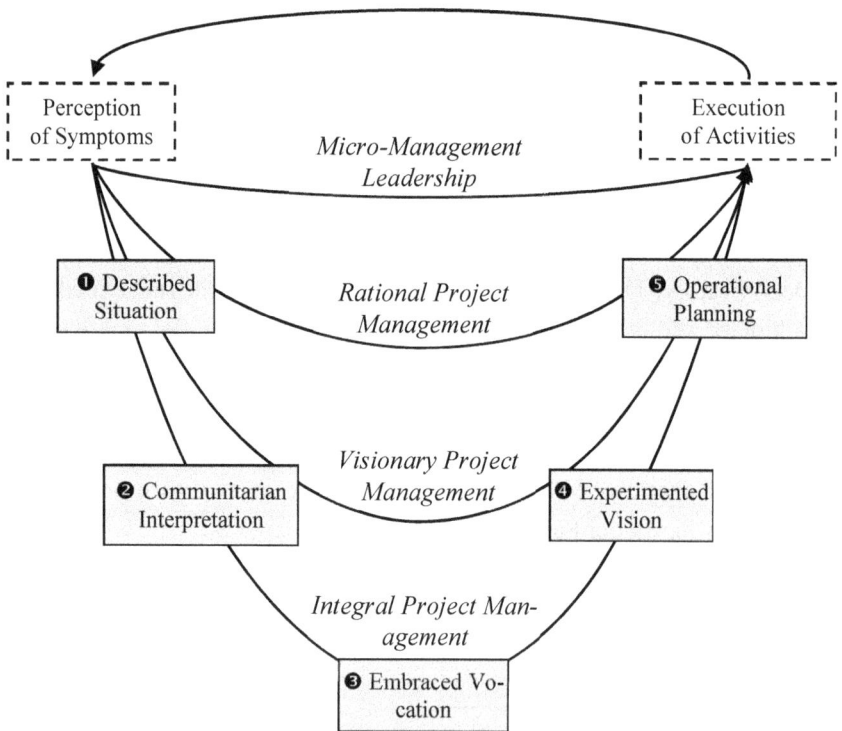

Scheme X: Application of the SEPP Integral Methodology

To make a more realistic proposal, we will introduce four types of project management that respect the demands of the real challenges and of the Educative and Pastoral Community situation (Scheme X):

1. *Micro-management leadership*, which does not imply any kind of real projects. The leaders' decisions are based on the personal perceptions of symptoms and tend towards an immediate execution of the orders. Almost every decision is made by the leader;

2. *Rational project management*, which is similar to the curriculum design theories of the 1960-70s. A rational analysis of the situation determines the needs and then switches directly to operational planning, establishing objectives, interventions and activities which are executed afterwards;

3. *Visionary project management* that deepens the description of the situation with an interpretation in order to get to a stimulating and positive vision of the future that fuels the next stage of operational planning;

4. *Integral project management*, proposed in the presented chapter. It is centered in the integration of rational, emotional and spiritual dimension and its central stage is the discernment of the vocation of the whole Educative and Pastoral Community.

The described project management types are more or less suited to different situations and to the EPC's levels of maturity. We propose the ideal of integral project management, but considering the principles of realism and of the graduality of the human growth, we see the necessity of less integral solutions adapted to the context. It resembles Don Bosco's principle of "the better is enemy of the good". It is an Italian proverb used by Don Bosco to indicate the realistic necessity to do the good in any setting, without waiting to have better or ideal conditions.[200]

In a situation of crisis, conflict or danger of total anarchy, where there is no real EPC, it is understandable and necessary that the hierarchical

---

[200] See the concluding section of Braido's biography of Don Bosco called "The desire for the excellent and the search for the possible good" in BRAIDO, *Don Bosco prete dei giovani*, vol. 2, pp. 680-683.

(or charismatic) leadership takes immediate decisions. However, perpetuating this micro-management style for a long time leads to non-productive patterns of thought and action. Management action is reactive and without a long-term vision or the vision is linked directly to the leader that does not favor the creation of an EPC. If there is an EPC, it is often either formal or built by loyal people close to the leader.

Where there is an EPC that works well on a practical and a professional level in a structure without alarming symptoms, the rational project management is generally adopted. The skillful conversation likely leads to compromises produced with a democratic mindset. There is generally a good working environment, but it lacks the sense of community, a shared vision or vocation. In order to grow as a community, it is suitable that the leader or the process facilitator proposes deeper dialogues and tries to question some of the unproductive paradigms. In this way the whole planning can be a formative process and can increase the maturity of the involved people building mutual trust in the EPC.

An Educative and Pastoral Community with a good level of trust and reflective dialogue can venture into the visionary project management. It is an investment both in the quality of community relationships within the EPC and in the operational effects of a vision that creates an interpretive framework for objectives, activities and actions. There are multi-religious or agnostic contexts, where a discernment of the vocation can be difficult. In those settings two paths can be followed. The first is to propose a deeper stage of embraced vocation to the core of the EPC. The second proposal can be to see the vocation as a universal human experience and build on the processes described by Scharmer and Senge.

There are situations where an integral project management is required: after many years of rational planning; after substantial changes in the current reality or in the group dynamic within the EPC; after a change of persons in key leadership positions, or after some significant achievements or failures. If there is a real potential to do so, it is optimal to start the whole planning cycle in all five stages.

In all situations, where the EPC is not able to adopt the integral project management, it is advisable to create integral planning experiences in small teams, such as the animating nucleus of the EPC. In this way the "inside-out" principle is followed and the quality change is diffused from small systems to larger ones; from the person to the group and finally to the community. Even where the impact of such small experiences could be limited on an operational level, one should not underestimate the formational potential of integral planning that can lead to deepening of faith, to spiritual conversions and, last but not least, to the maturation of operational virtues.

Appendix 1 – SDB General Chapters (1958-2014)

Year	Rector Major	Members	Days	Topic
GC27 (2014)	Ángel Fernández Artime	253	50	Work & Temperance
GC26 (2008)	Pascual Chávez Villanueva	222	50	Da Mihi Animas Cetera Tolle
GC25 (2002)	Pascual Chávez Villanueva	231	51	Salesian Community Today
GC24 (1996)	Juan Edmundo Vecchi	208	62	Salesians & Lay People
GC23 (1990)	Egidio Viganò	205	62	Education to Faith
GC22 (1984)	Egidio Viganò	186	120	Renewed Constitutions
GC21 (1977/8)	Egidio Viganò	184	103	Evaluation & Perspectives
GCS (1971/2)	Luigi Ricceri	202	206	New Constitutions
GC19 (1965)	Luigi Ricceri	151	53	Adaptation & Renewal
GC18 (1958)	Renato Ziggiotti	119	13	Religious Observance

Appendix 2 – Theories, their Relations and Evolution

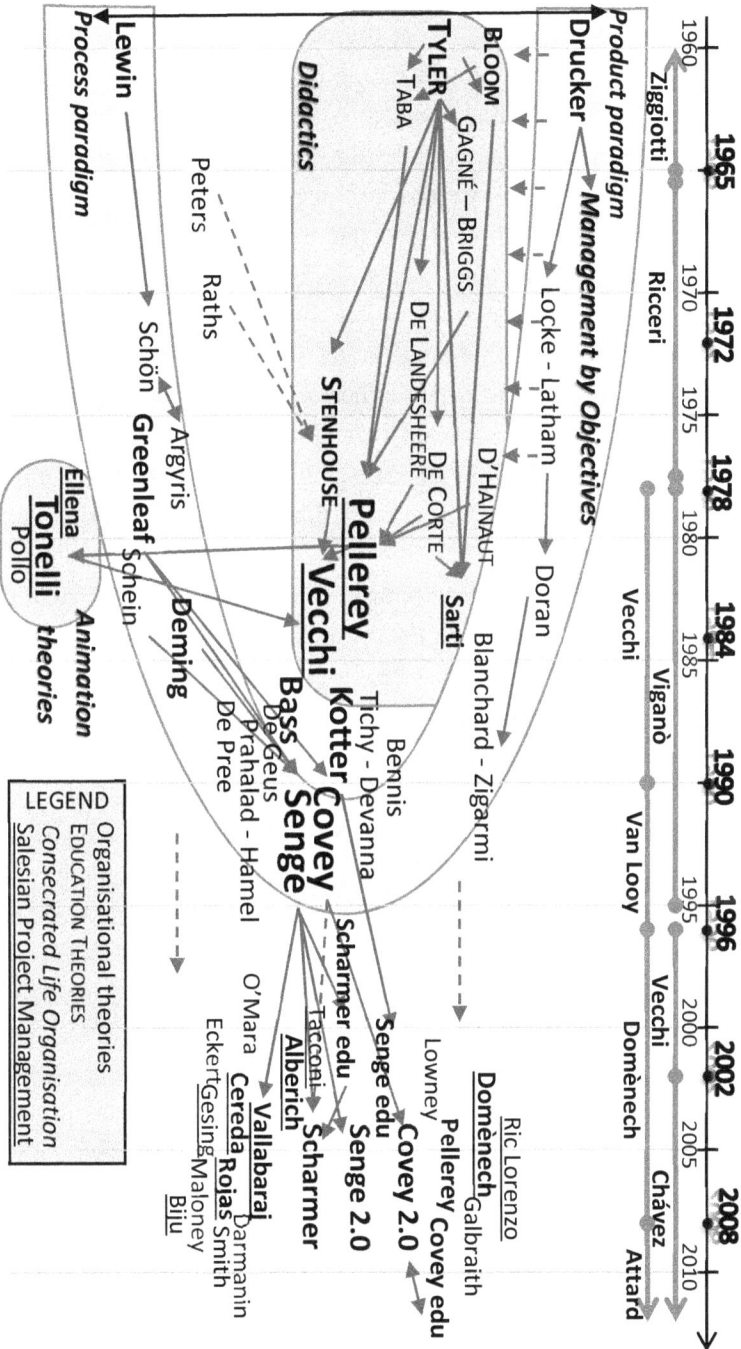

Timeline: 1960 · 1965 · 1970 · 1972 · 1975 · 1978 · 1980 · 1984 · 1985 · 1990 · 1995 · 1996 · 2000 · 2002 · 2005 · 2008 · 2010

Ziggiotti · Ricceri · Vecchi · Viganò · Van Looy · Vecchi · Domènech · Chávez · Attard

Process paradigm
Lewin

Product paradigm
Drucker — *Management by Objectives*
Locke - Latham
D'HAINAUT → Doran
Blanchard - Zigarmi

Didactics
TYLER
BLOOM
TABA
GAGNÉ – BRIGGS
DE LANDESHEERE
DE CORTE
STENHOUSE
Sarti
Pellerey
Vecchi

Peters · Raths · Schön · Argyris · Schein · Greenleaf

Ellena
Tonelli
Pollo

Deming
De Geus
Prahalad - Hamel
De Pree
Tichy - Devanna
Bennis
Bass
Kotter
Covey
Senge

Scharmer edu
Senge edu
Senge 2.0
Covey 2.0
Ric Lorenzo
Domènech Galbraith
Lowney
Pellerey Covey edu

O'Mara
Vallabarai
Cereda Rojas
Alberich
Scharmer
Tacconi
Eckert Gesing Maloney Smith Darmanin
Biju

Animation theories · **Consecrated Life Organisation** · **Salesian Project Management**

LEGEND
Organisational theories
EDUCATION THEORIES
Consecrated Life Organisation
Salesian Project Management

Appendix 3 – Feedback from a Pilot Project

The community of Borgo Ragazzi Don Bosco in Rome is a complex work involving three educational areas: A Vocational Training Center, an Oratory and a work for unsettled youngsters called "Put the Wings Back". In 2010, the community embarked on a difficult path of designing a shared Educative and Pastoral Project that would integrate the different areas more. After a complicated process, in 2012, we concluded the design of the next four-year period project. It was divided into general objectives and according to age-range target groups. In the course of implementation, numerous verification indicators were added. This project was well designed, but it also proved difficulties to interpret the complex linguistic formulations. For the same reason it was hard to implement by the same educators that designed it. In 2016, at the end of the execution of this SEPP, the path for drafting the new project began with a shared key-word asked by our operators: simplification. We were entrusted to the guidance of Prof. Michal Vojtáš towards a simpler project. It was clear that we would like to get to a basic inspirational vision, constructed through a process of discernment. Omitting the excessive level of detail would not hurt the process, of course.

We have therefore tried to simplify the project with respect to the past, without forgetting the important results achieved, such as the mentalization on a common project and the awareness about the importance of coordination between educators, operators at different levels of leadership.

The stages of the situation analysis and interpretation were decisive. The EPC members were really active, also thanks to creative dialogue methodologies, like "World Café", which favored the exchange without falling into superficial talk. The challenge of discernment has been fascinating, although it has not always been easy to distinguish a purely human discernment from a genuine spiritual discernment, especially when you bring together sixty / seventy very different people that operate in different services and areas.

It is normal to perceive the lack of motivation during the process, but this news type of operational design has made people feel involved because everyone's ideas found their place within a shared framework without being put aside.

The vision has been synthesized in a visual image with only one title and four key words. These have been specified in priorities (each one of them was declined in indicative processes and interventions). Just the visual image, along with the four priorities, helped the assembly to tune into the newly completed project and to find the right interventions for their specific educative areas.

Stefano Aspettati
Rector of the Borgo
Ragazzi Don Bosco, Rome

Index

List of Abbreviations
Sdb: Salesian Studies Author/Scholar
Edu: Education Sciences Author/Scholar
Org: Management and/or Leadership Author/Scholar
Cons: Consecrated Life Author/Scholar

292

List of Schemes

Bibliography

A servizio dell'educazione. La Facoltà di Scienze dell'Educazione dell'Università Pontificia Salesiana, a cura di G. Malizia ed E. Alberich, LAS, Roma 1984.

Acts of the 19th General Chapter. 8th April to 10th June 1965 Rome, in «Acts of the Superior Council of the Salesian Society» 47 (1966) 244.

ALBERDI R. – SEMERARO C., *Società Salesiana di San Giovanni Bosco*, in G. PELLICCIA – G. ROCCA (Eds.), *Dizionario degli istituti di perfezione*, vol. 8, San Paolo, Roma 1988, pp. 1682-1714.

ALBERICH E., *Catechesi*, in J.E. VECCHI – J.M. PRELLEZO (Eds.), *Progetto Educativo Pastorale. Elementi modulari*, LAS, Roma 1984, pp. 61-71.

ALBERICH E., *La catechesi oggi. Manuale di catechetica fondamentale*, LDC, Leumann (TO) 2002.

ALBERICH E. – VALLABARAJ J., *Communicating a Faith That Transforms. A Handbook of Fundamental Catechetics*, Kristu Jyoti Publications, Bangalore 2004.

ANDERSON D. – ANDERSON L.A., *Beyond Change Management. How to Achieve Breakthrough Results Through Conscious Change Leadership*, Pfeiffer, San Francisco [2]2010.

ANGELINI G., *Il vincolo ecclesiastico, la pratica religiosa, la fede cristiana*, in G. AMBROSIO et al., *Progetto pastorale e cura della fede*, Glossa, Milano 1996, pp. 15-39.

ARGYRIS C., *How normal science methodology makes leadership research less additive and less applicable*, in J.G. HUNT – L.L. LARSON (Eds.), *Crosscurrents in leadership*, Southern Illinois University Press, Carbondale IL 1979, pp. 47-63.

ARGYRIS C., *Flawed Advice*, Oxford University Press, New York 2000.

ATTARD F., *Ripensare la pastorale giovanile*, LAS, Roma 2013.

AUGUSTIN J.P. – GILLET J.C., *L'animation professionnelle. Histoire, acteurs, enjeux*, Harmattan, Paris Montréal 2000.

BAIRATI P., *Cultura Salesiana e società industriale*, in F. TRANIELLO (Ed.), *Don Bosco nella storia della cultura popolare*, SEI, Torino 1987, pp. 331-357.

BARSKY A., *Understanding the ethical cost of organizational goal-setting: A review and theory development*, in «Journal of Business Ethics» 81 (2008) 1, 63-81.

BASS B.M., *Leadership and Performance*, Free Press, New York 1985.

BASS B.M., *Bass and Stogdill's Handbook of Leadership. Theory, Research and Managerial Applications*, Free Press, New York [3]1990.

297

BATES R., *History of Educational Leadership/Management*, in P. PETERSON –
E. BAKER – B. MCGAW (Eds.), *International Encyclopedia of Education*, vol. 4,
Academic Press, Oxford ³2010, pp. 724-730.

BAY M., *Giovanni Bosco a Chieri 1831-1841. Scuola pubblica e seminario*,
LAS, Roma 2010.

BAZERMAN M.H. – CHUGH D., *Decisions without blinders*, in «Harvard Business Review» 84 (2006) 1, 88-97.

BEGLEY P.T., *Leadership: Authentic*, in P. PETERSON – E. BAKER – B. MCGAW
(Eds.), *International Encyclopedia of Education*, vol. 5, Academic Press, Oxford ³2010, pp. 7-11.

BENNIS W., *On Becoming a Leader*, Perseus Books, Reading MA 1989.

BENNIS W., *An Invented Life. Reflections on Leadership and Change*, Addison-Wesley, Reading MA 1993.

BENNIS W. – GOLDSMITH J., *Learning to Lead. A workbook on Becoming a
Leader*, Addison-Wesley, Reading MA 1997.

BENSON T. – IMMEDIATO C.S., *Educating the Next Generation of Systems Thinkers: An Interview with Tracy Benson*, in «Reflections. The SoL Journal on
Knowledge, Learning and Change» 10 (2011) 4, 13-22.

BERNHARD A. – KEIM W. (Eds.), *1968 und die neue Restauration*, Jahrbuch für
Pädagogik 2008, Peter Lang, Frankfurt am Main 2009.

BEYER J.M. – TRICE H.M., *The Utilization Process: A Conceptual Framework
and Synthesis of Empirical Findings*, in «Administrative Science Quarterly» 27
(1982) 591-622.

BIJU M. – LOCHRIE R.J., *Integrity. The Core of Leadership*, Tate Publishing,
Mustang OK 2009.

BLANCHARD K. – ZIGARMI P. – ZIGARMI D., *Leadership and the one minute
manager: Increasing effectiveness through situational leadership*, William
Morrow and Company, New York 1985.

BLOOM B.S. – KRATHWOHL D.R. et al., *Taxonomy of Educational Objectives.
The Classification of Educational Goals*, Handbook 1: *Cognitive domain*, David
McKay, New York 1956.

BOBBITT J.F., *Some general principles of management applied to the problems
of city-school systems*, National Society for the Study of Education, Bloomington 1913.

BOBBITT J.F., *The Curriculum*, Houghton Mifflin, Boston 1918.

BOPP K., *Kirchenbild und pastorale praxis bei Don Bosco. Eine pastoralgeschichtliche Studie zum Problem des Theorie-Praxis-Bezugs innerhalb der
Praktischen Theologie*, Don Bosco Verlag, München 1992.

298

BORREGO J. (Ed.), *La Patagonia e le terre australi del continente Americano [pel] sac. Giovanni Bosco*, in «Ricerche Storiche Salesiane» 7 (1988) 13, 255-291.

BORTOFT H., *Wholeness of Nature. Goethe's Way of Science*, Floris, Edinburgh 1996.

BOSCO G., *Vita del giovanetto Savio Domenico allievo dell'oratorio di San Francesco di Sales*, Tipografia e Libreria Salesiana, Torino 1880.

BOSCO G., *Opere edite*, 38 voll., LAS, Roma 1976-87.

BOSCO G., *Memoirs of the Oratory of Saint Francis de Sales from 1815 to 1855. The Autobiography of Saint John Bosco*, trans. Daniel Lyons, Don Bosco Publications, New Rochelle NY 1989.

BOSCO G., *Due lettere datate da Roma 10 Maggio 1884* in P. BRAIDO (Ed.), *Don Bosco educatore. Scritti e testimonianze*, LAS, Roma ³1997, pp. 344-390.

BOSCO G., *Tre lettere a salesiani in America*, a cura di Francesco Motto, in P. BRAIDO (Ed.), *Don Bosco educatore. Scritti e testimonianze*, LAS, Roma ³1997, pp. 439-452.

BOSCO G., *Vite di giovani. Le biografie di Domenico Savio, Michele Magone e Francesco Besucco*. Saggio introduttivo e note storiche, ed. Aldo Giraudo, LAS, Roma 2012.

BRAIDO P., *Il progetto operativo di Don Bosco e l'utopia della società cristiana*, LAS, Roma 1982.

BRAIDO P., *Pedagogia perseverante tra sfide e scommesse*, in «Orientamenti Pedagogici» 38 (1991) 899-914.

BRAIDO P., *"Memorie" del futuro*, in «Ricerche Storiche Salesiane» 11 (1992) 20, 97-127.

BRAIDO P., *Il Sistema Preventivo di Don Bosco alle origini (1841-1862). Il cammino del "preventivo" nella realtà e nei documenti*, in «Ricerche Storiche Salesiane» 14 (1995) 27, pp. 255-320.

BRAIDO P., *Don Bosco prete dei giovani nel secolo delle libertà*, 2 vols., LAS, Roma ²2003.

BRAIDO P., *Le metamorfosi dell'Oratorio Salesiano tra il secondo dopoguerra e il Postconcilio Vaticano II (1944-1984)*, in «Ricerche Storiche Salesiane» 49 (2006) 2, 295-356.

BRAIDO P., *Prevention not repression. Don Bosco's Educational System*, Kristu Jyoti Publications, Bengaluru 2013.

BRANCA P.G. – CONTESSA G. – ELLENA A., *Animare la città*, Istituto di Scienze Amministrative e di promozione sociale, Milano 1982.

BURNS J.M., *Leadership*, Harper&Row, New York 1978.

299

BURRELL G., *The Absent Centre. The Neglect of Philosophy in Anglo-American Management Theory*, in «Human Systems Management» 8 (1989) 307-312.

BUSH T., *Leadership and management development in education*, Sage, London ⁴2011.

CALLAHAN R., *Education and the Cult of Efficiency*, University of Chicago Press, Chicago 1962.

CAMPFENS H. (Ed.), *Community Development Around the World*, University of Toronto Press, Toronto 1997.

CARLONE D., *The Ambiguous Nature of a Management Guru Lecture. Providing Answers While Deepening Uncertainty*, in «Journal of Business Communication» 43 (2006) 2, 89-112.

CARNEY M. – CHINNICI J., *Implications for Governance from Franciscan Christology. Response to Zachary Hayes' presentation on Christology*, Franciscan Federation, Anaheim, LA 1995.

CASELLA F., *L'esperienza educativa preventiva di Don Bosco. Studi sull'educazione Salesiana fra tradizione e modernità*, LAS, Roma 2007.

CASELLE S., *Giovanni Bosco a Chieri 1831 – 1841. Dieci anni che valgono una vita*, Edizioni Acclaim, Torino 1988.

CENTRO INTERNACIONAL SALESIANO DE PASTORAL JUVENIL/ROMA, *Comunidad educativa en formación. Guiones para educadores*, 5 vols., CCS, Madrid 1985-86.

CEREDA F., *The Personal Plan of Life. Initial Formation*. Letter of 5 July 2003 addressed to Rectors and Members of Formation Communities, Provincials and Provincial Formation Delegates, in sdb.org/images/en/Formazione/ Documenti/zip/Personal_plan_Initial.zip.

CEREDA F., *The Personal Plan of Life. Ongoing Formation. A process of creative faithfulness towards holiness*. Letter of 21 June 2003 addressed to Provincials, Provincial Councils, Provincial Formation Delegates and Provincial Formation Commissions, in sdb.org/images/en/Formazione/Documenti/zip/Personal_plan_ ongoing.zip.

CEREDA F., *The Salesian Community Plan. A process of discernment and of sharing*. Letter of 13 December 2002 addressed to Provincials, Provincial Councils, Provincial Delegates for formation and Provincial Commissions for formation, in sdb.org/images/en/Formazione/Documenti/zip/Salesian_comm unity_plan.zip.

CERIA E., *Annali della Società Salesiana*, SEI, Torino 1941.

CERVONE D. – JIWANI N. – WOOD R., *Goal setting and the differential influence of selfregulatory processes on complex decision-making performance*, in «Journal of Personality and Social Psychology» 61 (1991) 2, 257-266.

300

CGS-COMMISSIONI PRECAPITOLARI CENTRALI, *Ecco ciò che pensano i Salesiani della loro congregazione oggi.* "Radiografia" delle relazioni dei Capitoli Ispettoriali speciali tenuti in gennaio-maggio 1969, 4 vols, Istituto Salesiano Arti Grafiche, Castelnuovo D. Bosco (AT) 1969.

CHÁVEZ VILANUEVA P., *Progetto di animazione e governo del Rettor Maggiore e del suo Consiglio per il sessennio 2002-2008*, in ACG 84 (2003) 380, 9-12.

CHÁVEZ VILLANUEVA P., *"And he took pity on them, because they were like sheep without a shepherd, and he set himself to teach them at some length" (Mk 6,34).* Salesian Youth Ministry, in ACG 91 (2010) 407.

CHÁVEZ VILLANUEVA P., *Lettere circolari*, in *Atti del Consiglio Generale 2002-2014* in digital.biblioteca.unisal.it/items/show/294.

CHENG M. – SUBRAMANYAM K.R. – ZHANG Y., *Earnings Guidance and Managerial Myopia*, in kellogg.northwestern.edu/accounting/papers/k.r%20subramanyam.pdf.

CHIOSSO G., *Carità educatrice e istruzione in Piemonte. Aristocratici, filantropi e preti di fronte all'educazione del popolo nel primo '800*, SEI, Torino 2007.

CLARK T. – SALAMAN G., *The management guru as organizational witchdoctor*, in «Organization» 3 (1996) 85-107.

COLLI C., *La direzione spirituale nella prassi e nel pensiero di Don Bosco: "memoria" e "profezia"*, in M. COGLIANDRO (Ed.), *La direzione spirituale nella famiglia Salesiana*, SDB, Roma 1983, pp. 53-77.

COLLINS J., *Good to great. Why Some Companies Make the Leap... and Others Don't*, HarperCollins Publishers, New York 2001.

COMBONI D., *Escritos*, Mundo Negro, Madrid 1996.

COMOGLIO M., *Abilitare l'animazione. Riflessioni teorico-pratiche sulle competenze dell'animatore*, LDC, Leumann (TO) 1989.

Constitutions of the Society of Saint Francis de Sales, SDB, Rome 1984.

CONTESSA G. – ELLENA A. – SALVI R., *Animatori del tempo libero*, Società Editrice Napoletana, Napoli 1979.

CONTESSA G. – ELLENA A., *Animatori di quartiere*, Società Editrice Napoletana, Napoli 1980.

COSTA G., *Don Bosco in terza pagina. La stampa e il Fondatore dei Salesiani*, Istituto Teologico S. Tommaso, Messina 1991.

COSTA G., *Pastorale giovanile in Italia. Un dossier,* La Roccia, Roma 1981.

Costituzioni della Società di S. Francesco di Sales 1874, in BOSCO, *Opere edite*, vol. 29, p. 201.

COVEY S., *The 7 Habits of Happy Kids*, Simon & Schuster Books for Young Readers, New York 2008.

COVEY S., *The 7 Habits of Highly Effective Teens*, Simon & Schuster, New York 1998

COVEY S.M.R. – MERRILL R., *The Speed of Trust. The One Thing That Changes Everything*, Free Press, New York 2006.

COVEY S.R., *Principle – Centered Leadership*, Free Press, New York 1992.

COVEY S.R. – MERRILL A.R. – MERRILL R.R., *First Things First*, Simon & Schuster, New York 1994.

COVEY S.R., *The 7 Habits of Highly Effective Families*, Simon & Schuster, New York 1999.

COVEY S.R., *The 7 Habits of Highly Effective People. Restoring the Character Ethic*, Simon & Schuster, New York ¹1989 and ²2004.

COVEY S.R., *The 8th Habit. From Effectiveness to Greatness*, Free Press, New York 2004.

COVEY S.R., *The Leader in Me. How Schools and Parents Around the World Are Inspiring Greatness, One Child at a Time*, Free Press, New York 2008.

D.J. SIMPSON – M.J.B. JACKSON, *John Dewey's View of the Curriculum in The Child and the Curriculum*, in «Education and Culture» 20 (2003) 2, 23-27.

D'HAINAUT L., *Des fins aux objectifs de l'éducation*, Labor, Bruxelles 1977.

"Da Mihi Animas, Cetera Tolle". Documents of the General Chapter XXVI of the Society of Saint Francis of Sales. Rome, 23 February – 12 April 2008, in ACG 89 (2008) 401.

DARMANIN A., *Governance in the Society of Jesus. What's New?*, in «Review of Ignatian Spirituality» 39 (2008) 3, 70-77.

DARMANIN A., *Ignatian Spirituality and Leadership in Organizations Today*, in «Review of Ignatian Spirituality» 36 (2005) 2, 1-14.

DAVID D. – REAM T.A. (Eds.), *Handbook for Secular Franciscan Servant Leadership*, in troubadoursofpeace.org/Documents/Formation/SFO Formation Resource Manual.pdf.

DAVIDSON FRAME J., *The New Project Management. Tools for an Age of Rapid Change, Complexity, and Other Business Realities*, Jossey-Bass, San Francisco CA ²2002.

DE GEUS A., *Planning as Learning*, in «Harvard Business Review» 66 (1988) 2, 70-74.

DE PREE M., *Leadership is an Art*, Michigan State University Press, East Lansing MI 1987.

DEL MONTE A., *Una Chiesa giovane per annunciare il vangelo ai giovani,* in «Il Regno-documenti» 3 (1979) 63-76.

Deliberazioni del terzo e quarto capitolo generale della Pia Società Salesiana. Tenuti in Valsalice nel settembre 1883-86, tip. Salesiana, S. Benigno Canavese 1887.

DEMARCHI F. – ELLENA A. (Eds.), *Dizionario di Sociologia,* Paoline, Roma 1976.

DEMING W.E., *Out of the Crisis,* MIT Press, Boston 1986.

DENG Z., *Curriculum Planning and Systems Change,* in P. PETERSON – E. BAKER – B. MCGAW (Eds.), *International Encyclopedia of Education,* vol. 1, Academic Press, Oxford ³2010, pp. 384-389.

DESRAMAUT F., *Don Bosco en son temps (1815-1888),* SEI, Torino 1996.

DESRAMAUT F. – MIDALI M., *L'impegno della Famiglia Salesiana per la giustizia.* Colloqui sulla vita Salesiana 7. Jünkerath 24-28 agosto 1975, LDC, Leumann (TO) 1976.

DEWEY J., *The Child and the curriculum,* The University of Chicago Press, Chicago 1902.

DEWEY J., *How We Think: A Restatement of the Relation of Reflective Thinking to the Educative Process,* D.C. Heath&Co., Boston 1933.

DEWEY J., *Experience and Education,* Macmillan, New York 1938.

DICASTERI PER LA PASTORALE GIOVANILE FMA-SDB, *Spiritualità Giovanile Salesiana. Un dono dello Spirito alla Famiglia Salesiana per la vita e la speranza di tutti,* [s.e.], Roma 1996.

DICASTERO PER LA PASTORALE GIOVANILE, *Progetto Educativo Pastorale. Metodologia,* Sussidio 1, [s.e.], Roma 1978.

DICASTERO PER LA PASTORALE GIOVANILE, *Elementi e linee per un progetto educativo pastorale Salesiano,* Sussidio 2, [s.e.], Roma 1979.

DICASTERO PER LA PASTORALE GIOVANILE, *Elementi e linee per un Progetto Educativo-Pastorale nelle parrocchie affidate ai Salesiani,* Sussidio 3a, [s.e.], Roma 1980.

DICASTERO PER LA PASTORALE GIOVANILE, *Lineamenti essenziali per un Piano Ispettoriale di Pastorale Vocazionale,* Sussidio 4, [s.e.], Roma 1981.

DICASTERO PER LA PASTORALE GIOVANILE, *Il Progetto Educativo-pastorale Salesiano. Rilettura dei progetti ispettoriali. Risultati dell'inchiesta ai delegati ispettoriali di PG e loro équipes sul "Progetto educativo-pastorale",* Dossier PG 8, SDB, Roma 1995.

DICASTERO PER LA PASTORALE GIOVANILE, *Il Progetto Educativo-Pastorale Salesiano. Raccolta antologica di testi,* Dossier PG 9, SDB, Roma 1995.

DICASTERO PER LA PASTORALE GIOVANILE, *Pastorale giovanile Salesiana*, SDB, Roma 1990.

DOMÈNECH A., *The Organic Provincial Plan*, in ACG 84 (2003) 381, 35-42.

DOMÈNECH A., *La formazione pastorale salesiana. Atteggiamenti e competenze da sviluppare*, in ACG 87 (2006) 393, 62-63.

DORAN G.T., *There's a S.M.A.R.T. way to write management's goals and objectives*, in «Management Review» 70 (1981) 11, 35-36

DRUCKER P.F., *The Practice of Management*, Harper & Row, New York 1954.

DRUCKER P.F., *Management. Tasks, Responsibilities, Practices*, Truman Talley Books, New York 1986

DUFFY M.F., *ZBB, MBO, PPB and their Effectiveness within the Planning/Marketing Process*, in «Strategic Management Journal» 10 (1989) 2, 163-173.

ECKERT J.C., *Dienen statt Herrschen. Unternehmenskultur und Ordensspiritualität: Begegnungen, Herausforderungen, Anregungen*, Schäfer Poeschl, Stuttgart 2000.

ECKERT J.C., *Die Kunst, sich richtig wichtig zu nehmen. Führungskompetenz aus dem Kloster*, Kösel, München 2012.

EDSON C.H., *Curriculum Change During the Progressive Era*, in «Educational Leadership» 36 (1978) 64-69.

EDWARDS G. et al., *Exploring power assumption in the leadership and management debate*, in «Leadership & Organization Development Journal» 36 (2015) 3, 328-343.

ELLENA A. (Ed.), *Enciclopedia sociale*, vol. 1: *Introduzione ai problemi sociali*, Paoline, Roma 1958.

ELLENA E. (Ed.), *Presenza educativa*, 2 vols, LDC, Leumann (TO) 1976-77.

ELLENA E., *Animatori*, in J.E. VECCHI – J.M. PRELLEZO (Eds.), *Progetto Educativo Pastorale. Elementi modulari*, LAS, Roma 1984, pp. 355-363.

ELLIOT A.J. – HARACKIEWICZ J.M., *Approach and avoidance achievement goals and intrinsic motivation: A mediational analysis*, in «Journal of Personality and Social Psychology» 70 (1996) 3, 461-475.

ELLIOTT J., *Education in the Shadow of the Education Reform Act*, in J. RUDDUCK, *An Education that Empowers. A collection of Lectures in Memory of Lawrence Stenhouse*, BERA, Clevedon (Avon) 1995, pp. 54-72.

FINE L.G., *The SWOT Analysis: Using your Strength to overcome Weaknesses, Using Opportunities to overcome Threats*, Kick it LLC, Charleston WV 2010.

FLEMING P. – ZYGLIDOPOULOS S.C., *The Escalation of Deception in Organizations*, in «Journal of Business Ethics» 81 (2008) 4, 837-850.

304

FORESTER J., *Planning in the Face of Power*, University of California Press, Berkeley CA 1989.

FREEBAIRN-SMITH L., *Abundance and Scarcity Mental Models in Leaders*, ProQuest, Ann Arbor MI 2011.

FRIGATO S., *Educazione ed evangelizzazione. La riflessione della Congregazione Salesiana nel Postconcilio*, in A. BOZZOLO – R. CARELLI (Eds.), *Evangelizzazione e educazione*, LAS, Roma 2011, pp. 39-90.

GALBRAITH C.S. – GALBRAITH O. III, *Benedictine Rule of Leadership*, Adams Media Corporation, Avon, MA 2004.

GALINSKY A.D. – MUSSWEILER T. – MEDVEC V.H., *Disconnecting outcomes and evaluations: The role of negotiator focus*, in «Journal of Personality and Social Psychology» 83 (2002) 5, 1131-1140.

GALTON M., *Big change questions: Should pedagogical change be mandated? Dumbing down on classroom standards. The perils of a technician's approach to pedagogy*, in «Journal of Educational Change» 1 (2000) 2, 199-204.

GANDEL S., *The 7 Habits of Highly Effective People (1989) by Stephen R. Covey*, in *The 25 Most Influential Business Management Books*, in «Time» (9 August 2011).

GARDINER J.J., *Transactional, Transformational, and Transcendent Leadership: Metaphors Mapping the Evolution of the Theory and Practice of Governance*, in «Kravis Leadership Institute Leadership Review» 6 (2006) 62-76.

GARDNER H., *Truth, Beauty, and Goodness Reframed: Educating for the Virtues in the Age of Truthiness and Twitter*, Basic Books, New York 2011.

GARDNER J.W., *On Leadership*, Macmillan, New York 1990.

GARLAND H., *Influence of ability, assigned goals, and normative information on personal goals and performance: A challenge to the goal attainability assumption*, in «Journal of Applied Psychology» 68 (1983) 1, 20-30.

GATTI G., *Dall'osservanza della legge alla crescita delle virtù. Lettura etica della "Vita"*, in A. GIRAUDO (Ed.), *Domenico Savio raccontato da Don Bosco. Riflessioni sulla Vita*. Atti del Simposio, Università Pontificia Salesiana, Roma 8 maggio 2004, LAS, Roma 2005, pp. 177-183.

GESING R. , *Das Mitbrudergespräch in einer Ordensgemeinschaft und das Mitarbeitergespräch im Unternehmen. Eine vergleichende Darstellung unter besonderer Bezugnahme auf das Mitbrudergespräch bei den SDB und das Mitarbeitergespräch bei RWE*, Manuscript in the series «Benediktbeurer Schriftenreihe zur Lebensgestaltung im Geiste Don Boscos», Benedikbeuern 2004.

GIACALONE R.A. – JURKIEWICZ C.L., *Handbook of workplace spirituality and organizational performance*, M.E. Sharpe, New York 2003.

GIANATELLI R. (Ed.), *Progettare l'educazione oggi con Don Bosco*, Seminario promosso dal Dicastero per la Pastorale Giovanile della Direzione Generale "Opere Don Bosco" in collaborazione con la Facoltà di Scienze dell'Educazione dell'Università Pontificia Salesiana Roma 1-7 giugno 1980, LAS, Roma 1981.

GILLILAND S.W. – LANDIS R.S., *Quality and quantity goals in a complex decision task: Strategies and outcomes*, in «Journal of Applied Psychology» 77 (1992) 5, 672-681.

GIRAUDO A., *Interrogativi e spinte della Chiesa del postconcilio sulla spiritualità Salesiana*, in C. SEMERARO (Ed.), *La spiritualità Salesiana in un mondo che cambia*, Salvatore Sciascia, Caltanissetta 2003, pp. 137-159.

GIRAUDO A., *L'importanza storica e pedagogico – spirituale delle Memorie delle Oratorio*, in G. BOSCO, *Memorie dell'Oratorio di S. Francesco di Sales dal 1815 al 1855*. Saggio introduttivo e note storiche a cura di Aldo Giraudo, LAS, Roma 2011, pp. 5-63.

GIRAUDO A., *Maestri e discepoli in azione*, in G. BOSCO, *Vite di giovani. Le biografie di Domenico Savio, Michele Magone e Francesco Besucco*. Saggio introduttivo e note storiche a cura di Aldo Giraudo, LAS, Roma 2012, pp. 5-35.

GLASER R. – LUMSDAINE A.A. (Eds.), *Teaching Machines and Programmed Learning. A Source Book*, National Education Association, Washington DC 1961.

Going on Learning Journeys, in J. JAWORSKI – A. KAHANE – C.O. SCHARMER, *Presence workbook. A companion guide of capacity-building practices, practical tips, and suggestions for further reading from seasoned practitioners* in allegrosite.be/artikels/Presence Workbook.pdf.

GOODLAD J.I., *Improving Schooling in the 1980s: Toward the Non-Replication of Non-Events. We have learned some painful lessons about how not to achieve change*, in «Educational Leadership» 40 (1983) 4-7.

GORDON T., *P.E.T. Parent Effectiveness Training*, P.H. Wyden, New York 1970.

GORDON T. – N. BURCH, *T.E.T. Teacher Effectiveness Training*, P.H. Wyden, New York 1974.

GORDON T., *Leader Effectiveness Training L.E.T.*, Wyden Books, New York 1977.

GOTTEINER S., *The Optimal MBO. A Model for Effective Management-by-Objectives Implementation*, in «European Accounting and Management Review» 2 (2016) 2, 43-56.

306

GRANT R.M., *The Resource-Based Theory of Competitive Advantage: Implications for Strategy Formulation*, in «California Management Review» 33 (1991) 3, 114-135.

GRASSO P.G., *La Società Salesiana tra il passato e l'avvenire. Risultati di un'inchiesta tra ex allievi Salesiani*, Edizione extra-commerciale riservata, Roma 1964.

GREENLEAF R.K., *Servant Leadership. A Journey into the Nature of Legitimate Power and Greatness*. 25th Anniversary Edition, Paulist press, New York 2002.

GROPPO G., *Evangelizzazione e educazione*, in J.E. VECCHI – J.M. PRELLEZO (Eds.), *Progetto Educativo Pastorale. Elementi modulari*, LAS, Roma 1984, pp. 38-49.

GROPPO G., *Promozione integrale*, in J.E. VECCHI – J.M. PRELLEZO (Eds.), *Progetto Educativo Pastorale. Elementi modulari*, LAS, Roma 1984, pp. 113-131.

GRUNDY S., *Curriculum: product or praxis?*, Falmer Press, Lewes 1987.

HAIMES Y.Y., *Risk Analysis, Systems Analysis, and Covey's Seven Habits*, in «Risk Analysis» 21 (2001) 217-224.

HAIMES Y.Y., *Risk Modeling, Assessment, and Management*, Wiley & Sons, New Jersey ³2009.

HAMEL G. – PRAHALAD C.K., *Competing For the Future*, Harvard Business School Press, Boston 1994.

HARROW A.J., *A taxonomy of the psychomotor domain. A guide for developing behavioral objectives*, David McKay Company, New York 1972.

HARTLEY J., *Programmed Instruction 1954-1974. A Review*, in «Innovations in Education & Training International» 11 (1974) 6, 278-291.

HAVARD A., *Virtuous Leadership. An Agenda for Personal Excellence*, Scepter Publishers, New York 2007.

HEPP N., *Piano pastorale*, in K. RAHNER et al. (Eds.), *Dizionario di Pastorale*, Queriniana, Brescia 1979, pp. 567-569.

HINDLE T., *Guide to Management Ideas and Gurus*, The Economist, London 2008.

HIRSCHHORN L., *Reworking Authority: Leading and Following in the Post-Modern Organisation*, MIT Press, Cambridge MA 1997.

HIRSCHHORN L., *The Psychology of Vision*, in E.B. KLEIN – F. GABELNICK – P. HERR (Eds.), *The Psychodynamics of Leadership*, Psychosocial Press, Madison CT 1998, pp. 109-126.

HOFMEISTER B., *Werte im Management*, VDM Verlag, Saarbrücken 2006.

HOSKING D.M. – MORLEY I.E., *The skills of leadership*, in J.G. HUNT – B.R. BALIGA – H.P. DACHLER – C.A. SCHRIESHEIM (Eds.), *Emerging leadership vistas*, Lexington Books, Lexington MA 1988, pp. 89-106.

Il sistema educativo di Don Bosco tra pedagogia antica e nuova. Atti del convegno europeo Salesiano sul Sistema Preventivo di Don Bosco, svoltosi a Roma dal 31 dicembre 1973 al 5 gennaio 1974, LDC, Leumann (TO) 1974.

ISAACS W., *Dialogue. The Art of Thinking Together*, Doubleday, New York 1999

ISTITUTO DI TEOLOGIA PASTORALE UNIVERSITÀ PONTIFICIA SALESIANA, *Dizionario di Pastorale Giovanile*, a cura di Mario Midali e Riccardo Tonelli, LDC, Leumann (TO) [1]1989 e [2]1992.

Itinerari di educazione alla fede. Un confronto interdisciplinare: orizzonti e linguaggi, Intervista a C. Bissoli, A. Domènech, G. Ruta, D. Sigalini, R. Tonelli, G. Venturi a cura di G. De Nicolò, in «Note di Pastorale Giovanile» 39 (2005) 8, 5-24.

IVANCEVICH J.M. – MATTESON M.T., *Organizational Behavior and Management*, McGraw Hill/Irwin, New York [6]2002.

JACKSON B., *Management Gurus and Management Fashions. A Dramatistic Inquiry*, Routledge, London 2001.

JAMES M., *An alternative to the objectives model. The process model for the design and development of curriculum*, in J. ELLIOTT – N. NORRIS (Eds.), *Curriculum, Pedagogy and Educational Research. The Work of Lawrence Stenhouse*, Routledge, London 2012, pp. 64-83.

JAMESON D.A., *Narrative Discourse and Management Action*, in «The Journal of Business Communication» 38 (2001) 4, 476-511.

JULIEN D., *Clare's Model of Leadership*, in «The Cord» 51 (2001) 4, 184-198.

KAHNEMAN D. – A. TVERSKY, *Prospect Theory: An Analysis of Decision Under Risk*, in «Econometrica» 47 (1979) 2, 263-291

KAHNEMAN D. – SLOVIC P. – TVERSKY A. (Eds.), *Judgment under uncertainty: Heuristics and biases*, Cambridge University Press, Cambridge 1982.

KAHNEMAN D., *Thinking Fast and Slow*, Farrar Straus and Giroux, New York 2011.

KÄUFER K. – SCHARMER C.O., *Universität als Schauplatz für den unternehmenden Menschen, Hochschulen als "Landestationen" für das In-die-Welt-Kommen des Neuen*, in S. LASKE – T. SCHEYTT – C. MEISTER-SCHEYTT – C.O. SCHARMER (Eds.), *Universität im 21. Jahrhundert. Zur Interdependenz von Begriff und Organisation der Wissenschaft*, Rainer Hampp Verlag, Mering 2000, 109-134.

KEMMIS, *Some Ambiguities in Stenhouse*, in J. RUDDUCK, *An Education that Empowers. A collection of Lectures in Memory of Lawrence Stenhouse*, BERA, Clevedon (Avon) 1995, pp. 73-115.

KERZNER H., *Project Management. A Systems Approach to Planning, Scheduling, and Controlling*, Wiley, New Jersey ¹⁰2009.

KING W.R. (Ed.), *Knowledge Management and Organizational Learning*, Springer, New York 2009.

KLOSTERMANN S., *Management im kirchlichen Dienst. Über Sinn und Sorge kirchengemäßer Führungspraxis und Trägerschaft*, Bonifatius-Verlag, Paderborn 1997.

KNIGHT D. – DURHAM C.C. – LOCKE E.A., *The Relationship of Team Goals, Incentives, and Efficacy to Strategic Risk, Tactical Implementation, and Performance*, in «The Academy of Management Journal» 44 (2001) 2, 326-338.

KOFFKA K., *Zu den Grundlagen der Gestaltpsychologie – Ein Auswahlband*. Herausgegeben von Michael Stadler, Verlag Wolfgang Kammer, Wien 2008.

KOLB D.A., *Experiential learning: experience as the source of learning and development*, Prentice Hall, Englewood Cliffs NJ 1984.

KONDRASUK J.N., *Studies in MBO Effectiveness*, in «The Academy of Management Review» 6 (1981) 3, 419-430.

KOSNIK C. – BECK C. – CLEOVOULOU Y. – FLETCHER T., *Improving Teacher Education Through Longitudinal Research: How studying our graduates led us to give priority to program planning and vision for teaching*, in «Studying Teacher Education» 5 (2009) 2, 163-175.

KOTTER J.P., *The Leadership Factor*, Free Press, New York 1988.

KOTTER J.P., *A Force for Change: How Leadership Differs from Management*, Free Press, New York 1990.

KOTTER J.P., *Accelerate. Building Strategic Agility for a Faster Moving World*, Harvard Business Review Press, Boston 2014.

KRATHWOHL D.R. – BLOOM B.S. – MASIA B.B., *Taxonomy of Educational Objectives. The Classification of Educational Goals*. Handbook 2: *Affective domain*, David McKay, New York 1964.

KRIDEL C. (Ed.), *Encyclopedia of Curriculum*, Sage, Thousand Oaks CA 2010.

KROGERUS M. – TSCHÄPPELER R., *The Decision Book. Fifty models for strategic thinking*, Profile Books, London 2011.

KRUGLANSKI A.W. et al., *A Theory of Goal Systems*, in M.P. ZANNA (Ed.), *Advances in Experimental Social Psychology*, vol. 34, Academic Press, San Diego CA 2002, pp. 331-378.

KÜHL S., *Sisyphos im Management. Die vergebliche Suche nach der optimalen Organisationsstruktur*, Wiley, Weinheim 2002.

La Società di san Francesco di Sales nel sessennio 1984-1990. Relazione del Rettor Maggiore don Egidio Viganò, SDB, Roma, 1990.

La Società di san Francesco di Sales nel sessennio 1990-1995. Relazione del Vicario del Rettor Maggiore don Juan E. Vecchi, SDB, Roma 1996.

La Società di san Francesco di Sales nel sessennio 1996-2002. Relazione del Vicario del Rettor Maggiore don Luc Van Looy, SDB, Roma 2002.

La Società di san Francesco di Sales nel sessennio 2002-2008. Relazione del Rettor Maggiore don Pascual Chávez Villanueva, SDB, Roma 2008.

LANGLOIS L., *The Anatomy of Ethical Leadership. To Lead Our Organizations in a Conscientious and Authentic Manner*, AU Press, Edmonton AB 2011.

LATHAM G.P., *Work motivation: History, theory, and practice*, Sage, Thousand Oaks CA 2007.

LATHAM G.P – LOCKE E.A., *Has Goal Setting Gone Wild, or Have Its Attackers Abandoned Good Scholarship?*, in «Academy of Management Perspectives» 23 (2009) 1, 17-23.

Le principali difficoltà emerse dal dibattito sulla relazione di don J.E. Vecchi, in ISPETTORIA SALESIANA LOMBARDO-EMILIANA [ILE], *Convegno sul Sistema Preventivo*, Milano-Bologna 3-4 novembre 1978, [s.e.], [s.l.] [s.d.].

LEITHWOOD K., *Transformational School Leadership*, in P. PETERSON – E. BAKER–B. MCGAW (Eds.), *International Encyclopedia of Education*, vol. 5, Academic Press, Oxford ³2010, pp. 158-164.

LENTI A., *I sogni di Don Bosco. Esame storico-critico, significato e ruolo profetico-missionario per l'America Latina*, in C. SEMERARO (Ed.), *Don Bosco e Brasilia: profezia, realtà sociale e diritto*, CEDAM, Padova 1990, pp. 85-130.

LENTI A., *Don Bosco. History and Spirit*. Edited by Aldo Giraudo, 7 vols., LAS, Roma 2009-2010.

LEWIS R.D., *When Cultures Collide. Leading across cultures*, Nicholas Brealey International, Boston MA ³2006.

LICKONA T., *The return of Character Education*, in «Educational Leadership» 51 (1993) 6-11.

LICKONA T., *Character Matters. How to Help Our Children Develop Good Judgement, Integrity, and Other Essential Virtues*, Touchstone, New York 2004.

LOCKE E.A. – LATHAM G.P., *Goal setting: A motivational technique that works*, Prentice Hall, Englewood Cliffs NJ 1984.

LOCKE E.A. – LATHAM G.P., *A theory of goal setting and task performance*, Prentice Hall, Englewood Cliffs NJ 1990.

310

LOCKE E.A. – LATHAM G.P., *Building a practically useful theory of goal setting and task motivation. A 35-year odyssey*, in «American Psychologist» 57 (2002) 9, 705-717.

LOCKE E.A. – LATHAM G.P., *New Directions in Goal-Setting Theory*, in «Current Directions in Psychological Science» 15 (2006) 5, 265-268.

LOPARCO G. –ZIMNIAK S. (Eds.), *Don Michele Rua primo successore di Don Bosco. Tratti di personalità, governo e opere (1888-1910)*, Atti del 5° Convegno Internazionale di Storia dell'Opera Salesiana Torino 28 ottobre – 1° novembre 2009, LAS, Roma 2010.

LOWNEY C., *Heroic Leadership: Best Practices from a 450-Year-Old-Company That Changed the World*, Loyola Press, Chicago 2005.

MACINTYRE A., *After Virtue*, University of Notre Dame Press, Notre Dame 1981.

MAIOLI E. – VECCHI J.E., *L'animatore nel gruppo giovanile. Una proposta "Salesiana"*, LDC, Leumann (TO) 1988.

MALONEY R., *Ten seeds of systemic change in the life and works of St. Vincent*, in aic-international.org/pdf/publicationions/cahier13en.pdf.

McKERNAN J., *Curriculum and Imagination. Process theory, pedagogy and action research*, Routledge, London 2008.

MEZIROW J. et al., *Fostering Critical reflection in adulthood. A Guide to Trasformative and Emancipatory Learning*, Jossey-Bass, San Francisco 1990.

MEZIROW J. et al., *Transformative Dimensions of Adult Learning*, Jossey-Bass, San Francisco 1991.

MILANESI G., *L'utilizzo delle scienze dell'educazione nell'impegno dei Salesiani per i giovani "poveri, abbandonati, pericolanti"*, in VECCHI J.E. – PRELLEZO J.M. (Eds.), *Prassi educativa pastorale e scienze dell'educazione*, SDB, Roma 1988, pp. 87-120.

MILLER J.L., *Curriculum and Poststructuralist Theory*, in P. PETERSON – E. BAKER – B. McGAW (Eds.), *International Encyclopedia of Education*, vol. 1, Academic Press, Oxford ³2010, pp. 499-504.

MINER J.B., *The Validity and Usefulness of Theories in an Emerging Organizational Science*, in «Academy of Management Review» 9 (1984) 296-306.

MITCHELL T.R. – SILVER W.S., *Individual and group goals when workers are interdependent: Effects on task strategies and performance*, in «Journal of Applied Psychology» 75 (1990) 2, 185-193.

MOLINSKY A., *Global Dexterity. How to Adapt Your Behavior Across Cultures without Losing Yourself in the Process*, Harvard Business School Publishing, Boston MA 2013.

MORANTE G., *Progetto educativo*, in Z. TRENTI et al. (Eds.), *Religio. Enciclopedia tematica dell'educazione religiosa*, Piemme, Casale Monferrato (AL) 1998, pp. 752-753.

MOTTO F. (Ed.), *Costituzioni della Società di S. Francesco di Sales 1858-1875*, LAS, Roma 1982.

MOTTO F., *I "Ricordi confidenziali ai direttori" di Don Bosco*, in «Ricerche Storiche Salesiane» 3 (1984) 4, 125-166.

MOTTO F. (Ed.), *Memorie dal 1841 al 1884-5-6 pel Sac. Gio. Bosco a'suoi figli Salesiani (Testamento spirituale)*, LAS, Roma 1985.

MOTTO F., *Un sistema educativo sempre attuale*, LDC, Leumann (TO) 2000.

MOTTO F., *Start afresh from Don Bosco*, s.e., Roma 2006.

MUCZYK J.P. – REIMANN B.C., *MBO as a Complement to Effective Leadership*, in «The Academy of Management Executive» 3 (1989) 2, 131-138.

MUSSWEILER T. – STRACK F., *The "relative self": Informational and judgmental consequences of comparative self-evaluation*, in «Journal of Personality and Social Psychology» 79 (2000) 1, 23-38.

NONAKA I. – TAKEUCHI H., *The Knowledge-Creating Company. How Japanese Companies Create the Dynamics of Innovation*, Oxford Univesity Press, New York-Oxford 1995.

O'MALLEY D., *Christian Leadership in Education*, Don Bosco Publications, Bolton 2007.

O'MARA P., *The Franciscan Leader: A Modern Version of the Six Wings of the Seraph. An Anonymous Franciscan Treatise in the Tradition of St. Bonaventure*, Franciscan Institute Publications, St. Bonaventure, NY 2013.

O'MURCHU D., *Consecrated Religious Life. The Changing Paradigms*, Orbis Books, Maryknoll NY 2005.

ORDÓÑEZ L.D. – SCHWEITZER M.E. – GALINSKY A.D. – BAZERMAN M.H., *Goals Gone Wild: How goals systematically harm individuals and organizations*, in «Academy of Management Perspectives» 23 (2009) 1, 6-16.

ORDÓÑEZ L.D. – SCHWEITZER M.E. – GALINSKY A.D. – BAZERMAN M.H., *On Good Scholarship, Goal Setting, and Scholars Gone Wild*, in «Academy of Management Perspectives» 23 (2009) 3, 82-87.

PAZZAGLIA L., *Apprendistato e istruzione degli artigiani a Valdocco (1846-1886)*, in F. TRANIELLO (ed.), *Don Bosco nella storia della cultura popolare*, SEI, Torino 1987, pp. 39-46.

PELLEREY M. – GRZĄDZIEL D., *Educare. Per una pedagogia intesa come scienza pratico-progettuale*, LAS, Roma ²2011.

PELLEREY M., *Progettazione didattica*, SEI, Torino 1979.

312

PELLEREY M. (Ed.), *Progettare l'educazione nella scuola cattolica*, LAS, Roma 1981.

PELLEREY M., *Itinerario*, in J.E. VECCHI – J.M. PRELLEZO (Eds.), *Progetto Educativo Pastorale. Elementi modulari*, LAS, Roma 1984, pp. 188-196.

PELLEREY M., *Obiettivi*, in J.E. VECCHI – J.M. PRELLEZO (Eds.), *Progetto Educativo Pastorale. Elementi modulari*, LAS, Roma 1984, pp. 93-100.

PELLEREY M., *Processi formativi e dimensione spirituale e morale della persona. Dare senso e prospettiva al proprio impegno nell'apprendere lungo tutto l'arco della vita,* CNOS-FAP, Roma 2007.

PETERS R.S., *Ethics and Education*, George Allen and Unwin, London 1966.

PETERS R.S. (Ed.), *The Philosophy of Education*, Oxford University Press, Oxford 1973.

PETERSON C. – SELIGMAN M.E.P., *Character strengths and virtues. A handbook and classification*, American Psychological Association Press – Oxford University Press, Washington DC – New York 2004.

PICKARD M.J., *The New Bloom's Taxonomy: An Overview for Family and Consumer Sciences*, in «Journal of Family and Consumer Sciences Education» 25 (2007) 1, 45-55.

PLASCENCIA MONCAYO J.L., *Costituzioni della Società di san Francesco Di Sales. Processo diacronico dell'elaborazione del testo*, vol. 1: Articoli 1-95, manuscript, Roma-Guadalajara 2007.

POLLO M., *L'animazione culturale: teoria e metodo. Una proposta*, LDC, Leumann (TO) 1980.

POLLO M., *L'animazione culturale: teoria e metodo*, LAS, Roma 2002.

POLLO M. – TONELLI R., *Animazione*, in J.E. VECCHI – J.M. PRELLEZO (Eds.), *Progetto Educativo Pastorale. Elementi modulari*, LAS, Roma 1984, pp. 285-309.

POPHAM W.J., *Instructional Objectives Exchange rationale statement*, UCLA Center for the Study of Evaluation, Los Angeles CA 1970.

POPHAM W.J. – BAKER E.L., *Systematic instruction*, Prentice-Hall, Englewood Cliffs NJ 1970.

PRAHALAD C.K. – HAMEL G., *The core competence of the corporation*, in «Harvard Business Review» 68 (1990) 3, 79-91.

PRAHALAD C.K. – HAMEL G., *Competing for the Future*, Harvard Business School Press, Boston MA 1994.

PRELLEZO J.M., *Valdocco nell'Ottocento tra reale ed ideale (1866-1889). Documenti e testimonianze*, LAS, Roma 1992.

PRELLEZO J.M., *Sistema educativo ed esperienza oratoriana di Don Bosco*, LDC, Leumann TO 2000.

PRELLEZO J.M. – MALIZIA G. – NANNI C. (Eds.), *Dizionario di Scienze dell'Educazione. Seconda edizione riveduta e aggiornata,* LAS, Roma 2008.

QUAGLINO G.P. (Ed.), *Leadership. Nuovi profili di leader per nuovi scenari organizzativi,* Raffaello Cortina, Milano 2005.

QUAGLINO G.P., *La vita organizzativa. Difese, collusioni e ostilità nelle relazioni di lavoro*, Fabbri, Milano 2007.

RAHNER K. et al. (Eds.), *Dizionario di Pastorale*, Queriniana, Brescia 1979.

RATHS J.D., *Teaching without specific objectives*, in «Educational Leadership» 28 (1971) 714-720.

RAWSTHORNE L.J. – ELLIOT A.J., *Achievement Goals and Intrinsic Motivation: A Meta-Analytic Review*, in «Personality and Social Psychology Review» 3 (1999) 4, 326-344.

REAM D.D. – REAM T.A. (Eds.), *Handbook for Secular Franciscan Servant Leadership*, in troubadoursofpeace.org/Documents/Formation/SFO Formation Resource Manual.pdf.

REAMS J., *Illuminating the Blind Spot: An Overview and Response to Theory U*, in «Integral Review» 3 (2007) 5, 240-259.

Regolamento dell'Oratorio di S. Francesco di Sales per gli esterni, in G. BOSCO, *Opere edite*, vol. 29, LAS, Roma 1977, pp. 31-92.

Regolamento per le case della Società di S. Francesco di Sales, in in G. BOSCO, *Opere edite*, vol. 29, LAS, Roma 1977, pp. 97-196.

Regole o Costituzioni della Società di S. Francesco di Sales secondo il decreto di approvazione del 3 aprile 1874, Torino 1877 in G. BOSCO, *Opere edite*, vol. 29, LAS, Roma 1977, pp. 199-288.

Relazione Generale sullo stato della Congregazione, SDB, Roma 1971.

RIC LORENZO F. , *Management of Governance structures in Religious Institutes of active life. Applied to the Salesian Society of St. John Bosco*, Salesian Pontifical University; thesis no. 0810D; director: J.M. Graulich; date of discussion: 3. 4. 2006.

RICCERI L., *Lettere circolari di don Luigi Ricceri ai Salesiani*, Direzione Generale Opere Don Bosco, Roma 1996.

RODGERS R. – HUNTER J.E., *Impact of Management by Objectives on Organizational Productivity*, in «Journal of Applied Psychology» 76 (1991) 2, 322-336.

ROSCH E. – LLOYD B.B. (Eds.), *Cognition and categorization*, Erlbaum, Hillsdale NJ 1978.

314

SALESIAN YOUTH MINISTRY DEPARTMENT, *Salesian Youth Ministry. Frame of Reference*, SDB, Rome [1]1998, [2]2001, [3]2014.

Salesians and Lay People. Documents of 24th General Chapter of the Society of St Francis de Sales. Rome, 19 February - 20 April 1996, in ACG 77 (1996) 356.

SARTI S., *Valutazione*, in J.E. VECCHI – J.M. PRELLEZO (Eds.), *Progetto Educativo Pastorale. Elementi modulari*, LAS, Roma 1984, pp. 310-321.

SCHARMER C.O., *Kopf, Herz und Hand. Die Anforderungen eines zukunftsfähigen Wohlstandsmodells an die Universitäten*, in «Politische Ökologie» 39 (1994) 51-54.

SCHARMER C.O., *Neues Wohlstandsmodell als Bildungsaufgabe*, in F-T. GOTTWALD et al. (Eds.), *Bildung und Wohlstand, Auf dem Weg zu einer verträglichen Lebensweise*, Wiesbaden 1994, pp. 14-25.

SCHARMER C.O. – SENGE P. – JAWORSKI J. – FLOWERS B.S., *Presence. Exploring Profound Change in People, Organizations, and Society*, Currency Doubleday, New York 2004.

SCHARMER C.O., *Theory U. Leading from the Future as it Emerges. The Social Technology of Presencing*, SoL, Cambridge MA 2007.

SCHEIN E.H., *Organizational Culture and Leadership*, Jossey-Bass, San Francisco [1]1985, [3]2004.

SCHÖN D.A., *The Reflective Professional. How Professionals Think in Action*, Basic Books, New York 1983.

SCHWAB J.J., *Science, curriculum and liberal education*, The University of Chicago Press, Chicago 1978.

SCHWEITZER M.E. – ORDÓÑEZ L. – DOUMA B., *Goal Setting as a Motivator of Unethical Behavior,* in «Academy of Management Journal» 47 (2004) 3, 422-432.

SCILLIGO P., *Gruppo*, in J.E. VECCHI – J.M. PRELLEZO (Eds.), *Progetto Educativo Pastorale. Elementi modulari*, LAS, Roma 1984, pp. 386-398.

SENGE P.M., *The Fifth Discipline. The art and practice of the learning organization*, Doubleday, New York [1]1990, [2]2006.

SENGE P.M. et al., *The Fifth Discipline Fieldbook. Strategies and Tools for Building a Learning Organization*, Doubleday, New York 1994.

SENGE P.M. et al., *The Dance of Change. The Challenges of Sustaining Momentum in Learning Organizations*, Doubleday, New York 1999.

SENGE P.M. et al., *Schools That Learn. A Fifth Discipline Fieldbook for Educators, Parents, and Everyone Who Cares About Education*, Doubleday, New York 2000.

SENGE P.M. et al., *The Necessary Revolution. How Individuals and Organizations Are Working Together to Create a Sustainable World*, Doubleday, New York 2008.

SHAH J.Y. – FRIEDMAN R. – KRUGLANSKI A.W., *Forgetting all else: on the antecedents and consequences of goal shielding*, in «Journal of Personality and Social Psychology» 83 (2002) 6, 1261-1280.

Sintesi dei lavori e conclusioni, in J.E. VECCHI – J.M. PRELLEZO (Eds.), *Prassi educativa pastorale e scienze dell'educazione*, SDB, Roma 1988, pp. 321-328.

SMITH M.K., *Curriculum theory and practice*, in *The encyclopaedia of informal education*, in infed.org/biblio/b-curric.htm.

SMITH P., *Franciscan Leadership: Mutual Love Generating a Future. Keynote presentation at the Franciscan Federation Annual Conference 2009*, in franfed.org/Keynote - AFC2009, PatSmithOSF.pdf.

SMITH T.K., *What's so effective about Stephen Covey? The author of The Seven Habits of Highly Effective People sells a message of moral renewal, and corporate America is buying it. Is this a good thing?*, in «Fortune Magazine» 12 December 1994, in money.cnn.com/magazines/fortune/fortune_archive/1994/12/12/80049/index.htm.

SNYDER B.R., *The hidden curriculum*, Knopf, New York 1971.

STAW B.M. – BOETTGER R.D., *Task revision. A neglected form of work performance*, in «The Academy of Management Journal» 33 (1990) 3, 534-559

Special General Chapter of the Salesian Society, Rome 10 June 1971 – 5 January 1972, SDB, Rome 1972.

STELLA P., *Don Bosco nella storia economica e sociale (1815-1870)*, LAS, Roma 1980.

STELLA P. , *Don Bosco. Life and Work*, Don Bosco Publications, New Rochelle NY 1985.

STELLA P., *Don Bosco. Religious Outlook and Spirituality*, Salesiana Publishers, New Rochelle NY 1996.

STELLA P., *Don Bosco's Dreams. A historic-documentary analysis of selected samples*, Salesiana Publishers, New Rochelle NY1996.

STELLA P., *Don Bosco*, Il Mulino, Bologna 2001.

STENHOUSE L., *The Humanities Curriculum Project*, in «Journal of Curriculum Studies» 1 (1968) 1, 26-33.

STENHOUSE L., *An Introduction to Curriculum Research and Development*, Heinemann, London 1975.

Storia dell'Oratorio de S. Francesco di Sales, in «Bollettino Salesiano» 7 (1883) 97-98.

SZAMEITAT A.R. – NESTLER H., *Intuition as a Key Factor for Implementing Theory U*, in «The Systems Thinker» 21 (2011) 8, pp. 8-10.

TABA H., *Curriculum development: theory and practice*, Burlingham: Harcourt, Brace & World, New York 1962.

TACCONI G. , *Alla ricerca di nuove identità. Formazione e organizzazione nelle comunità di vita apostolica attiva nel tempo di crisi*, LDC, Leumann (TO) 2001.

TASSAN R., *Leadership & Analisi Transazionale. Come migliorare le proprie capacità manageriali*, Franco Angeli, Milano 2004.

TAYLOR F.W., *The Principles of Scientific Management*, Harper & Brothers, New York 1911.

TENBRUNSEL A.E. et al., *Understanding the Influence of Environmental Standards on Judgments and Choices*, in «The Academy of Management Journal» 43 (2000) 5, 854-866.

The Salesian Community Today. Documents of 25th General Chapter of the Society of St Francis de Sales. Rome, 24 February – 22 April 2002, in ACG 83 (2002) 378.

THIBODEAUX M.E., *Reimagining the Ignatian Examen. Fresh Ways to Pray from Your Day*, Loyola Press, Chicago 2015.

TICHY N.M. – DEVANNA M.A., *Transformational Leader*, Wiley, New York 1986.

TOLOMELLI M., *Il Sessantotto. Una breve storia*, Carocci, Roma 2008.

TONELLI R., *Riunioni di verifica*, in «Note di Pastorale Giovanile» 2 (1968) 8-9, 60-65.

TONELLI R., *Punti fermi per una programmazione valida*, in «Note di Pastorale Giovanile» 3 (1969) 8-9, 43-59.

TONELLI R., *Per fare un progetto educativo*, in «Note di Pastorale Giovanile» 14 (1980) 6, 57-66.

TONELLI R., *Impostazione della comunità educativa in un contesto pluralista*, in R. GIANATELLI (Ed.), *Progettare l'educazione oggi con Don Bosco*, Seminario promosso dal Dicastero per la Pastorale Giovanile della Direzione Generale "Opere Don Bosco" in collaborazione con la Facoltà di Scienze dell'Educazione dell'Università Pontificia Salesiana Roma 1-7 giugno 1980, LAS, Roma 1981, pp. 43-88.

TONELLI R., *Un itinerario di educazione dei giovani alla fede*, in «Note di Pastorale Giovanile» 18 (1984) 8, 57-88.

TONELLI R., *Itinerari per l'educazione dei giovani alla fede*, LDC, Leumann (TO) 1989.

TONELLI R., *Progetto Educativo-Pastorale*, in ISTITUTO DI TEOLOGIA PASTORALE UNIVERSITÀ PONTIFICIA SALESIANA, *Dizionario di Pastorale Giovanile*, a cura di Mario Midali e Riccardo Tonelli, LDC, Leumann (TO) ²1992, pp. 903-906.

TONELLI R., *Ripensando quarant'anni di servizio alla pastorale giovanile*, intervista a cura di Giancarlo De Nicolò, in «Note di Pastorale Giovanile» 43 (2009) 5, 11-65.

TSOUKAS H., *Do we really understand tacit knowledge?*, in M. EASTERBY-SMITH – M. LYLES (Eds.), *The Blackwell handbook of organizational learning and knowledge management*, Blackwell Publishing, Cambridge MA 2003, pp. 411-427.

TVERSKY A. – KAHNEMAN D., *Extensional versus intuitive reasoning: The conjunction fallacy in probabilistic reasoning*, in «Psychological Review» 90 (1983) 293-315.

TYLER R.W., *Basic Principles of Curriculum and Instruction,* The University of Chicago Press, Chicago 1949.

VALLABARAJ J., *Empowering the Young Towards Fullness of Life*, Kristu Jyoti Publications, Bangalore 2003.

VALLABARAJ J., *Animazione e pastorale giovanile. Un'introduzione al paradigma olistico*, LDC, Leumann (TO) 2008.

VALLABARAJ J., *Educazione catechetica degli adulti. Un approccio multidimensionale*, LAS, Roma 2009.

VAN J.E. AKEN, *Management Research Based on the Paradigm of the Design Sciences: The Quest for Field-Tested and Grounded Technological Rules*, in «Journal of Management Studies» 41 (2004) 2, 219–246.

VAN LOOY L., *Mentalità di itinerario*, in ACG 74 (1993) 345, 50-56.

VAN LOOY L., *Il Progetto Educativo Pastorale nelle Ispettorie*, in ACG 75 (1994) 349, 33-41.

VARELA F.J., *Ethical Know-How: Action, Wisdom and Cognition.* Edited by Timothy Lenoir and Hans Ulrich Gumbrecht, Stanford University Press, Stanford CA 1999.

VARELA F.J. – THOMPSON E. – ROSCH E., *The embodied mind. Cognitive science and human experience*, MIT Press, Cambridge MA 1991.

VECCHI J.E., *Per riattualizzare il Sistema Preventivo*, in ISPETTORIA SALESIANA LOMBARDO-EMILIANA, *Convegno sul Sistema Preventivo*, Milano-Bologna 3-4 novembre 1978, [s.e.], [s.l.] [s.d.].

VECCHI J.E., *Verso una nuova tappa di PG Salesiana*, in *Il cammino e la prospettiva 2000*, Documenti PG 13, SDB, Roma 1991, pp. 39-106.

VECCHI J.E., *Pastorale, educazione, pedagogia nella prassi Salesiana*, in *Il cammino e la prospettiva 2000*, Documenti PG 13, SDB, Roma 1991, pp. 123-150.

VECCHI J.E., *I guardiani dei sogni con il dito sul mouse. Educatori nell'era informatica*, Rettore Maggiore dei Salesiani di Don Bosco intervistato da Carlo di Cicco, LDC, Leumann TO 1999.

VECCHI J.E., *Progetto educativo pastorale*, in J.E. VECCHI – J.M. PRELLEZO (Eds.), *Progetto Educativo Pastorale. Elementi modulari*, LAS, Roma 1984, pp. 15-25.

VECCHI J.E., *Sistema Preventivo*, in J.E. VECCHI – J.M. PRELLEZO (Eds.), *Progetto Educativo Pastorale. Elementi modulari*, LAS, Roma 1984, pp. 72-89.

VECCHI J.E., *Educatori appassionati, esperti e consacrati per i giovani. Lettere circolari ai salesiani di don Juan E. Vecchi*. Introduzione, parole chiave e indici a cura di Marco Bay, presentazione di don Pascal Chávez Villanueva, LAS, Roma 2013.

VECCHI J.E. – PRELLEZO J.M. (Eds.), *Progetto Educativo Pastorale. Elementi modulari*, LAS, Roma 1984.

VECCHI J.E. – PRELLEZO J.M. (Eds.), *Prassi educativa pastorale e scienze dell'educazione*, SDB, Roma 1988.

VIGANÒ A., *Alcuni punti fondamentali riaffermati dal convegno sul Sistema Preventivo* in ISPETTORIA SALESIANA LOMBARDO-EMILIANA [ILE], *Convegno sul Sistema Preventivo*, Milano-Bologna 3-4 novembre 1978, [s.e.], [s.l.] [s.d.].

VIGANÒ E., *The Letter of the Rector Major Rev. Fr. Egidius Viganò on the Preventive System*, The Salesian Publication – The Citadel, Madras.

VIGANÒ E., *Lettere circolari di don Egidio Viganò ai Salesiani*, Direzione Generale Opere Don Bosco, Roma 1996.

VOJTÁŠ M., *Progettare e discernere. Progettazione educativo-pastorale Salesiana tra storia, teorie e proposte innovative*, LAS, Roma 2015.

VOJTÁŠ M., *Implicazioni metodologiche del principio religioso nell'educazione salesiana*, in «Orientamenti Pedagogici» 64 (2017) 1, 11-37.

WEINSCHENK R., *Grundlagen der Pädagogik Don Boscos*, Don Bosco Verlag, München 1987.

WENGER E., *Communities of Practice. Learning, Meaning, and Identity*, Cambridge University Press, Cambridge 1998.

WENGER E. – MCDERMOTT R. – SNYDER W.M., *Cultivating Communities of Practice*, Harvard Business School Press, Boston MA 2002.

WERNERFELDT B., *A Resource-Based View of the Firm*, in «Strategic Management Journal» 5 (1984) 2, 171-180.

WHITLEY R., *The Management Sciences and Managerial Skills*, in «Organization Studies» 9 (1988) 1, 47-68.

WILDAVSKY A., *If Planning Is Everything, Maybe It's Nothing*, in «Policy Sciences» 14 (1983) 4, 127–153.

WILSON A.L. – CERVERO R.M., *Program Planning*, in P. PETERSON – E. BAKER – B. MCGAW (Eds.), *International Encyclopedia of Education*, vol. 1, Academic Press, Oxford ³2010, pp. 53-57.

WIRTH M., *Da Don Bosco ai nostri giorni. Tra storia e nuove sfide (1815-2000)*, LAS, Roma 2000.

"Witnesses to the radical approach of the Gospel" Work and temperance. Documents of the General Chapter XXVII of the Society of Saint Francis of Sales. Rome, 22 February - 12 April 2014, in ACG 95 (2014) 418.

WITZEL M., *A History of Management Thought*, Routledge, Abingdon 2012.

WOLF N. – ROSANNA E. , *Die Kunst Menschen zu führen*, Rowohlt Taschenbuch, Hamburg 2007.

WRIGHT P.M. – GEORGE J.M. – FARNSWORTH S.R. – MCMAHAN G.C., *Productivity and extra-role behavior: The effects of goals and incentives on spontaneous helping*, in «Journal of Applied Psychology» 78 (1993) 3, 374-381.

XXI General Chapter of the Salesian Society. Chapter documents. Rome 31 October 1977 – 12 February 1978, SDB, Roma 1978.

XXII General Chapter of the Salesian Society. Chapter documents. Rome 14 January – 12 May 1984, SDB, Roma 1984.

ZIGGIOTTI R., *Tenaci, audaci e amorevoli. Lettere circolari ai Salesiani di don Renato Ziggiotti*. Introduzione, parole chiave, indici e appendici statistiche a cura di Marco Bay, LAS, Roma 2015.

Contents

www.ingramcontent.com/pod-product-compliance
Lightning Source LLC
Chambersburg PA
CBHW060247100426
42742CB00011B/1666